# MARGO NASH

# THE POLITICS OF MURDER

## THE POWER AND AMBITION BEHIND "THE ALTAR BOY MURDER CASE"

SECOND EDITION

WILDBLUE PRESS

WildBluePress.com

*POLITICS OF MURDER published by:*
*WILDBLUE PRESS*
*P.O. Box 102440*
*Denver, Colorado 80250*



*ISBN 978-1-970361-40-7 Trade Paperback*
*ISBN 978-1-970361-39-1 Hardcover*
*ISBN 978-1-970361-38-4 eBook*

*Interior Formatting/Book Cover Design by Elijah Toten*
*www.totencreative.com*

*Cover Photograph Courtesy of The Boston Herald*

ACKNOWLEDGEMENTS

I want to thank my brother, Jim Nash, for his painstaking first edit of this manuscript. His advice was invaluable in shaping the story and giving me direction and focus. My sister, Anne Marie McCall, read every word of the book and gave me support and feedback throughout the writing process. Eddie and the entire O'Brien family opened their hearts and their home to me and included me in their Christmas, Easter and family celebrations.

Jeannette de Beauvoir appeared just when I needed a professional editor, and, with patience and grace, taught me how to use simpler words and make the prose flow naturally. After thirty-odd years of legal brief writing, I'd forgotten how to do this.

# CONTENTS

# PROLOGUE

In July of 1995, they charged Eddie O'Brien, a fifteen-year-old boy from Somerville, with first-degree murder for the brutal and bloody slaying of his best friend's mother.

I'd been a practicing trial lawyer in Massachusetts for twelve years. I also appeared as "bar counsel" for indigent adult criminal defendants and juveniles in delinquency proceedings. "Bar counsel" were private attorneys, approved by the local bar association to accept court appointments at reduced fees. We were, if you will, private public defenders. The program was necessary because there were never enough public defenders to meet the demand. Through the same program, I also served as a guardian *ad litem* in various courts in the Boston, Somerville and Cambridge courts.

I received a telephone call that October from the Somerville District Court, asking me if I would accept an appointment from Judge Paul P. Heffernan to act as guardian *ad litem* for Eddie O'Brien. Guardian *ad litem* literally means guardian "for the proceeding." GALs are often appointed in parental custody disputes, where they're expected to advocate for the child's best interests, which are not necessarily the child's expressed desires. I had never been appointed before as a GAL in a delinquency proceeding.

My role with Eddie was not so clearly defined. I was the designated adult with whom Eddie could discuss his questions and concerns regarding his legal representation. His lawyers were supposed to be consulting me regarding their legal strategies, opinions, and decisions, as if I were

Eddie's parent.

Eddie had never been in any trouble before. He was a sophomore at Don Bosco, a private Catholic high school in Boston. He was an altar boy at his local parish—St. Joseph's in Somerville—until he turned thirteen. He babysat for neighborhood children. He was a sports fanatic; he loved hockey, basketball, and baseball. He was a sports card collector; the Boston Celtics' Larry Bird was his idol.

He hadn't made the varsity football team in high school because he wasn't aggressive enough. He had a part-time job stocking drink coolers and putting together the Sunday newspapers at Mid-Nite Convenient, a corner store that sold newspapers, soda, magazines, and snacks.

The case was an immediate headline grabber, and Eddie's face—and stories about him—appeared almost daily in the local and national media.

I remember the day he was arraigned. It happened in the main adult open courtroom, not in a closed juvenile session. That was unusual. The elected district attorney himself appeared for the Commonwealth. That was unheard of. I'd been in the courtroom that day on one of my cases, and I'd certainly heard about the O'Brien case. I'd actually seen Eddie down in the lockup earlier that morning speaking with a private investigator. I was there when the investigator emerged from the cell, looked up and said, "This kid did not commit this crime."

I looked over at Eddie O'Brien in that cell, a scared boy who looked about twelve years old. He was tall but hadn't yet lost his baby fat. His cheeks were flushed red.

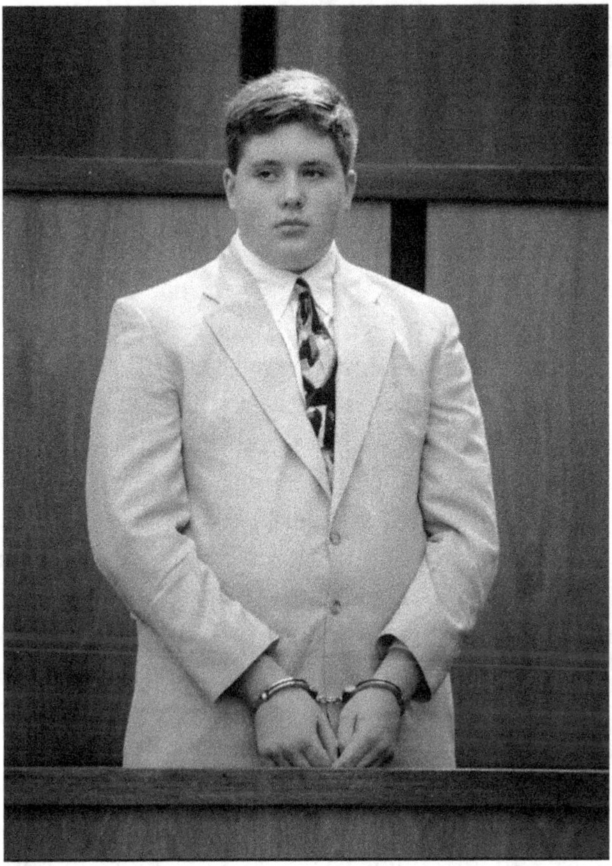

*Eddie O'Brien at his arraignment. Photo courtesy of The Boston Herald.*

I accepted the judge's appointment, but secretly I was worried about exactly how I could protect this kid and his legal rights. Looking back now, so many years later, I know with absolute certainty that I could *never* have protected him or his legal rights.

I couldn't, Judge Paul P. Heffernan couldn't, the judicial system of Massachusetts couldn't, his parents couldn't.

Even the truth couldn't.

Eddie O'Brien fell directly into a political maelstrom brewing since 1991. Lawmakers and politicians were waiting for a case like this to come along, and Eddie's case became the catalyst that changed juvenile law in Massachusetts and sent children to adult prisons for the rest of their natural lives. It also catapulted political careers and perverted the orderly administration of justice that we'd all once believed in.

I've remained involved with Eddie and his parents over the years he's spent in state prison, serving a life sentence. He is middle-aged now; he has grey hair and a wonderful sense of humor. He is such a good man, a spiritual man, a forgiving man. "I don't need that kind of drama and negativity in my life," he frequently says. "I'd rather focus on what's positive." If his cellblock has been in lockdown because of a fight or a shortage of guards, he shrugs, "This is prison. It happens. There's nothing I can do about it, so there's no point in getting upset about it." During those long stretches locked up in his cell he reads, watches news programs, writes letters to friends, and works on his case.

Eddie doesn't trust easily, especially lawyers. Once burned, twice cautious. He spars with me over legal theories of his case, about which issues are the most important to appeal, about whom he can and cannot rely on for help. Eddie does get angry, sometimes with me, his siblings, his legal team. He's a normal man with normal responses and emotions. He's no longer the complacent teenager who blindly believed that right beats might and the truth will set you free.

In a recent letter he wrote:

*Before the trial I couldn't wait for it to begin. I thought that I would finally be able to clear my name, but it didn't happen. Years later after the trial I'm still anxious to clear my name. No one whoever hasn't gone through something like this could ever know what it feels like to want to clear your name. I'm not that 15-year-old boy who didn't understand what was going on anymore. I fully understand what I want and what I need to do this time around and what it takes.*[1]

In 2015, Eddie and I spent a lot of time talking, reading old transcripts, and putting the pieces of a fractured puzzle together. I cringe about having completely missed the big picture so many years ago.

To be fair, the big picture took years to develop and emerge into a legible image. When these events were actually going on, I was focused on far more immediate issues: his detention, the integrity of the police investigation, his transfer hearings, the appeals, the removal of judges, and the central question: Who really murdered Janet Downing?

Today I finally understand what actually happened to Eddie O'Brien and why he has spent more than half of his life behind bars.

## A NOTE ON MY ROLE AS GUARDIAN AD LITEM

The appointment of a GAL in a delinquency proceeding is rare. In Eddie's case, the Commonwealth intended to call Eddie's father as a witness. Since his father was listed as a witness for the prosecution, Eddie's lawyers (Ralph Champa and Maria Curtatone at that time) felt he needed a GAL to act as a neutral "parental" advisor to him. They asked the court to appoint me. The Commonwealth never called his father to the witness stand, and, looking back, I'm sure they never intended to do so. It was most likely part of a strategy to divide the family and further isolate Eddie from everything he knew and loved in hopes that he would capitulate and admit to a crime he didn't commit.

1 Letter to Margo Nash from Edward O'Brien, June 14, 2016

Although Eddie instructed his new lawyer, Bob George, to keep me informed of developments and decisions in the case, Bob and I hardly spoke during his two years of representation. Eddie's parents were similarly uninformed, told that everything was fine, and that they were in expert hands. Perhaps I should have pushed harder to be included in the decision-making. I believe now that there was only one person making legal decisions for Eddie: Bob George. I don't think he shared decision-making with anyone, not even the lawyers working for him.

I trusted that Eddie's lawyer knew what he was doing. He was more informed in murder cases than I. He was well-known in the Boston area. I didn't question him. I should have. I know that now. I don't know if he would have shared anything more with me, but at least I would know that I'd tried to protect Eddie.

My times with Eddie were limited. We attended his grandfather's wake, accompanied by two correctional officers, Eddie in handcuffs and leg irons. I saw him before the court day started, down in lockup for a few minutes, longer if there was a delay. I often brought a second lunch for him, to compensate for the lousy food the detainees got in the courthouse lockup and to remind him of home. We talked when the sheriff didn't take him directly back to the Plymouth Correctional Facility at the end of the day.

I visited him at the juvenile facility in Plymouth and at the Cambridge jail where he was housed during his trial. I sat through his psychological examination by the Commonwealth's expert, Dr. Donald Condie. I think I knew him as well as an adult non-family member could.

Eddie was emotionally and psychologically a young adolescent. He clearly didn't understand the proceedings or the gravity of what was happening. He got angry when a witness lied, but didn't understand how that lie might impact him. He was grateful and happy to see friends and hear them say good things about him in their testimony; he didn't understand their testimony would never affect the outcome. He was excited when an FBI profiler testified at his transfer hearing, someone who had written a book—Eddie talked about that a lot. He didn't grasp that this was a really bad development in his case.

Our talks revolved around the lies witnesses told, and how his lawyer "caught" the lie. He completely believed in Bob George. Eddie never thought for a minute that he would be convicted of murder. It was inconceivable to him. He hadn't killed Janet Downing. He had nothing to hide. He couldn't be convicted, because he didn't commit the crime. His grandfather was a cop. Cops were good guys. The truth would come out eventually.

I went to counsel's table during breaks in the proceedings to put my hands on Eddie's shoulders: I wanted to show everyone (including the TV audience in news reports and later Court TV coverage) that I wasn't afraid of him. Often he and one of the lawyers would be playing hangman or tic-tac-toe on a yellow pad in front of him. Eddie would be giggling and fooling around with them.

I never saw Eddie take one note during those two years. He was either engaged in a game with someone at the table, or was staring off into the distance, a blank look on his face.

I'd say, "What did you think about what Dr. Such-and-Such said?" He'd often reply, "Oh, I wasn't listening then. She was really boring."

He was a *kid.* His life was at stake, and he understood very little of what was happening around him.

I didn't understand everything that was happening, either. I didn't have access to DNA and blood evidence documents, police reports, the very things that with hindsight show the truth and the extent to which the Commonwealth went to obfuscate that truth to win this case.

Eddie wrote in June 2016:

*I had trust in my lawyers that they were doing the right thing by me. From the first day my parents hired Bob George, I felt that he had my best interests in mind. Before the trial I couldn't wait for it to begin. I thought that I would finally be able to clear my name, but it didn't happen.*

*I thought that I was going to take the stand and be able to speak for myself and defend myself, but then Bob George advised against it. He felt that the Commonwealth didn't prove that I was guilty and he didn't want me to take the stand. On his advice I didn't. In hindsight, I came to believe he only cared about the money and the publicity he received from the case. It was like he gave up after the transfer hearings, and couldn't wait to get rid of my case. I didn't see it at the time, but he could have done so much more, especially since he promised me so much more.*

A tsunami of politics, incompetence, and misconduct was swirling around him, and Eddie O'Brien was thinking, when this is all over, I can't wait to get home and play street hockey again.

*Eddie O'Brien in 2014*

# CHAPTER 1
## JUST ANOTHER SUNDAY

Eddie O'Brien's alarm went off at 6:30 a.m.; he would go to work by 7:00. Today he would put the Sunday newspapers together at the neighborhood variety store across the street from St. Joseph's Church in Union Square in Somerville, his hometown. Eddie had been working at the store for about two years.

He got ready for work. He had no other plans for the day.

It had been a difficult summer so far in the O'Brien home. His grandfather, "Papa" to Eddie, was home from a month-long stay at the Somerville Hospital: he had late-stage lung cancer. Papa refused further treatment or second opinions: he just wanted to go home.

Papa's room was the former dining room in the modest single-family Victorian house on Boston Street. Just the week before, on July 16, 1995, Eddie's parents had thrown a party for Papa's 80th birthday. All the neighbors dropped by because Papa—also known as T.J. or Chief—was a fixture in the neighborhood. He'd lived in that same house for thirty-six years, through two marriages and a long, distinguished career with the Somerville police. He had retired as chief the same year Eddie was born.

The family took the opportunity while Papa was in the hospital to clean out the attic: it was filled with boxes of things Papa had accumulated from his years with the Somerville Police Department. His youngest son, Ed, Ed's wife, Trisha, and the three children they had then—Jeannie,

Eddie, and Jessica—had moved into Papa's house in 1985, but this was the first opportunity they'd had to sort through things. Among the files and papers and ledger books they found, there were also guns, swords, knives, old billy clubs, police badges, and all the pins that had decorated Papa's old uniform jacket.

It was a treasure trove to a fifteen-year-old boy.

Eddie packed them into a box and brought them across the street to his friend Ryan Downing's house to show all his friends. This was a group of approximately six boys who hung out together, often at the Downing home. Ryan was Eddie's closest friend; they'd known each other since they were toddlers. The guys passed the knives and clubs around and imagined where they came from—and what they'd been used to do.

That Sunday in July 1995, Eddie worked all morning at the store with Walter Golden, the owner, and Walter's son-in-law, Frank Kling. He got a ride home from his sister Jeannie. He brought copies of the *Boston Globe* and the *Boston Herald* for his parents and a big Tootsie Roll for his three-year-old sister, Mary. He went back to bed and slept for a few hours.

It was a hot and humid summer day, hovering around 85 degrees, and the house wasn't air-conditioned. Eddie got up, ate a sandwich, and watched TV until it was time for the 5:30 Mass at St. Joe's. He told his parents he was going to church and left with his sister Jeannie and her friend Paul Downing, Ryan Downing's twin brother, and they dropped him off in Union Square.

When he got to the square, Eddie saw Frank Golden, Walter's son, working at the variety store, and went in to chat instead. The store was a familiar and safe place; even when he wasn't working, he liked to go there and read sports magazines, hang with his co-workers, and have a cold drink and a snack. Most of Eddie's friends dropped in to Mid-Nite at some point in their day.

He left the shop around 6:30, stopping briefly at the park to talk to some friends. After that he headed home again, running into Ryan Downing and two of their friends, Joey Dion and Chris Ford, outside Ryan's house. The boys went into the Downing home and hung out until almost 8:00, when everyone but Eddie left to go swimming in yet another friend's pool.

Eddie didn't want to join them; he was sensitive about his weight. At fifteen he still had the chubbiness of a pre-adolescent; he wasn't even shaving yet.

Eddie joined his father and three of his sisters—Jessica, twelve, Mary, three, and Megan, the baby—on the O'Briens' front porch. A neighbor, John Roberts, stopped by with his baby daughter and two-year-old son, Timothy, to chat. Eddie's grandfather was in the house. His sister Jeannie was out with Paul Downing. His mother was out.

It was getting darker outside. Eddie was thinking about going to his friend Garvey Salomon's house; Garvey had called earlier to see what everyone was up to. He didn't want to go swimming, either, and said he was going to stay home.

Jeannie pulled up in her car with Paul Downing and told her father that they were going to change and go to Revere Beach for a swim. Paul went into his house, and Jeannie came up to the O'Brien house. Eddie stayed outside in the street talking to Michelle Cameron, another of Jeannie's friends, who was waiting for Paul and Jeannie to get ready for the beach. The three left for Revere Beach at about 8:30.

Eddie returned to the porch and then went into the kitchen to get some popsicles for Timothy. At about 8:45, John decided it was time to go home; Eddie put the two-year-old on his shoulders and walked him across the street to his house. Then he went back and rewound and restarted a

Disney videotape for toddler Mary in the living room.

At about 9:15, after listening to the radio for a while in his room, Eddie decided to grab something to eat at the Burger King in Union Square and then go to his friend Garvey's house. On his way out, Eddie glanced over at the Downing house, wondering whether Ryan and the others had returned from their swim yet. He decided to check in there on his way down the hill to Union Square.

That decision changed the course of his life.

# CHAPTER 2

## JANET DOWNING

Janet Downing was a forty-two-year-old divorced mother of four children: Kerriann, twenty; Erin, nineteen; and twins Ryan and Paul Jr., sixteen. They lived on the corner of Hamlet and Boston Streets, at 71 Boston St. The house is a duplex, and Downing's family lived on the right side, along Hamlet Street. Janet rented the other half of the house to Barry and Virginia Reckley.

Janet Downing had known Eddie O'Brien almost all his life, as he and her son Ryan were best friends. The O'Briens moved from just down the Hamlet Street hill to across the street at 74 Boston St. when Eddie was five years old.

Most of the information I gathered about Janet Downing came from interviews with a neighbor, Gina Mahoney, who'd known her since they were both in their teens. Mahoney had grown up in the house at 70 Boston St. and raised her five children there. Although the two women lost touch with each other during the early years of their marriages, the friendship was rekindled when Janet and her husband, Paul, bought the duplex across the street from Mahoney in 1977. Mahoney said she and Downing did not "run in the same circles" as married adults, but were close neighbors. They borrowed and shared and talked the way neighbors often do. They watched out for each other.[2]

---

2 In addition to our interviews, Gina Mahoney provided me with digital media on which she had recorded all she remembered about Janet's murder many years ago.

Downing spent the last ten hours of her life on July 23, 1995, at Mahoney's house. She arrived at 7:00 that morning and left at 5:00 that evening to go grocery shopping. She was murdered in her own house sometime between 8:00 and 10:00 that night.

Downing had been living at 71 Boston St. for eighteen years, first with her husband and after the divorce with their children. She was a clerical worker at Harvard Health, in Medford, the next town over from Somerville.

Her oldest daughter, Kerriann, was living temporarily in a shelter with her baby. Kerri had a difficult adolescence complicated by emotional problems and substance abuse. "Janet and Paul did everything they could possibly do to help her. It broke Janet's heart to tell Kerri to get out of the house," said Mahoney.

Kerri's bedroom on the second floor was now empty. Erin also had a bedroom on the second floor of the house, near her mother's. Ryan and Paul, the sixteen-year-old twins, shared an attic room.

Janet Downing was born and raised in North Cambridge, one of five children. Mahoney remembers that two of Downing's brothers had mental health issues and that one of them spent time in and out of hospitals. Downing told her that both of her parents had also had mental health issues. When they were teenagers together, though, she and Downing never talked in depth about these things.

Downing's parents were very religious, born-again Christians, Mahoney said, though she didn't know the denomination. The parents "shunned" Downing after she converted to Catholicism. Downing loved them and wanted their approval, and was upset and hurt when they refused to speak to her. Downing was quiet and "meek," disliking confrontation and arguments. "A raised voice was violence to her," Mahoney said.

The neighborhood along Boston Street was family-oriented and filled with kids, with noise, bustle and life. No one rang a doorbell; people just walked in the door and yelled "Hello?" Mahoney said she'd never once locked her front door.

In the summer, people lived on their front porches and moved freely between houses, visiting one another. When someone came home with groceries, whatever kids were outside would help unload them. "It didn't matter if it was your kid or the neighbor's. You called for them, and they came," recalled Mahoney.

On that fateful day in 1995, "no sooner had I made my cup of coffee and gone out to the porch, when I saw Janet coming over with her cup of coffee." That was at 7:00 a.m. Downing left once to take Erin to a tanning booth, and again later to take young Paul to work. Both times she returned directly to Mahoney's house. She didn't leave until about 5:00, when she realized she had to get to Market Basket before it closed.

Downing had a lot on her mind that day. Primarily she was worried about her job; she thought her employer was trying to terminate her. She'd received an unfavorable performance review. She knew Mahoney had worked in a "union shop" all her life and wanted to get her opinion and advice. Downing described what was happening at work, a reorganization forcing her to apply for other positions for which she wasn't qualified.

Mahoney told her that the review seemed designed to give cause to terminate her rather than to portray her performance truthfully. She said she didn't know if filing a grievance would make any difference in the decision. Downing understood, but wanted to save her job if at all possible. Mahoney offered to write the letter disputing the performance review and give it to Downing the following morning. Downing seemed relieved, and they passed a few hours after that just chatting on the porch.

Eventually they went into the house for a cold drink. When Mahoney's daughter Danni, who was seventeen, asked about having a later curfew that night, Downing pointed out that there'd been a young girl murdered in Somerville the previous March. Danni abruptly left the room. Mahoney explained that she'd been close to the murdered girl, Deanna Cremmin, and was traumatized by the event. They discussed the murder investigation and how there were still no suspects after four months.

Downing then stunned Mahoney: she said that if anything like what happened to Cremmin ever happened to her, she wanted Mahoney to promise that she would make the police "investigate, investigate, investigate." She pounded her fist into her palm each time she said *investigate*. "No matter what it looks like, Gina, even a car accident, make sure it is thoroughly investigated. I would never kill myself!"

Mahoney asked the obvious questions. Why was she so adamant about this? Why had she even thought about it at all? Had someone threatened her?

Downing went back to her house and returned with a book called *A Guide for the Divorced Woman*. She told Mahoney that she had been reading this book every night. She kept it on her night table, and one night it was gone, though it had been there when she left that morning. A few days later, her brother-in-law, Artie Ortiz, appeared beside her car in the parking lot as she was leaving work with the book in his hand. He gave it to her and said he'd found it in a parking lot somewhere and knew it was Downing's. His sudden appearance holding her book terrified Downing.

Downing had been afraid of Ortiz to begin with. In the winter of 1994 she'd allowed him and her younger sister, Carol, and their baby, AJ, to move in with her and the kids.

Ortiz drove a taxi for Green Cab of Somerville.

Downing remodeled the downstairs den to accommodate Carol's family, even though it wasn't an ideal situation given Downing's struggles with Kerri and some recent acting out by Paul Jr. Artie and Carol fought constantly. The situation became untenable when Downing discovered Ortiz was dealing drugs out of her basement, so in March she asked Carol and Artie to leave the house. They'd been living with her for about a year by then.

Ortiz was angry with Downing for asking them to move out.

Other "scary" things had been happening in the house, Downing told Mahoney. Clothes would disappear and reappear days later in odd places. Christmas decorations were left in various rooms on the main floor. Downing believed Ortiz was following her and was doing these things to frighten her.

"Let me tell you a story, Gina," she said. One dark evening after Carol and her husband moved out, Downing said she was driving home from work and realized that she was suddenly surrounded by Green Cab taxis: one behind her, one on either side of her, and one in front. They kept beeping their horns at her. They had her boxed in as she drove slowly down the street. "I was shaking so hard, I couldn't look over at them, I had to just focus on not hitting them." She asked Mahoney if she'd ever seen a Green Cab taxi in the neighborhood.

"There's a Green Cab in your driveway almost every day when I get home from work at 3:30, Janet. He's there all the time. I thought you knew."

Downing had come home several times to find Ortiz inside the house. She repeatedly asked him to stay away and return her house keys, which he hadn't done when they moved out. Ortiz claimed he didn't have the keys, that he lost them and that the kids had let him in. When she asked the kids about it, each one denied it happening, and often said they hadn't seen him that day.

Once, Downing had forgotten to bring in a bottle of cooking oil from her car for a few days. When she finally brought it in, it was unsealed and she smelled perfume in it. Another time, someone poured windshield-washing liquid all over her car's interior, seats and rugs.

"Call the police," Mahoney advised her friend at once. "Get a restraining order! If you're afraid of this guy, and he's coming in and out of your house like that, you should call the police!"

Downing demurred. She didn't want to go to the police because it might look as if she was "crazy," and her ex could use that information if they had to go back to court. Downing was afraid that her family's history of mental illness would be used against her.

Mahoney told her to call if she ever felt she was in any danger. She promised to look for Ortiz's cab, and the next time she saw it in the driveway, she'd go confront him herself. Downing thanked Mahoney and left to do her grocery shopping.

Mahoney saw her neighbor return from Market Basket at about 6:15. Downing parked in front of the house rather than in the driveway, because it was easier to unload the groceries from there. Sometime after that, Mahoney went into her own house to make salad for dinner. When her husband got home from the racetrack, Mahoney sent him to the backyard to grill some steaks. They ate dinner, and she cleaned up.

It was after that she noticed Downing's car still sitting in front of the house, which was unusual; Downing always moved her car to the driveway after she brought the groceries in.

Later, Mahoney remembers, she was watching an HBO

movie about a riot at Attica prison. Just as the TV was showing sirens and lights, she could see straight through the dining room to the living room windows, where lights were also flashing. For a moment she couldn't distinguish between the TV sirens and the sirens in the street. When she realized something was happening outside, she jumped up and ran to the door. Police cars, a fire truck, and ambulances were everywhere.

# CHAPTER 3

## VIRGINIA RECKLEY

In 1995, Virginia Reckley and her husband, Barry, had been renting the other half of Janet Downing's duplex for five years. They knew Downing and her family well, and considered them good friends; they also knew the O'Briens and the Mahoneys. It was a close-knit neighborhood.

Virginia and Barry were home all day on July 23, 1995, babysitting their granddaughter. Their daughter, Christine, joined them at about 6:00 when she finished work. The family had a pasta dinner together and then went into the backyard to put the baby in the wading pool to cool her off.

Both Virginia and Christine remember clearly that they looked at the kitchen clock and it was 8:15 when they decided to come inside and get the baby dressed. Virginia took the baby to the dining room table to change her; the table stood against the wall that her side of the duplex shared with Janet Downing's stairwell.

Just then both women heard a loud booming sound from the bottom of the stairwell. More precisely, they heard what sounded like someone falling down hard the last four or five stairs to the bottom.

Christine was alarmed. "Mom, what was that? Should we check to see if anything is wrong?" They listened for a minute and heard nothing. The Downings' dog, a constant barker, wasn't barking, so Virginia said she thought it was okay, and they continued with what they were doing. It was Barry's birthday, and they were about to celebrate with a cake. They served it at 8:30; Christine remembers looking at the clock again to check on the time. After they finished, she packed her granddaughter's things; Christine and the baby left shortly before 9:00.

After Christine left, Virginia went into the kitchen to do the dishes and noticed there was no water pressure. This happened often if the Downings were using the water. It took forever to fill up the big pasta pot to soak. She washed the dishes and, again, noticed that it took a long time with so little water coming out of the faucet. When she finally finished, she dried her hands, wiped the counters, and went into the living room. Barry was lying on the floor, watching television, and Virginia sat down on the couch.

Virginia next remembers that Ed O'Brien, Trish's husband, came running by the front window yelling for help.

She thinks that was shortly after she'd finished the dishes, but isn't sure of the exact time. Virginia jumped up off the couch, and she and Barry ran with Ed into the Downing home.

The first thing she saw was Janet Downing lying on the dining room floor; then she noticed the hallway powder room's sink was running full force, water slopping over the edge of the sink. *So that's why I had no water*, she thought.

Her feet were bare, and she stepped on a framed picture lying on the floor. Luckily, the glass didn't break. Just then she saw Ryan coming in the front door with his rollerblades on. She grabbed him and took him outside. Barry stayed inside the house for over an hour after the police arrived.

As it turned out, Virginia and Barry Reckley were never interviewed by the Somerville police. Not that night, not the next week, not the next year. They were never interviewed by the State Police CPAC Unit, the Crime Prevention and Control Unit attached to the District Attorney's Office that investigated all murders in Middlesex County. It was not until about two weeks before she was to testify for Eddie O'Brien's defense in late September 1997, more than two years after Janet Downing's murder, that the DA interviewed her.

It seems incredible and indefensible that the first people on the scene, people who actually shared a common wall with the murder victim, were not included in the police investigation.

The problem with Virginia and Barry Reckley, from the prosecution's point of view, was that their testimony would establish a serious commotion happening on Downing's stairs at about 8:15. This would exclude Eddie O'Brien as a suspect, and was inconsistent with the case the prosecution was building against him. They knew where Eddie was at 8:15—he was on his own front porch.

The Reckleys also could establish that the Downings' hallway sink apparently was running full force at 9:00 when Virginia was trying to wash the dishes. Eddie's whereabouts were clearly accounted for between 8:00 and 9:15.

The elected district attorney, Thomas Reilly, chose to prosecute this case himself. He "vehemently defended the probe, saying Reckley had nothing 'new' to offer," according a statement made to reporters Ann Donlan and Bill Hutchinson just a few weeks after the murder.[3]

Eddie O'Brien's first attorney hired an investigator immediately after he was arrested. He took Virginia Reckley's statement in August 1995. District Attorney Reilly had that report since 1995. He knew what Virginia Reckley heard and saw that night. Yet he chose not to follow up on that information.

Notwithstanding the unequivocal observations of the next-door neighbors, Reilly would ask a jury to believe that

3 Donlan, Ann E. and Bill Hutchinson, "Cops Failed to Quiz Two Witnesses in Brutal Slaying," The Boston Herald, August 10, 1995

Eddie O'Brien went into the Downing home at about 9:15 and, between that time and a knock at the front door by his friends at approximately 9:20, brutally attacked Downing, dragged her from the front den through the living room, up the stairs, down the stairs, while stabbing her ninety-eight times. In the midst of this killing spree, he removed her bra, sliced it thirty-six times, and placed it back on her body. Eddie allegedly also spent some time inflicting some twenty-two slicing wounds on the victim's neck, wounds inflicted after she was unconscious or immobile.

Reilly would ask the jury to believe that Eddie then turned on the hallway sink and washed himself clean, but somehow left huge smears of blood on both sides of the basement stairwell walls, on the post at the bottom of the stairs, on the clothes on the line, and on the latch and surface of the cellar door to the backyard. This was the DA's theory of the case at this point.

Virginia Reckley had very important information that would need to be ignored if DA Reilly was to convince a jury that Eddie was the murderer.

# CHAPTER 4

## GINA MAHONEY

Seeing all the commotion at the Downing house, Gina Mahoney immediately thought there must be a crisis with Kerri. "I went out the front door and saw several emergency vehicles parked around Janet's house," she explained. "I assumed that her daughter Kerri had come by and that they were in a confrontation. This was a frequent event when Kerri was there, and Janet's way to handle it was to call the police. My temper flared, and I decided that with all of the other problems Janet had told me about, I would go over and lay into Kerri. I walked past the policeman standing on Janet's walkway and went into the foyer. I could see the EMTs working on Janet and I couldn't see Kerri anywhere around so I went back out."[4]

Mahoney said she returned to her porch to watch what was happening. She was there only a minute when she saw Artie Ortiz walking from Hamlet Street toward her porch. He looked, she reported, "as fresh as a daisy." Everyone else was wilted from the humid summer heat, but Ortiz looked like he'd just stepped out of a cool shower, with wet and freshly combed hair. Ortiz told her that his dispatcher had radioed him to say that his sister-in-law had been murdered.

Mahoney wondered how he could have known that when Downing was still inside with the EMTs.

Mahoney saw Ortiz's Green Cab parked the wrong way on Hamlet Street beside Downing's backyard (facing toward

4 Information taken directly from disks Gina Mahoney made on her computer on May 24, 2003, to have a record of everything she remembered about that night.

the bottom of the hill, on the left side of the street instead of the right side). She noticed that it was blocked in by a fire engine, police car, and ambulance, which meant that Ortiz had been parked there before the first responders even arrived. And he certainly didn't look like he'd been driving a cab all night.

Ortiz asked if he could use the phone to call his wife, Janet's sister. Mahoney's daughter went inside to get it for him.

"He stepped off of the porch and was leaning against the car at the curb. He turned back to us and announced, 'Well, she's officially dead now.'[5] He handed me back the phone and reached into his pocket, then he started patting himself down, looking in pockets, and kept saying, 'Oh, shit, oh, shit,' then he shouted that he'd lost his keys and that he had to find them right now. He took off at a run across the street toward Janet's house. The police had begun to put the yellow tape around the property. Artie was searching around the back and sides of the cab, then he sprinted across Janet's lawn and a cop stopped him. He told the cop that he lost his keys and wanted to go in the backyard of the house and look for them. The cop told him that he couldn't come beyond the tape until it was removed. The cop also told him that if his keys were found, they would be returned to him.

"Artie came back and was repeatedly saying that he *had* to find those keys *now*. He asked me if I thought that the police would be leaving soon, and I explained that I thought that the procedure would be to leave a cop on the site to keep people from getting in past the tape. Artie was very upset and said that he needed to get over there to look for his keys, that he couldn't leave them behind. He again went across the street and asked the cop if he could search for his keys but

5 In fact, Janet Downing was not pronounced dead until after her arrival at Massachusetts General Hospital.

he came back to my house and said that the cop wouldn't let him go into the backyard to look for his keys. He asked to use the phone again, to call the company to have the cab towed away."

A few minutes later, Jessica O'Brien, Eddie's twelve-year-old sister, came running out of the O'Brien house, calling for her father. Mahoney told her he was inside Downing's house. Mahoney went with Jessica to the Downing house and asked one of the cops to get "Big Ed."

Jessica told her father, "Little Ed got hurt. He just called from Mid-Nite."

Mahoney returned to her house. She later found out that her daughter had been up in her bedroom smoking a joint with Ortiz.

Eventually, Ortiz's cab was towed. Ortiz remained around the crime scene for hours afterward. "He was frantic about having lost his keys, he kept commenting on what trouble he was going to be in for losing them *over there*," wrote Mahoney in her recollections. "I remember saying that it probably was a common happening and that they would have duplicate keys at the dispatch office. He just said, 'You don't understand, this is really bad, I'm fucked now.'"

As the hours passed, Paul Downing and Jeannie O'Brien returned from Revere Beach. Janet's ex-husband, Paul, also arrived, as did Erin and Kerriann, their two daughters. Mahoney sat on the curb and held young Paul in her lap while he cried and cried. His father was also crying.

None of what Downing told Mahoney on the last day of her life would ever be heard by a jury. Similarly, what Ortiz told Mahoney about Downing being murdered and "officially dead now," or how he had managed to lose his keys in Downing's backyard, would not be disclosed to the jury in Eddie's trial. All of these statements were deemed "inadmissible hearsay" by Judge James McDaniel, a former

Middlesex County assistant district attorney who presided over the trial.[6] Hearsay is considered unreliable in terms of proof because there's no opportunity to cross-examine the person who actually said the words. There are many exceptions to the hearsay rule, but only one ineffective attempt to get this testimony in through one of those exceptions was made by the defense.

No detectives or investigators would testify about what Downing told Mahoney that day because the CPAC investigators refused to interview Mahoney. Her information would not appear in any police reports or narratives of the investigation into the murder. When the Somerville police first came to Mahoney's house on Monday morning, the day following Downing's murder, they asked only two questions: "When was the last time you saw Janet Downing?" and "When did she leave your house?" Mahoney made it clear she had additional information, but the police said that was all they needed at that time.

The DA, the CPAC Unit, and the Somerville police had already decided who had committed this murder. They believed they had their bad guy and weren't interested in considering any alternative perpetrator.

When investigators discovered that Eddie O'Brien had a cut on his hand and had been taken to Somerville Hospital that Sunday night, they didn't believe him when he said that he'd been mugged in Union Square. They immediately connected Downing's murder with Eddie's lacerated right hand. Local and state police arrived at the hospital and asked the nurse to swab a small drop of blood from Eddie's right shin.

---

6 Judge James McDaniel was the head of the Civil Rights Division while working at the District Attorney's Office and supervised a young ADA named Thomas Reilly. A motion to recuse the judge was filed and argued by Eddie O'Brien's attorney and denied by Judge McDaniel.

Eddie and his father were brought to the Somerville police station that night and questioned at length. Eddie's clothes and sneakers were seized. His fingerprints were taken. Early Monday morning, Eddie was released into his father's custody, but it was clear that he was a suspect. He would be formally arrested in the slaying one day later.

Seasoned homicide detectives say that the worst mistake investigators can make is to focus too quickly on one suspect.

Over the course of the next year, Mahoney repeatedly called the detective bureau to say that she wanted to tell them what Downing had said on the day she died. Each time Mahoney was told that the detectives had all the information they needed about Downing.

Eventually Mahoney just stopped calling the police.

# CHAPTER 5

## EDDIE O'BRIEN

Just before 9:15 that Sunday night, Eddie closed his bedroom door and walked down to the first floor. On the way, he yelled to his father in the kitchen that he was going to Burger King. Jessica was in the living room watching TV. Papa was in his room. Eddie's mother was at a musical event.

Eddie headed across the street to Ryan's house. He was still wearing the same white "Over the Rim" T-shirt, black sneakers, and green shorts he'd worn all day. He went up to the Downing house and knocked on the window as he always did. He heard a loud bang as though someone had fallen.

He thought he heard someone say, "Help!" The front door was ajar, so he stepped into the small foyer, opening the second door leading to the hallway. The house was dimly lit inside.

Eddie saw blood on the stairs, blood in the front hallway. The bathroom door was closed. He looked to his right and saw Downing lying on her side on the dining room floor. Thinking she had fainted or fallen, he ran to her; when he put his hand on her he realized she wasn't conscious. He saw blood all over the floor. He couldn't understand how she could get hurt that badly by falling down.

Eddie turned Downing over onto her back and saw the extent of her injuries. There was blood all over the front of her blouse and cuts on her neck going ear to ear. He saw her eyes half-open. She wasn't breathing.

Eddie shook her and called her name. Nothing happened, and he stood up to run out the front door for help. That was when he saw a tall male, with dark hair and dark clothes, standing in front of the door. The man moved into the hallway, stepped up to Eddie, and said, "Close the door!" He had a knife and held it to Eddie's throat; Eddie reached back and closed the inside front door. He didn't recognize the voice. Then the man grabbed him by the arm and said, "If you say anything, I'll kill you and your family, and I'll have time before the police catch me. Now get the fuck out of here."

Eddie tried to see who he was, but he couldn't make out his features; the man was wearing a nylon stocking over his face with a tear on the left side close to his ear. He was wearing "like surgical gloves," Eddie reported to Dr. Paul A. Spiers, a clinical neuropsychologist, in an interview with the defense's expert witness in October 1995.[7]

There was a knock at the front door. Time seemed to stop. The man said again, "Get the fuck out of here!"

Eddie ran through the dining room past Downing's apparently lifeless body and into the kitchen, grabbed the knob on the cellar door and pulled the door open. He couldn't bring himself to look back. He worried that the guy might leave by the front door as he went down to the basement. He flew down the steep cellar stairs, and hit a pillar at the bottom. There was laundry hanging on lines in the damp

---

7 Evaluation of Dr. Paul A. Spiers, Ph.D., dated January 5, 1996. Eddie was interviewed both before and after administration of sodium amytal, often called "truth serum," by this doctor at his attorney's request. A videotape was made of the entire interview and formed the basis of the defense's contention that Eddie happened upon the scene as the murder was taking place, and ran for his life. This videotape was made available to the prosecution as well. The district attorney had full knowledge of what Eddie's story was regarding the murder of Janet Downing very early on in the case.

basement. He pushed his way past it and headed for the door to the backyard. It was wide open, and he ran out. That door, he said, was always latched closed. "A couple of years ago, Janet put—um—like a bolt on the door because—um—her younger daughter's boyfriend—ah—used to break in the house and sleep downstairs, so she put the bolt on, and that bolt was open."[8]

He does remember hitting the bushes outside and falling into them, but he doesn't remember any pain or feeling scratched by the sticker bushes. He remembers not wanting to go directly to the right out the door onto Hamlet Street, because the guy might have been there, so he went through the bushes in the back.

Eddie made his way to the sidewalk on Hamlet Street and heard voices calling him. Determined to get away from the man inside the house—and the memory of seeing Ryan's mother lying in a pool of blood—he headed down Hamlet Street toward Highland Avenue.

He was terrified. He couldn't think. He'd never been so scared in his life. He'd never seen anyone seriously injured, let alone stabbed. Eddie completely believed that the man would harm him and his family if he told anyone what he had just seen. He never considered calling the police. He was afraid to tell his parents. His whole family would have to move someplace else, go into hiding.

He could tell no one, because he had to protect his family.

What Eddie really wanted was to go back to his house and start all over again, this time without stopping at Ryan Downing's house. He wanted to pretend that none of this had happened. He wished he'd gone swimming. He wished he'd gone over to Garvey's house. His heart was beating out of his chest and he didn't know what to do or where to go. He felt trapped, frozen, and alone.

---

8 Ibid.

Eddie next remembers going into the Burger King to wash his face. He was sweating profusely. He doesn't remember his hand being cut at that time. He doesn't recall any pain in his hand or blood in the sink. He splashed water on his face and tried to think what to do. He told Dr. Spiers in 1995, "I was in there for about 15, 20 minutes—and just thought everything over, and I couldn't believe what just happened, and I washed up a little bit from when I went through—ah—the wooded area. I had scratches on me."

He left Burger King and was on Somerville Avenue when he said two teenagers suddenly confronted him, demanding his money and flashing a knife. He handed over the $17.00 in his pocket and looked at the kid who took it. "Now I'm gonna have to cut you 'cause you saw my face," the kid said and lunged at him. Eddie sidestepped and reached out to shield himself from the knife. It cut his right hand. At least that's when Eddie believes he got cut; the first he remembers knowing he was cut was when he went inside Mid-Nite Convenient a few minutes later.

As a lawyer, or even as a layperson, at this point, one has to ask: What are the odds that a fifteen-year-old kid would see a murder and then get robbed both within one half-hour? A zillion to one? It's just not believable. A jury will never buy it. Lose this story, Eddie, you will never convince a jury that this happened, I thought.

Again, retelling it to me, the same story he told years ago, he says, "I wish I could tell you that it didn't happen, that I made it up out of fear. I wish I could tell you absolutely that it was here that my hand got cut. But it did happen, and I don't remember actually getting cut by that knife, either. I just remember being in complete shock and handing them my money."

Eddie reminds me again he's had twenty years to come up with a story that would be more believable or consistent with the evidence. Yet in our interviews inside the Souza-Baranowski Correctional Center in July 2015 he told the same things to me that he told Spiers in 1995. "Don't you think that I could have come up with a better story by now?"

The only difference I can detect is that he remembers less now than he did then. That's not unusual: Every witness I've re-interviewed remembers less now than twenty years ago. Trauma erases memories.

I pressed Eddie about how he'd cut his hand. "If they found traces of your blood at the scene, then you must have gotten cut at Janet's house. Did you grab for the knife, Eddie?" In reliving those horrific moments with me, over twenty years later, he lamented: "I wish I could just tell you, 'Yes, I tried to grab his knife, and I must have gotten cut.'"

That would so easily explain why his blood and DNA were found in four places[9] in the house: inside the inner front door, the right door jamb of the dining room, the wooden post at the bottom of the cellar stairs, and on the pink dress on the laundry line in the basement. But he doesn't remember getting cut in that house. He doesn't remember feeling any pain, and he doesn't remember bleeding. He's had twenty years to come up with a plausible story, but he refuses say he remembers something that he doesn't, even if it would help his case.

How could his blood have been detected at the scene if he didn't get cut there? The only possible explanations for finding his blood in the four swabbed samples are:

1. The swabs were contaminated somewhere between the police gathering the evidence, logging them into evidence, and transporting the swabs to the State Police

9 These samples were the only four of almost ninety collected at the scene that were not sent to the FBI lab. They remained in custody at the state lab before being sent for DNA testing on September 6, 1996, fourteen months after the murder.

forensic lab for blood typing tests.
2. The swabs were contaminated during transport from the State Police Crime Laboratory to Cellmark Diagnostics in Maryland for DNA testing.
3. The swabs were contaminated in the State Police lab or at Cellmark Diagnostics; or
4. Eddie's blood was deliberately placed on those swabs to implicate him.

All of these scenarios would need to be investigated to make sure that the blood evidence found at the scene had not been contaminated, either intentionally or inadvertently.

Still, I wanted Eddie to remember every detail, and I became frustrated and annoyed when he said, "Margo, I *don't remember*."

Eddie does remember that he ran into the Mid-Nite Convenient store, his safe place, and told them he'd been "jumped." He didn't elaborate. Frank, the clerk, dialed the police and handed Eddie the phone. The police and EMTs arrived about fifteen minutes later and looked at the cuts on his right hand. There was a cut in the top crease of his pinky finger; another was located in the fleshy pad on his palm about an inch under his pinky finger. Another cut was on the tip of his right thumb, starting at the middle of the thumb and going straight down toward his palm, about half an inch long. His hand wasn't bleeding, and the EMTs didn't believe Eddie needed any further medical attention. The Somerville police drove Eddie home.

Papa wanted Eddie to go to the Somerville Hospital to get a tetanus shot and be evaluated. While they were there waiting for the doctor to stitch up his hand, the police arrived and asked the nurse to swab a drop of dried blood on Eddie's shin. Eddie recalls this happened before his father arrived, but he's not 100 percent sure. No consents or Miranda waivers were signed. Eddie's father didn't object to the swabbing of his son's shin.

Of course he didn't. If it helped determine who mugged Eddie, why would he object?

The police asked Ed and Eddie to come to the station to be interviewed. Ed was concerned by now that his son was being considered a suspect in the Downing murder, but he was assured that local and state police were only investigating the mugging. At the station, both Ed and Eddie signed Miranda waivers and cooperated fully. They had nothing to hide. Eddie hadn't done anything wrong.

Eddie hadn't yet told his parents what he'd seen that night and didn't tell them until two weeks after his arrest. He was still fearful of jeopardizing his family's safety. He was sure the police would figure out he hadn't killed Downing and would release him.

Eddie was photographed at the Somerville Police Department that night; he still had on the same clothes he'd had on all day. The photos show that there was no visible blood on him. His shirt had a faint watery blood smear consistent with his hand wound. All these items were later tested by the police. He did have visible scratches over his arms and legs from the sticker bushes.

Janet Downing had been stabbed approximately ninety-eight times. Some sixty-six of these wounds were deep stab wounds, some four to five inches deep, to her chest, torso, back, neck, skull, ear, legs, and arms. The rest were slash wounds on her neck and body. Some were long superficial cuts inflicted deliberately while she was unconscious or dead.

Blood was everywhere at the scene. It was visible on the first five stairs and walls of the stairway that led up to the bedrooms; it was on the hallway walls, on doors and woodwork in the dining room, and in the kitchen. There was a huge puddle of blood on the dining room floor where

Downing lay. Blood drops were on the hallway floor, the kitchen floor, and blood was smeared all the way down both sides of the cellar stairway walls. There was blood all over the cellar door and iron latch leading out to the backyard.

You don't need to be a forensic expert to understand that it would have been impossible for Eddie to commit that homicide, a homicide that included a struggle traversing three rooms and a flight of stairs, and not get a single drop of blood on his white shirt, green shorts, or black sneakers.

And yet the police charged Eddie O'Brien with murder on the night of July 25, 1995. The fact that police found no blood on his clothes, in the creases of his hands, under his fingernails, or on his size 15 sneakers was just an inconvenient truth. The fact that he had no motive to harm his best friend's mother was of no consequence. The DA could—and would—fill in those blanks later.

Why this rush to arrest? Why not a more thorough investigation first? After all, Eddie wasn't a flight risk. He was about to enter his sophomore year in high school, his family was firmly entrenched in the local community. There was no need to arrest him less than forty-eight hours after the murder before any real investigation had begun.

This was no longer a search for the truth; it was a search for evidence that would convict Eddie O'Brien.

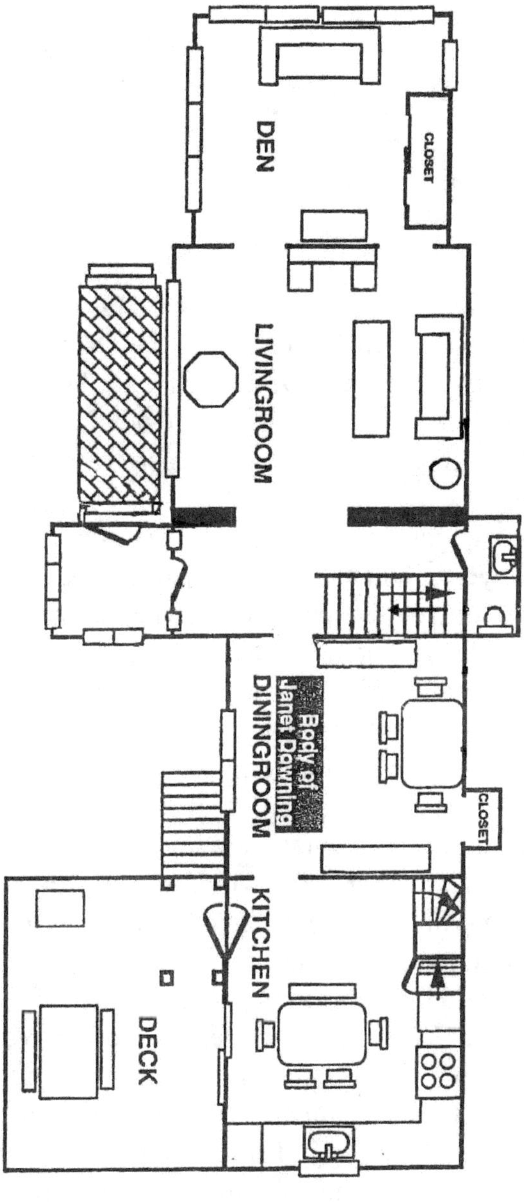


First Floor – 71 Boston Street, Somerville, MA

# CHAPTER 6

## ARTIE ORTIZ

Aristides J. Ortiz was the husband of Carol Ortiz, Janet Downing's younger sister. In March 1994, the Ortizes and their toddler, AJ, moved into the Downing home. Downing and her children reported to many friends and neighbors that the couple fought constantly and that it wasn't a pleasant living environment.

Although the arrangement was supposed to be temporary, it lasted almost a year. When Downing learned that Ortiz was dealing drugs out of the basement of her house, she demanded that they leave; she told Gina Mahoney that Ortiz kept the drugs in a small refrigerator in the basement.

Ryan Downing, in one interview with the police, reported that several weeks before the murder, he came home from school and saw the outside basement door wide open. Had Ortiz continued dealing drugs? Mahoney said that Ortiz was at the Downing home often while Downing was at work and the children were in school. Downing said he had keys to the house that he refused to return to her.

Janet Downing told three different people (her best friend Jean McGeary, Gina Mahoney, and her co-worker Mary Madeline Riveira) about the Green Cab taxis surrounding her on Summer Street, about things being moved around in her house and clothes appearing in Erin's closet that weren't Erin's, about Christmas ornaments being found around the house, about her book disappearing from her nightstand and being returned to her in the parking lot by Ortiz several weeks later, about windshield washer fluid being poured on her car seats. All of these events had occurred since Ortiz moved out in March.

Not once did Downing mention to any of these people that she suspected Eddie O'Brien of these things. She told Mahoney that she suspected Ortiz.

Reporter Margery Egan wrote in the *Boston Herald* that "Jean McGeary, Janet Downing's closest friend, says that Downing was upset, unnerved by the odd appearances, and disappearances, in her home. The bag of strange clothes that materialized out of nowhere. Her daughter Erin's house keys, missing since Christmas. But never, ever did Downing tell McGeary of any suspected connection to Eddie O'Brien."[10]

Every witness interview is required to be documented in a police report. That is standard police procedure. There was no police report filed of the interviews with Jean McGeary and Artie Ortiz. Why? Was something discovered that was harmful to the Commonwealth's case?

The theory District Attorney Tom Reilly would present depended on jurors believing that Eddie O'Brien, secretly obsessed with Janet Downing, was the one sneaking in and out of the Downing home. In both Juvenile Court transfer hearings that were held, Reilly suggested—through well-prepared witnesses Paul and Ryan Downing—that Eddie O'Brien might have been breaking into the Downing house and moving things around, making Eddie appear predatory and obsessed, and providing a motive for the killing. Although Reilly didn't have to prove motive, it's very difficult to convict someone of first-degree murder when no motive is apparent. All Reilly needed to do was suggest that it could have been Eddie.

Police refused, over and over again, to interview Gina

---

10 Egan, Margery, "When Tragedy Hits Home," Boston Herald, July 30, 1995

Mahoney. They seemed intent on avoiding having any reports containing contradictory evidence in the official investigation file. Statements of a witness like Jean McGeary, who would not have agreed with the Commonwealth's theory, could have been ignored in a different way: If the interview weren't documented in writing, the defense would not have access to the information.

The Brady Rule[11] requires prosecutors to disclose to the defense any materially exculpatory evidence the government possesses. "Brady material," or evidence the prosecutor is required to disclose under this rule, includes any evidence favorable to the accused: evidence that goes toward negating a defendant's guilt, that would reduce a defendant's potential sentence, or that goes to a witness's credibility.

The only way to get around the Brady Rule is to not have the information in your possession. If there's no written report, there is no possession. Even though standard police procedure, especially in a murder investigation, requires that all interviews be documented in a formal report, it's not always done.

We know Ortiz was interviewed because on Tuesday afternoon, July 25, 1995, two days after the murder, he surprised Mahoney by returning to her house. He told her he'd been questioned by the police and they'd told him that the investigation was concentrated on Little Ed. He showed Mahoney a drawing of a knife that the police made during the questioning. To Mahoney, it appeared to be a common kitchen knife, used for chopping vegetables. Ortiz reported that the police asked him if Little Ed knew where Downing kept her kitchen knives.

And then Ortiz added that he and Downing had talked many times in the past and Downing had insisted, if anything ever happened to her, that she wanted him and Carol to have

---

11 Named for Brady v. Maryland, 373 U.S. 83 (1963)

her car.

Her *car*? His sister-in-law is brutally murdered, and two days later he wants her *car*? And it didn't stop there. Downing also, Ortiz continued, wanted him and Carol to move into her house, raise her children, and take care of her property. Needless to say, this was hardly credible, since he'd been thrown out of the house three months before.

Eddie didn't recognize the man who threatened him at the Downing home as Artie Ortiz. However, Ortiz had been able to enlist the help of others in the taxicab incident. It is not inconceivable that he could have done so again. Or Eddie could have been mistaken.

When interviewed by Dr. Spiers in October 1995, Eddie said the basement door was wide open when he ran out. Paul Downing told police that his mother had been sleeping on the couch when he closed the front door and left the house to go to Revere Beach at 8:30. He claimed that the door locked automatically when closed. Downing would have been alone in the house after Paul left at 8:30.

When Eddie arrived at approximately 9:15, the front door was unlocked and ajar. Only the inside door to the house was closed. Someone had opened the front door.

Marco Abreu, John Fitzpatrick, and Joey Dion, Ryan Downing's friends, knocked at the door at 9:20. They all said the outside front door was open. No one answered the inner door when they knocked.

Ryan said he came home and discovered his mother's body at 9:55. He reported that he had to open the front door with a key because it was closed and locked. Someone had to have locked that door between Eddie fleeing the house at 9:20 after the boys knocked and Ryan's return home at 9:55.

The police determined that there was no forced entry to the house. The back door was locked. Downing's purse and keys were on the kitchen counter. There was no robbery.

Someone had opened the front door between when Paul left his mother napping on the couch and when Eddie arrived. Someone had been in the basement and opened the basement door to the backyard sometime between 8:30 and 9:15. Eddie was at his home across the street during all of that time.

Whose taxicab was parked beside the backyard? Ortiz's. Whose taxi was unable to move because it was surrounded by the emergency vehicles that arrived at 9:56? Ortiz's. Who said he lost his keys in the backyard of 71 Hamlet St. that night? Ortiz. The keys were reportedly found in the backyard and returned to him, but there's no mention of the keys in the investigatory file that was turned over to the defense.

Mahoney said that for more than one year after the murder, Ortiz repeatedly appeared wherever she happened to be. She would see him in his cab behind her as she drove. She would see him on Boston Street, driving by her house after she came home from work, or at the shopping mall, grocery store, post office. One day she went to the O'Briens' home to meet with Eddie's lawyers. They stood in the front window as Mahoney said, "Okay, he should be right along soon," and they watched Ortiz go by in the cab, slowing down as he looked out the window. I asked her to estimate how many times she found him following her that next year, and Mahoney said, "at least 200 to 300 times."

Why? And more importantly, why weren't the police and District Attorney Tom Reilly in the least bit interested to hear about any of this?

# CHAPTER 7

## CHANGES IN THE JUVENILE LAW

When Eddie O'Brien entered the juvenile justice system in July 1995, it had already changed significantly in the prior four years. Legislative amendments had been enacted in a flurry of angry and fearful responses to two incidents involving three particularly horrific homicides, all committed in the city of Boston by juveniles. These were the murders of Kimberly Rae Harbour, Charles Copney, and Korey Grant.

Before that, the Massachusetts juvenile justice system was based on a model that mandated educational, social, clinical, and diagnostic services to kids adjudicated as delinquent. This system replaced the earlier "reform school" or "training school" model, which was punitive, physically abusive, and lacking in any meaningful rehabilitation. The new system was based on the premise that kids younger than seventeen years old found guilty of crimes should be treated differently than their counterparts were treated in the adult criminal justice system. Adolescents were not able to make wiser, more thoughtful choices. They were impulsive and often unable to consider the consequences of their actions. They were heavily influenced by both their peers and their environment.

Before 1991, in order to be tried as an adult, a youth between the ages of fourteen and seventeen had to have been charged with an offense that, for an adult, would be punishable by incarceration in state prison (as opposed to county jail) and they had to have been previously found delinquent in Juvenile Court and placed in the custody of the Department of Youth Services. Under those narrow exceptions, the prosecution could request a hearing to have that adolescent moved to adult court. At that hearing the judge had to find, by clear and convincing evidence, both that the juvenile presented a significant danger to the public and that he was not amenable to rehabilitation through treatment in the juvenile justice system.[12]

The two amendments to the law in 1990 and 1991 changed the standards by which adolescents could be tried in adult court. They also reflected the new political agenda regarding violent juveniles emerging in the early 1990s around the country. Politicians, social scientists, and conservative legislators were clamoring for more punishment and less rehabilitation.

## THE HARBOUR AMENDMENT

On October 31, 1990, Kimberly Rae Harbour, a twenty-six-year-old mother, was dragged into Franklin Field in the Dorchester section of Boston by a group of teens. She was beaten, repeatedly raped, stabbed 132 times and left for dead. Three sixteen-year-olds and two fifteen-year-olds, thought to be gang members, were arrested shortly after. Three "adult" suspects (a seventeen-year-old, an eighteen-year-old, and a nineteen-year-old) were also arrested. The victim and all of the suspects were African-American.

Governor William F. Weld believed in retribution, not rehabilitation. [13]

---

12 Massachusetts General Laws, c. 119, sec. 61 et seq.

13 Oddo, Danielle R., "Removing Confidentiality Protections and the 'Get Tough' Rhetoric: What Has Gone Wrong with the Juvenile Justice System?" 18 B.C. Third World L.J. 105 (1998) - See Also Task Force on Juvenile Justice, "The Massachusetts Juvenile Justice System of the 1990s: Re-Thinking a National Mode," 21 J. CRIM. & CIV. CONFINEMENT 339, 350-51 (1995)

On December 5, 1990, long before any of the defendants would go to trial, the Massachusetts Legislature amended the juvenile transfer laws. The amendment declared that any adolescent between the ages of fourteen and sixteen charged with murder was presumed not to be amenable to rehabilitation in the juvenile justice system. The incoming Republican governor, Weld, who took office just two days after the law became effective, enthusiastically supported this new amendment.

## THE COPNEY-GRANT AMENDMENT

One year after Harbour's murder, Charles Copney, age eleven, and Korey Grant, age fifteen, were shot and killed while playing in front of Charles' house in the Roxbury section of Boston. Two fifteen-year-olds and one sixteen-year-old were arrested almost immediately. Both the victims and the three suspects were African-American. Prosecutors announced at the arraignment two days later that they would seek to have the youths tried as adults. This case would test the effectiveness of the new Harbour Amendment in getting adolescents into adult court.

At the transfer hearings in Juvenile Court, two of the three were transferred to adult court, where they were tried on two counts of first-degree murder. A jury found them not guilty of murder, but guilty of possession of a gun. One had his conviction overturned shortly after (due to false testimony by a police officer) and all charges against him were dismissed. Thc othcr, Willie Dunn, was sentenced to not more than five years in prison.

Ironically, fifteen-year-old Damien Bynoe, who actually fired the gun, wasn't transferred to adult court. He waived a trial, admitted to the murders, and was sent to juvenile lockup until his twenty-first birthday, the maximum allowed under the juvenile law at that time.

The Weld administration and outraged legislators, in response to Bynoe's sentence, passed the Copney-Grant Amendment, giving a prosecutor the right to appeal when a judge refuses to transfer an adolescent charged with murder to adult court. The amendment also established minimum sentences for youths convicted of murder in Juvenile Court: fifteen years with eligibility for parole for first-degree murder, and ten years with eligibility for parole for second-degree murder. This meant that juveniles convicted of murder in Juvenile Court would first serve their sentences in a juvenile facility until age eighteen, after which they would move over to an adult facility to serve out the rest of their sentences. This became known as "split-sentencing."

These cases and changes in the juvenile law in Massachusetts set the stage for the explosion of what can only be described as hysteria around Eddie O'Brien's case. Between 1991 and 1995, when Eddie entered the juvenile justice system, there was a growing movement in Massachusetts (and the United States) of people who believed that our inner cities were about to become war zones for a juvenile population of "superpredators." Social scientist James A. Fox, a criminologist, warned of "a bloodbath of violence" that could soon wash over the land.[14]

Politicians from both major parties picked up the cry. "Superpredator dread had a racial component: it focused on young male African-Americans."[15] Boston already had a nationwide reputation for racism and racial unrest. It is no coincidence that the three murders that prompted the knee-jerk-response amendments passed by the legislators in 1990 and 1991 were crimes committed by young inner-city African-American males on young inner-city African-

14 Haberman, Clyde, "When Youth Violence Spurred 'Superpredator Fear,'" The New York Times, April 6, 2014

15 All quotes from Haberman's article above.

American victims.

Two of the staunchest proponents of superpredator laws in Massachusetts, Weld and Thomas Reilly, the Middlesex County district attorney, both were white men. The African-American district attorney for the inner city (Suffolk County), Ralph Martin, in whose county the three murders had actually taken place, remained silent on the issue.

In the early 1990s, Boston was still reeling from the school busing debacle of the 1970s when hundreds of white parents and their children marched in the streets, pelted school buses full of black children with rocks, and protested the forced busing of African-American children into their white neighborhoods. State Police troopers were called in and remained on duty in South Boston for the next three years. In 1974, the federal court took over the administration of the entire city school system; control was returned to the school committee only in 1988.

Images from that era are imprinted in the minds of Bostonians. Who could ever forget the 1976 photograph of a white teenager attacking an African-American man on City Hall Plaza with a pole holding the American flag?

*The Soiling of Old Glory*
*Pulitzer Prize 1977 - stanleyformanphotos.com*

But the case that most shamed Boston racially was that of Charles Stuart. In 1989, Stuart and his pregnant wife, Carol, were shot after attending a birthing class in the Mission Hill section of Boston, which, though racially mixed, contained a predominately African-American housing project. Charles Stuart reported that a black man had shot them. He lived; his wife did not.

Hundreds of police officers scoured the housing project, as well as the Mattapan, Roxbury, and Dorchester (i.e. African-American) sections of the city for the thirty-year-old, six-foot-tall black man in a tracksuit that Stuart had described. Two months later the police arrested Willy Bennett, age thirty-nine. He was vilified in the press. Seventy-three days after Bennett's arrest, Stuart jumped off the Tobin Bridge and the real story unfolded; Stuart had murdered his wife for the insurance money.

In any domestic crime, the police always suspect the husband or wife first, apparently unless you said you were shot and robbed by a black man. The city of Boston was indelibly tarnished by the way the police and the white population readily accepted Charles Stuart's version of events.

United States Attorney Wayne Budd initiated a federal inquiry into the arrest of Willy Bennett for the Stuart murder to investigate the "stop and search" tactics used by the Boston police. Budd was an African-American Republican who'd been appointed U.S. attorney by President Ronald Reagan shortly after Carol Stuart's murder. He was also a close friend and former law partner of Democrat Thomas Reilly, the Middlesex County district attorney. In fact, the two had formed Budd & Reilly, a Boston-based law firm and the largest minority-dominated firm in New England. Ralph Martin, who would become the Suffolk County district attorney, worked there as an intern, then later for Budd at the U.S. Attorney's Office. Budd put Martin in charge of the federal investigation into the Boston Police Department racism accusations.

In 1992, Governor Weld (who had preceded Budd as U.S. attorney in Massachusetts) appointed Ralph Martin to the Suffolk County District Attorney's Office. Fox Butterfield of *The New York Times* opined that the appointment was "a move intended to improve race relations in the city and shake up Boston's entrenched political and law enforcement worlds,"[16] adding that "aides to Governor Weld said he had become convinced of the need to appoint a black to the district attorney's post after the Los Angeles riots (following the Rodney King police beating). He was also heavily influenced by Wayne A. Budd." Butterfield characterized Ralph Martin as "a protégé of Mr. Budd."[17] Budd would, in 1997, become the campaign manager for Tom Reilly in his run for attorney general.

On July 26, 1995, Thomas F. Reilly walked into the courtroom in Somerville District Court for Eddie's arraignment and announced that he would personally be trying the Commonwealth's case against Edward S. O'Brien.

Never before had a sitting Middlesex County district attorney personally tried a case, and certainly not a "juvie" case. Middlesex is the largest county in New England, encompassing fifty-four cities and towns. Over 250 assistant district attorneys try more than 35,000 cases a year in nineteen courts. Reilly's decision to be the lead attorney in the O'Brien case was seen by political pundits and newspaper reporters alike as his first public move to position himself for a run for state attorney general. This case would draw national attention to the entire juvenile reform and

16 Butterfield, Fox, "Black Republican Is Appointed District Attorney for Boston Area," The New York Times, July 31, 1992

17 Ibid.

superpredator debate that was Weld and Reilly's agenda. It affected Martin because he was the DA in Suffolk County now, where the other teen murders had occurred.

What many people didn't know in July 1995 was that Weld also had political aspirations, and they were much more immediate. In November 1995, he announced his resignation as governor in order to run for the U.S. Senate against sitting Senator John Kerry.

By personally trying the O'Brien case, Tom Reilly became the public face of the fight for new and tougher laws for juvenile offenders. He would become the first prosecutor to use the Copney-Grant Amendment to appeal the initial decision to keep Eddie in Juvenile Court. He and Weld were both planning runs for new offices. They were united in their fight to change the juvenile justice laws. Reilly and Weld would both benefit politically from this case. The stakes were very high for both of them. Reilly had to succeed in sending Eddie to adult court and securing a first-degree murder conviction.

The bonus for them was that Eddie O'Brien was a Caucasian boy. Reilly would show the critics that white semi-urban juveniles charged with murder were prosecuted just like their African-American inner-city counterparts.

Reilly was prosecuting one of his own: a white, Irish, Catholic altar boy. Weld and Reilly could not have asked for a better scenario.

# CHAPTER 8

## THE FIRST TRANSFER HEARING

Eddie O'Brien was indicted by the grand jury in August 1995, just one month after his arraignment in Juvenile Court, with the district attorney presenting the case himself. Imagine what weight it carries for jurors to see the official they voted for, the elected district attorney for the largest county in Massachusetts, up there in person!

It's rare that a "true bill" (indictment) would *not* be handed down by a grand jury; Tom Reilly hardly needed to present this case himself. Usually there's one assistant district attorney who presents all the cases to the grand jury.

The indictment removed the need for the first part of the Juvenile Court transfer hearing (known as Part A) in which the Commonwealth had to prove that there was probable cause to hold the accused over for trial. The proceedings skipped directly to the second part of the transfer hearing (known as Part B), in which his amenability to rehabilitation was at issue, with Judge Paul Pierce Heffernan presiding.

Under the new Copney-Grant Amendment to the juvenile law, there was a presumption that Eddie was *not* amenable to rehabilitation within the juvenile justice system. It was up to Eddie to prove that he could be rehabilitated. Since he had the burden of proof, his part of the case was presented first.

With Eddie proclaiming his innocence in Janet Downing's murder, how was he to prove he was amenable to a program of rehabilitation for a crime he hadn't committed?

As is customary for these hearings, a psychiatric specialist was appointed by the court to do an in-depth evaluation of the juvenile defendant to determine whether he was a candidate for rehabilitation. For the purposes of these evaluations, the expert evaluator assumes that the youth committed the crime in order to determine if he would be amenable to the services offered in order to rehabilitate him.

In Eddie's case, his attorney made it clear in his instructions to Eddie and in his comments to the court that Eddie had a Fifth Amendment privilege against self-incrimination and that he had instructed Eddie not to discuss any aspect of the crime itself with the evaluator. The judge reiterated, over the Commonwealth's objection, that Eddie in fact did have the same constitutional rights as any other defendant, and he directed the psychiatrist not to inquire about the crime itself when meeting with Eddie.

His attorney's decision to press this Fifth Amendment issue would create more problems than it solved. Eventually it would give the Commonwealth reason to appeal the judge's final decision in the case.

Secondly, an important part of what is assessed by the psychiatrist is the level of remorse exhibited for the crime. Every time he could, the district attorney drove home the fact that the psychiatrist said Eddie expressed no remorse.

More importantly, though, allowing Eddie to tell his story would have put into evidence his version of what he saw that night. The Commonwealth already knew Eddie's version. Investigators had a copy of the "sodium amytal" interview with Dr. Spiers during which he discussed finding his best friend's mother slain that night. Eddie had told the same story both before and after the sodium amytal was administered.

There was just no reason for Bob George to instruct Eddie not to talk about what happened that night. It only hurt him in the end.

Judge Paul Heffernan was a well-respected jurist and the presiding judge of Somerville District Court. He'd spent a lifetime in the juvenile justice system and had heard hundreds of juvenile transfer hearings since his appointment to the bench in 1979. This was most likely District Attorney Tom Reilly's first transfer hearing and first foray into the world of juvenile delinquency proceedings.

The district attorney and Eddie's lawyer both stipulated that the court would appoint Dr. Richard Barnum, a child and adolescent forensic psychiatrist, to evaluate Eddie and present his recommendations to the court.

Dr. Barnum had an impressive résumé and had worked in the Juvenile Court system for many years also. He received his medical degree from Albert Einstein College of Medicine at Yeshiva University in New York City in 1974. He had directed the Boston Juvenile Court Clinic since 1982, conducting evaluations of thousands of children and families involved in Juvenile Court. He was formerly on the faculty of the University of Massachusetts and Harvard Medical Schools and was published widely on issues of forensic assessment of children and families and mental health concerns in the juvenile justice system.

Dr. Barnum presented a forty-one-page report on December 20, 1995. In addition to seven hours of face-to-face interviews with Eddie, he had met with Eddie's family for nine hours and reviewed dental, medical, and educational records, as well as grand jury minutes. He had telephone conversations with Reilly, Eddie's first and second lawyers, his grade school and high school teachers and administrators, his sports coaches, and the staff at the correctional facility. He also directed Dr. Lynda Field, a well-known child and adolescent psychologist, to conduct a full battery of psychological testing.

Addressing the nine statutory factors on which the court

is required to make findings of fact, Dr. Barnum reached the following conclusions:

- *Maturity: actual cognitive and emotional functioning is much more like that of a preteen or early adolescent than like that of a late adolescent or early adult.*
- *Prior court record: no prior court involvement or history of delinquency charges.*
- *Family and social history: came from a stable, intact, loving family in which there is no reported history of violence, abuse, neglect, or substance abuse.*
- *School: no indications of conduct problems in school, and his academic record has been generally consistent with his average cognition.*
- *Social: maintained successful peer relationships and has been involved in a number of prosocial activities involving service to the community.*
- *Success or lack of success with any past treatment efforts: The only specific treatment with which Edward has been involved is speech therapy in early childhood (ages three to five).*
- *Services available through the juvenile justice system: The nature of services available to him is not entirely clear at this time. Juveniles committed on murder charges would remain at the Plymouth Correctional Facility to age 21. Clinical services to this population have been in flux, and are currently under review and redevelopment.* (Because of the recent changes in the law made by the Harbour and the Copney-Grant Amendments, the entire juvenile system was in flux, trying to accommodate the legislative changes. So, not only did Eddie have to prove he was amenable to rehabilitation for a crime he didn't commit, he also had to prove he was amenable to a treatment program that didn't yet exist.)
- *Adequate protection of the public: The uncertainty*

*regarding the actual nature of Edward's involvement in the current offense raises some questions regarding whether long term incarceration is required. (*Eddie's lawyer's decision that Eddie shouldn't tell Dr. Barnum how and why he came to be in the house that night and what he had seen made it impossible for the evaluator to make a clear determination that might have helped Eddie's cause in the final analysis. Instructing Eddie not to tell his story prevented Dr. Barnum from concluding that the public would be adequately protected if Eddie were released.)

- *Nature, circumstances, and seriousness of the alleged offense: Available information regarding the killing of Ms. Downing suggests that it involved a struggle and took place over some period of time. The specific events leading up to and including the killing remain a matter of speculation, as does the motive.*

In determining whether Eddie was a likely candidate for rehabilitation, Dr. Barnum stated his opinion that Eddie did not "currently present with any clear psychiatric disorder for which treatment is indicated."[18] Again, the evaluator noted that he was at a loss to be more definitive because Eddie did not provide information either about his involvement in the offense or about his own emotional reactions. Dr. Barnum couldn't infer either the presence or absence of a more serious personality pathology. His clinical impression based on his interviews was that "it is more likely that he does not in fact have a serious personality disorder than that he does."[19]

Dr. Barnum's opinion was that Eddie's prognosis for

---

18 Court-ordered psychiatric evaluation of Edward S. O'Brien by Richard Barnum, M.D., December 20, 1995, p. 38

19 Id., p. 39.

successful treatment within the juvenile justice system was good. Now it was the district attorney's chance to show Eddie was *not* amenable to treatment.

DA Reilly's case at the first transfer hearing consisted of presenting all the evidence regarding the horrific nature of this crime. He presented Trooper Joseph Duggan from the district attorney's CPAC Unit, Somerville Police Detective Charles Femino (a first responder that night), and one of the EMTs from Cataldo Ambulance Service. He elicited long and detailed testimony from the state medical examiner, Dr. Leonard Atkins, who did the autopsy. He called three of Eddie's friends—Ryan and Paul Downing, and Marco Abreu—to testify about some fairly benign things Eddie had said in the past.

When Eddie was arrested, the police told reporter Ann Donlan, "We don't have a motive at this point. We can't even think of one."[20] Reilly added, "It's much too early to speculate on what the motive may have been. We've got a lot of work to do before we make a judgment on that."[21]

The Downing sons' testimony was intended to lay the foundation for the emerging "motive" the Commonwealth was trying to develop: that Eddie had a peculiar interest in their mother.

Marco Abreu testified that he'd seen Eddie on Hamlet Street coming out of the bushes the night of the murder. He originally told the police that he wasn't sure whom he had seen. The day after the murder, he was overheard saying he was still unsure. By the third day, after Eddie's father told him he now was unwelcome at their house, Marco's mother called the police so he could make a third statement: He was

---

20 Heaney, Joe, and Ann E. Dolan: "Altar Boy Held in Savage Murder," Boston Herald, July 26, 1995

21 Dolan, Ann E.: "The Boy Next Door: Well-Liked Teen Denies Horrific Murder," Boston Herald, July 27, 1995

now 100 percent sure he saw Eddie coming out of the bushes behind the Downings' house that night.

None of this evidence went to the amenability of Eddie O'Brien to rehabilitation within the juvenile justice system, the only purpose of the first transfer hearing.

When he read Dr. Barnum's report in December 1995, Reilly had to be very worried by the absence of motive in the case. Two weeks after Dr. Barnum submitted his report, the district attorney met with him and "conveyed information that he had not conveyed in our telephone conversations prior to the submission of my original report."[22]

Reilly told Barnum that a newspaper article had been discovered in Eddie's bedroom describing another murder by adolescent perpetrators. (This "article" would become the subject of much confusion at trial.) He also told Barnum that Eddie had obtained a key to St. Joseph's school and entered the school illicitly, both alone and with friends. (The subsequent testimony at the transfer hearing regarding the key and the school proved to be very different from what Reilly suggested to Barnum on January 5, 1996. In fact, Eddie's friends testified that Eddie and his friends played hide-and-seek in the closed and abandoned school.)

In addition, Reilly told Barnum that:

1. Eddie had been stealing money from his grandfather in the six months prior to Janet Downing's murder. (This was never verified by anyone nor was ever raised at trial.)
2. Downing had begun to report missing money after Eddie's grandfather's money went missing. (This also was never verified and was never raised at trial.)
3. Eddie told friends about looking through Downing's window and watching her undress shortly before the murder. (Ryan Downing alleged that Eddie told him that

22 Addendum to Clinical Report, January 8, 1996, Richard Barnum, M.D., p. 2

he once saw her undressing in her bedroom window. Eddie denies he ever saw this or told Ryan he saw it.)

4. Eddie did have prior police involvement: He had been questioned once by the Medford police regarding a burning mailbox but was never charged in the case. (Reilly implied that he had been guilty but got away with it.)

Eddie's attorney objected to the admission of this "Addendum" to Dr. Barnum's report at the transfer hearing, due to the unverified statements and the fact that the DA only thought to inform Dr. Barnum about these allegations *after* the forensic psychiatrist had noted that Eddie had no known motive. Reilly's efforts with Dr. Barnum seemingly were to show that Eddie had a propensity to commit the crime and may also have had a motive. Judge Heffernan didn't allow the addendum into evidence.

Reilly meanwhile engaged the services of a former FBI special agent, Gregg McCrary. He tried to call him to the stand as an expert in criminal investigative analysis. Reilly told Judge Heffernan that McCrary would testify to "the sexual nature of this crime, and that component, that very serious component, when sex and violence come together. He will testify as to the behavior, the planning, the things that Dr. Barnum pointed out in his report: the planning, the aggressiveness, the exploitation is another word he used … And he will testify in all of those—on all of those subjects."[23]

As an offer of proof to the judge of what McCrary would say on the witness stand, Reilly said, "In short, Your Honor, Edward O'Brien, at his own choice, has made a decision in terms of the degree of cooperation with Dr. Barnum and Dr. Field that has resulted in an incomplete picture with respect to motive and intent in this case. That is his own choice.

23 Transfer hearing, Volume VIII, January 19, 1996, pp. 44, 45

We will fill in those blanks for you as the Trier of Facts in this case, so that you will understand and have a complete understanding of motive, of intent, which goes directly … to the issue of rehabilitation."[24]

So, five months after the murder, Reilly had finally produced a motive. He wanted the court to allow McCrary, based on his review of the crime scene photographs, the grand jury testimony, and the autopsy report, to give his opinion as to why the crime occurred, how it was premeditated and carefully planned out, and what Eddie's motivation and intent were in committing the crime.

The court didn't permit McCrary to testify. The judge determined that this testimony could be relevant to Eddie's ultimate guilt or innocence at trial, but it was not the kind of testimony to be considered at a Part B transfer hearing. (The statute is quite clear as to what the court must consider: those are the nine factors outlined in Dr. Barnum's report.)

The last of the nine factors, the nature and seriousness of the crime, was undisputed. The judge did not need an expert to tell him that this was a vicious and brutal homicide. Dr. Leonard Atkins had done that quite well.

Dr. Atkins testified that he performed Janet Downing's autopsy at 11:41 a.m. on July 24, 1995. She suffered sixty-six stab wounds and thirty-two incised wounds for a total of ninety-eight distinct knife wounds. An incised wound is a cutting, slashing-type wound longer than it is deep. In the doctor's thirty-nine-year career, he said, he could not recall seeing that many wounds on a single victim.

Downing had fought. She had defensive knife wounds on both hands, her wrist, her left arm, and two fingers of her left hand. She had a stab wound on the upper part of her left forearm and an abrasion of her elbow.

She had been assaulted virtually everywhere. In the head

24 Id., pp. 45,46

area, she suffered a total of five wounds, two stab wounds to the back of her skull, an incised wound above her left ear, a scrape to her head and bruising to her ear. Her neck had three stab wounds and twenty-two incised wounds ear to ear across her neck, inflicted, in the coroner's medical opinion, after she was unconscious. There was another stab wound one inch deep below her left ear, and a slashing to her chin.

She had thirty-eight stab wounds in the center of her chest below her breasts; the wounds were from one-eighth inch deep to over four inches deep, going into her chest cavity and beyond to an unknown depth. One wound was used seven times to inflict seven separate injuries to her lungs, sever a rib, and perforate her liver.

She suffered five stab wounds to her upper back, shoulder blade, and lower left back area. Two of these were two inches deep.

In addition to the stab wounds all over her body, she had blunt-force injuries with bruising on the bridge of her nose, her lower lip, her chin, near the stab wounds under her right and left breasts, her upper back, the back of her left arm, elbow, and the top of her left wrist.

Dr. Atkins said the knife wounds to her lungs and liver were fatal. It took several minutes for her to die from those wounds. It was not possible to tell how long it would have taken the perpetrator to inflict all of these injuries, but it certainly took "some time."[25]

The level of brutality is staggering and incomprehensible. The abundance of blood that would be scattered from ninety-eight knife wounds and a severe beating is obvious, even if one never saw the photographs of the autopsy and the crime scene. The perpetrator would have been saturated in Janet Downing's blood. It defies logic to think that Eddie could have committed this crime without getting more than one

25 Id., p. 46

drop of blood consistent with her AB blood type on his right shin. Many witnesses had seen Eddie in the same clothes all day and all night. Although the district attorney would make attempts during the trial to suggest that Eddie changed his clothing (presumably both before the crime and then somewhere between leaving the scene and arriving at Mid-Nite Convenient, he was not able to provide a scintilla of evidence to support this theory.

# CHAPTER 9

## WHAT THE COMMONWEALTH KNEW

Trial testimony would reveal that Eddie became a "person of interest" in Janet Downing's murder the moment he reported the mugging. The police made him their prime suspect after interviewing him that night, seizing his clothes and sneakers, photographing and fingerprinting him. They arrested him just thirty-eight hours later.

What evidence against Eddie O'Brien did the Commonwealth have on July 25, 1995, before they arrested him?

**Eyewitnesses:** Three boys, friends of Eddie and Ryan, had gone to Ryan's house at approximately 9:20 p.m. to see if Ryan was home yet. Marco Abreu, Seth Dion, and John Fitzpatrick knocked at the front door, but got no answer. The front door was ajar, but the inner door to the house was closed. Seth went to the back door on the deck, and got no answer. Marco, standing in the backyard, noticed the cellar door was wide open.

Just then, they heard a rustle in the bushes and saw a six-foot-two, 220-pound white male jump onto Hamlet Street and continue walking down the hill. Marco called to him: "Hey, Ed!" "Nice hiding place, Ed." Their accounts varied as to whether or not this person turned to look at them. But none of the boys positively identified the man as Eddie O'Brien. Marco said he saw the man smile but couldn't be 100 percent sure; he didn't positively identify Eddie until after the arrest.

John said the man never stopped and continued walking.

Despite the lack of positive identification, the district attorney believed he had eyewitnesses who put Eddie O'Brien at the scene of the crime.

**Alleged murder weapon:** The police found a piece of metal they believed to be the hilt of a small pocketknife in the shag carpet on the third stair in the Downing home. They never found a "murder weapon." The hilt they found was substantially similar to a small green knife Eddie owned. The green knife had a matching red knife. Eddie had found the knives while cleaning out the attic when his grandfather was in the hospital that June and brought them over to the Downing home to show his friends. Eddie also brought the green knife into Mid-Nite Convenient to show one of the clerks (Jack Arnold, coincidentally also a court officer in the Somerville District Court) the night before the murder. The clerk said he noticed that the hilt was loose. Eddie left the knife at Mid-Nite that Saturday night with Jack Arnold. The green knife was never found.

**Fingerprints:** Eddie O'Brien's left thumb, index finger, and middle finger prints were found on the post at the foot of the cellar staircase. Prints from his right index finger and right middle finger were found on the inside of the interior front door, above the door handle.

The district attorney had Eddie's fingerprints at the scene of the crime. That's it—the only "hard" evidence implicating Eddie O'Brien as the perpetrator of the horrific murder of his best friend's mother that the district attorney had before arresting Eddie. No blood testing had been done yet, and Marco Abreu had not yet changed his story to being 100 percent sure it was Eddie he saw. No comparison had been done between the metal piece and any similar knife with a hilt.

The Commonwealth eventually learned that Eddie had indeed been inside the Downing house that night and that he said he had seen the perpetrator. But that wasn't until they learned from the defense team about Eddie's interview with Dr. Paul Spiers.

Eddie had been in custody for at least two weeks when he wrote a note in mid-August to his attorney Ralph Champa, telling him he'd been in the house and seen the attacker. His attorney arranged for Eddie to undergo the forensic interview under the influence of sodium amytal (so-called "truth serum") by Dr. Spiers. Like a lie detector test, this is a useful tool in gathering additional information or corroborating known information, but it is not admissible at trial. Like a lie detector test, it is not considered scientifically reliable.

The test indicated that Eddie was being truthful about what happened to him that night.

The report was shared with the district attorney. Notwithstanding the test, or the fact that Eddie had no detectable blood on his clothing, sneakers, hands, or under his fingernails right after the murder (and had been wearing the same clothing all day), the Commonwealth proceeded to build its case around Eddie O'Brien to the exclusion of any other possible suspect.

The DA knew that the Reckleys, Janet Downing's common-wall neighbors, had heard a sound that could have been someone falling down the stairs at exactly 8:15 p.m. Investigators knew that part of what they believed was the "murder weapon" and blood were found on the lower five steps of that staircase. They knew that there was almost no water pressure at the Reckleys' home at 9:00. They knew that this often happened if the water was running at Downing's house. They knew that Downing's water was still running full force in the powder room when the first responders arrived at the scene at 10:00. They knew Eddie O'Brien was at home in his own house between 8:15 and 9:15 that night.

The testimony of the Commonwealth's own witnesses—Marco Abreu, Seth Dion, John Fitzpatrick, and Michelle Cameron—made it impossible for Eddie to have committed the slaying within the time frame available to him. The testimony of the coroner alone illustrated the enormous amount of time the murderer spent with Janet Downing: struggling across three rooms and the stairway, beating her, killing her, undressing and redressing her, and then inflicting post-mortem wounds. The "window of opportunity" for Eddie O'Brien would have been between 9:15, when he was known to have left his house, and about 9:20, after the boys knocked and saw someone jumping out of the bushes.

District Attorney Tom Reilly himself was present during witness interviews the morning after the murder. Reilly's CPAC Unit had taken over the case from the Somerville police detectives at 2:30 a.m., just hours after the murder.

Decisions had already been made about how this investigation would proceed. Who told the troopers not to interview the Reckleys? Why weren't they interviewed until two years after the murder? Was it because their observations completely conflicted with what little evidence the Commonwealth had against Eddie O'Brien?

Every prosecutorial decision made along the long legal journey in this case placed the blame squarely on the shoulders of a fifteen-year-old boy to the exclusion of any other possible suspect. It appeared that no one else was ever seriously considered as a possible suspect. Eddie had to be guilty. Tom Reilly's credibility and career depended on it.

# CHAPTER 10

## THE DECISION

The first transfer hearing spanned nine trial days and ended on January 22, 1996. Judge Paul Heffernan, on the final day of the hearing, allowed DA Tom Reilly to present two psychiatrists, Dr. Robert Kinscherff and Dr. Donald Condie, to offer their opinions about the "overkill" nature of the crime.

Overkill is the infliction of many more wounds than are necessary to incapacitate or kill a victim. It is suggestive of rage rather than panic, since a perpetrator who is in a state of panic flees at the first opportunity. Both psychiatrists felt the crime was sexual in nature: Downing's bra was cut thirty-six times, sixteen in the left cup, nine in the right cup, and fourteen in the rear. These cuts didn't correspond to the cuts in her blouse or on her body. This suggested that the killer had removed her bra, sliced it thirty-six times, and then replaced it; it was unfastened but under her blouse and covering her breasts when the EMTs arrived. Both doctors suggested the perpetrator was a sexually sadistic predator, due to the mutilation of the bra and the fact that numerous gratuitous incised wounds were inflicted when Downing was either unconscious or otherwise incapacitated.

Neither psychiatrist had interviewed Eddie O'Brien, his family, or any of the witnesses. They made it clear they were offering no opinion as to Eddie, his past or current functioning, or his amenability to rehabilitation. They agreed that the reports from Dr. Barnum and his associate Dr. Field provided no evidence of sexual, violent, or sadistic behavior in Eddie's past or present.

However, the additional doctors were crucial to the DA because they enabled him to get his theory of the murder into evidence. Reilly's theory seemed to be that Eddie O'Brien was a raging, sexually sadistic predator who had hidden his dark side from everyone in his life. This was quite a leap from the immature altar boy with no propensity for violence and no motive to harm Downing of the Barnum and Field reports just five months before.

There was no dispute that a very deranged killer had murdered Janet Downing. The evidence was overwhelming. But Eddie O'Brien, a deranged madman? Eddie would have had to have been a highly sophisticated psychopath to pass a lie detector test, go through a full battery of psychological testing, and endure seven hours of interviews with a psychiatrist without anyone picking up any sign of mental illness.

Judge Heffernan took just fifteen days to render his decision. On February 6, 1996, he found that Edward S. O'Brien was indeed amenable to rehabilitation in the juvenile justice system and ordered him retained in Juvenile Court for trial.

In his twelve-page decision the judge noted the "conundrum" the defendant faced: any statements Eddie made to clinical personnel to support his retention in the juvenile system could be used against him in his upcoming trial for first-degree murder. Heffernan found it was "exacerbated by a suggestion that rehabilitation could only be undertaken if the defendant implicated himself and demonstrated 'remorse' for the crime" which had not yet been proven.[26]

26 Findings and Order of the Court, Paul P. Heffernan, Presiding Justice, February 6, 1996, p. 4

The judge was attaching great weight to the forensic testimony and evidence regarding dangerousness and amenability to treatment.[27] He noted that the testimony of Drs. Kinscherff and Condie, though not case-specific (they didn't evaluate the defendant), was considered in light of other forensic evidence offered by the prosecution. He ordered Eddie held without bail due to his potential dangerousness. However, he pointed out, "Dr. Barnum, after an exhaustive evaluation, concluded that Edward O'Brien was not afflicted with any mental illness or defect."[28]

The judge ruled that the credible testimony regarding the clinical, social, and legal factors, coupled with the security systems in place to deal with children found delinquent of murder, led him to believe that Eddie should remain in the juvenile system.

My reading of this decision? Judge Heffernan was convinced that if Eddie *had* committed this murder, it wasn't because he was a depraved and sexually sadistic predator: he was a child with no prior propensity for any criminal conduct, let alone a brutal murder. Therefore, in his opinion, even if guilty, Eddie was "capable of growth which will allow him to make free moral decisions when he ponders the enormity of his involvement and the ramifications thereof."[29]

If found delinquent by reason of murder in Juvenile Court, Eddie would serve his sentence in a Division of Youth Services facility getting treatment until he reached the age of twenty-one; he would then serve fifteen more years in an adult prison (a split sentence). He would be released at age thirty-six. If convicted in adult court, however, he would

27 Id., p. 11. The judge's interchanging of the words "treatment" and "rehabilitation" would provide DA Tom Reilly with a basis for appealing the decision.

28 Id., p. 12

29 Id., p. 12

serve a life sentence without any possibility of parole.

The public had been following this case on television and in the media for almost seven months, and Reilly had been promising them that Eddie would be tried in adult court and put away for the rest of his natural life. Reilly couldn't accept a nineteen-year sentence: his career was at stake. His successful prosecution of this case would lead to the Attorney General's Office, but he might not be elected if he so publicly lost a juvenile transfer hearing.

Supported by Governor Weld, Reilly immediately claimed the Harbour and Copney-Grant Amendments to the juvenile laws were proving insufficient. He filed a Notice of Appeal in late February 1996, asking the Massachusetts Supreme Judicial Court to overturn Heffernan's decision and remove the judge from the case.

On June 1, 1996, Weld stood flanked by families of victims allegedly killed by adolescents and called on the Massachusetts Senate to pass a bill requiring juveniles charged with murder to be tried as adults. "The public has a right to be protected from cold-blooded killers, and any system that fails to protect it is badly in need of repair."[30] Janet Downing's father and brother stood with Weld and were quoted in news reports.

On July 26, 1996, after momentum grew for the bill following the Heffernan decision, Weld signed into law sweeping juvenile justice reform legislation mandating that anyone ages fourteen, fifteen, or sixteen charged with murder must be tried as an adult and, if convicted of first-degree murder, must be sentenced to life without parole. Split sentencing died just four years after it began for children charged with first- and second-degree murder.

While Heffernan's decision was being appealed by Reilly

30 Page, Connie, "Gov. Pushes Bill to Try Teen Killers as Adults," Boston Herald, June 1, 1996

to the Supreme Judicial Court, the governor (who appoints all judges in Massachusetts) was publicly stating, in essence, that Heffernan's decision was a prime example of what was wrong with the law: it failed to protect the public. Weld urged legislators to take these decisions away from judges (who weighed all the evidence and considered all the factors involved in a child's life and the circumstances surrounding the crime) and deny juveniles charged with murder any chance at rehabilitation.

Just ten days before he signed this bill into law, Weld nominated Herbert P. Wilkins to the position of chief justice of the Supreme Judicial Court, which was still considering Eddie O'Brien's appeal. Wilkins had been an associate justice of the Supreme Judicial Court for fourteen years.

Judge Heffernan's decision stood little chance of being upheld by the upper court, given the visible and powerful political sentiment against it. Heffernan knew that, and he knew it long before Weld lobbied for and applauded the new legislation in July 1996.

In 2013, I had a conversation with Heffernan about the O'Brien case. I called him at home, as I'd done periodically since his retirement from the bench. He always asked how Eddie was, and was aware of my continued involvement with him and the O'Brien family. When he told me the following story in 2013, he asked me to "take it to the grave" with me. I assured him that I would.

Judge Heffernan related that, approximately one week after he issued his decision, he got a call from Judge Samuel Zoll, chief justice of the Trial Court. Heffernan and Zoll had been colleagues and friends for many years.

Zoll was calling him to congratulate him on the soundness of his decision and on having the courage to make the right decision in the face of so much public and political opposition. Zoll acknowledged the enormous wave of sentiment that was running against Heffernan, and said he wanted him to know he was proud of him for having the courage of his convictions.

The next week Zoll called Heffernan again. "I remember it like it was yesterday," Heffernan told me. "I was sitting in Waltham District Court that day. I answered the call without any ominous feelings or expectations. Sam said, 'Paul, you've got to change your decision in the O'Brien case.' I said, 'Sam, what are you talking about?' Then Sam told me that he'd been advised that if I didn't change my decision in the case, I'd be removed from the case. I couldn't believe what I was hearing."

This telephone conversation occurred before Tom Reilly had even filed any notice of appeal in the case.

I couldn't believe what Judge Heffernan was telling me, either. I knew that judges talked to one another about cases. Every once in a while someone got caught trying to get a nephew or son-in-law out of hot water. But I had never thought that judges could be told how to decide a case.

"I'm speechless," I said. "I can't believe what I'm hearing."

Judge Heffernan said that he'd answered Zoll without hesitation, "Sam, I would rather walk naked through Sullivan Square Station than change my opinion in that case." Zoll reiterated that he'd been told Heffernan would be removed from the case. Heffernan said he told Zoll, "Let them do what they have to do."

Sam Zoll and Paul Heffernan were good friends. They remained good friends. This directive didn't come from Zoll, and Heffernan knew that.

Not long after he was removed from the case, Heffernan was attending a party celebrating a colleague in the Boston Municipal Court. His friend met him at the elevator to alert him that Supreme Judicial Court Chief Justice Wilkins was at the party. Heffernan walked into the room with his head held high. He greeted the chief justice respectfully. Wilkins responded, "We could have handled that better, Paul," an awkward apology for besmirching Heffernan's reputation and removing him from the O'Brien case. It became a secret inside joke among Heffernan's friends.

*We could have handled that better, Paul.*

In the spring of 2015, I called Judge Heffernan to tell him that the Innocence Program had accepted Eddie's case for review. Heffernan was overjoyed. "I'm eighty-three-years old now. I hope I'm alive to see him walk out of jail."

I told him that I, too, was now retired and had decided to tell this story the way I saw and understood it, with all the unseemly political grandstanding, the obfuscation of evidence that didn't support the Commonwealth's case, the failures of his trial counsel, and my belief that Eddie was innocent and may have been set up by a district attorney who knew that he didn't kill Janet Downing. "I'm going to name names," I said. "I've got nothing to lose. I'm not practicing law anymore. What can they do to me now?"

The judge gave me permission to disclose what he'd told me two years before. "You can quote me about anything and everything I've told you, Margo. I trust you completely."

# CHAPTER 11

## THE SUPREME JUDICIAL COURT DECISION

The appeal of Heffernan's ruling took eight months to be decided.

The decision was released on December 6, 1996, written by Associate Justice Neil L. Lynch. Many politicians and pundits viewed Lynch as a conservative jurist. He had been an associate justice of the court for fifteen years, appointed by Republican Governor Ed King.

Lynch's opinion, in brief, concluded that Judge Heffernan:

1. Applied an erroneous standard in determining whether the defendant was amenable to rehabilitation, referring to the interchanging of the words "treatment" and "rehabilitation." The court noted, "during the course of the transfer hearing the judge, the experts, and the attorneys used the terms 'treatment' and 'rehabilitation' without differentiation. However, that does not relieve the judge of the obligation to indicate clearly that he found that the defendant could be rehabilitated as opposed to merely treated."[31]

2. Improperly relied on evidence not part of the record: Heffernan referred to Dr. Spiers' testimony that Eddie O'Brien did not suffer from any mental illness. Dr. Spiers testified at Eddie's bail hearing but not at the transfer hearing, so his testimony was technically not part of the transfer hearing record.

3. Improperly limited the admission of expert testimony.

---

31 *Commonwealth vs. Edward S. O'Brien*, 423 Mass. 841, December 6, 1996, p. 847

Heffernan excluded

Dr. Barnum's addendum, prepared at the behest of DA Tom Reilly.

While this third "error" was arguably a legitimate or defensible reason to send the case back to Heffernan for reconsideration, it was also the one error that permitted the higher court to order "further hearings" (not just reconsideration by the judge). An easy correction would be changing the word "treatment" to "rehabilitation" and striking Spiers' opinion. Instructing Heffernan to include Barnum's addendum meant that Heffernan had to reopen the case to take additional evidence.

The Supreme Judicial Court's decision to remand the case for further hearings was ridiculous; it was almost embarrassing how thin the reasoning was stretched to reach its conclusion.

Of course, I didn't know then what I know now: the justices (or was it only Wilkins?) intended to remove Heffernan from the case entirely. Reilly had requested Heffernan's removal in his appellate argument, but the high court declined to address that issue in their decision.

Reilly sent a three-page letter to Zoll requesting that he reassign the case to another judge for rehearing. Zoll responded by telling Reilly that such requests "are typically raised by a motion to recuse addressed to the trial judge himself or herself." Zoll believed that this would be the appropriate course; he reminded Reilly that he'd requested Heffernan's removal in his appellate brief, but the Supreme Judicial Court had refused to act on it. As chief justice of the Trial Court, Zoll didn't believe he had the authority to act on a request that the high court had declined to address.

Reilly must have been perplexed by the failure of the SJC to remove Heffernan. He must have known, as Heffernan himself knew, that the judge's refusal to change his decision would result in his removal. Did the justices mean to allow Heffernan to render yet another decision against Reilly before they removed him?

Perhaps Wilkins was hoping that when push came to shove, Heffernan would remove himself from the controversy rather than risk another public lashing by the SJC. I'm sure he didn't want the political embarrassment of removing Heffernan publicly, raising questions about the impartiality of the Supreme Judicial Court.

Heffernan denied the motion to recuse that was filed by Reilly. Like Zoll, Heffernan was not making it any easier to get a different judge more sympathetic to the Commonwealth. Reilly was forced to file yet another petition for extraordinary relief with the Supreme Judicial Court seeking Heffernan's removal from the case.

On March 3, 1997, the Supreme Judicial Court issued an order asking Chief Justice of the Trial Court Samuel E. Zoll to assign a judge to replace Judge Paul P. Heffernan in all further proceedings in the O'Brien case. The reasons for this extraordinary action were to "eliminate controversies and unnecessary issues in further proceedings and in any appeal."[32]

I've never read a decision with a vaguer ruling. Was this the new standard for the removal of judges? Can you imagine any respectable lawyer standing before the highest court in the Commonwealth and arguing, "This judge should be removed from my case, Your Honor, because it will eliminate controversies and unnecessary issues"? It screams of political maneuvering and judge-shopping.

What controversies was the court referring to? The only controversy in the case was that Reilly had lost the case and embarrassed himself and the governor. His political future

32 Order entered March 3, 1997, by the justices, signed by Jean M. Kennett, clerk

was in jeopardy. Weld's U.S. Senate race was looming, and he was scheduled to resign as governor in just three months in order to run. Reilly took a big chance grandstanding such a public and controversial position in the juvenile justice debate of the 1990s. It didn't pay off. That's politics, not controversy.

I couldn't have linked the governor's agenda and Wilkins' appointment to the bench at that time. Even if I had, I wouldn't have believed the connection. I also didn't know that Zoll had already told Heffernan the year before that he'd be removed from the case if he didn't change his opinion. Heffernan was making "them" do what they had to do. He refused to be complacent.

The same day as the order was issued, Zoll appointed Judge Gerald Alch, an associate justice of the Dedham District Court, to hear the O'Brien case.

Gerald Alch was a Harvard- and Boston University-educated defense attorney appointed to the District Court bench as a circuit judge by Democratic Governor Michael Dukakis in 1990. A circuit judge is not assigned to any one District Court, but moves among all the courts as needed.

Alch was famed criminal defense attorney F. Lee Bailey's former law partner and had worked many high-profile criminal cases. Eddie and his attorneys were thrilled with the appointment. However, just one day after his appointment, Alch wrote, "Since I accepted your request to preside over the matter of Commonwealth v. Edward S. O'Brien, I have recalled that prior to assuming the bench, I supported the candidacy of the current District Attorney for Middlesex County Thomas F. Reilly and I believe he spoke in support of my nomination to the bench. . . . Given the concern by the Supreme Judicial Court 'to eliminate controversies and unnecessary issues,' I feel that it would be appropriate that you assign another judge to the case and I respectfully request that you do so."[33]

A more transparent and commonly used course of action would have been to meet with DA Reilly and Eddie's lawyer, Robert George, and ask them if they saw a conflict. It's called full disclosure and is done every day in courtrooms around the country. If either attorney has an objection, then the judge recuses himself.

Are we to believe that, having been called by Zoll (with whom he discussed the case and the reasons for Heffernan's removal), Alch went home, smacked his forehead, and said, "Oh, no! I forgot that I supported Tom Reilly for DA six years ago! And I forgot Tom Reilly appeared on my behalf at the Governor's Council who approved my judgeship!"

Did Reilly or Weld advise Alch not to take the O'Brien case? Weld had just recently appointed Alch to the Dedham District Court after six years "riding the circuit." I do know that before Alch "remembered" he'd supported Reilly for DA and that Reilly spoke on his behalf in support of his nomination to the bench, attempts had been made by Alch's office to schedule the case for hearings in the Dedham District Court instead of the Somerville District Court. In other words, it took a long time for Alch to remember events that one would clearly not ever forget in the first place.

The next move in the case answered all those questions when Zoll appointed Judge Timothy H. Gailey to succeed Heffernan. His appointment came just one day later on March 5, 1996. Gailey was formerly assistant secretary for the Executive Office of Consumer Affairs and Business Regulation, and was later appointed insurance commissioner for the Commonwealth under Republican Governor Ed King. Governor Dukakis appointed him to the bench in 1990. Judge Gailey was the Dorchester District Court judge who'd transferred Willie Dunn, one of the defendants in the

33 Letter of Gerald Alch to Samuel Zoll dated March 5, 1996

Copney-Grant murder case, to adult court. Dunn had been acquitted of murder but found guilty of gun possession and served five years. In February 2005, Associated Press reporter Jeff Donn described Dunn as "beaming in a natty double-breasted suit accented by a red handkerchief, [as] he sat in First Lady Laura Bush's box for guests of honor, right next to a decorated Marine, during President George W. Bush's State of the Union address."[34] Dunn represented an example of the proof of rehabilitation to the nation. Gailey obviously had missed that when he transferred Dunn to adult court and found him *not* amenable to rehabilitation.

The judge had a nickname in the world of defense lawyers: "Guilty Gailey." It was rumored he'd never uttered the words "not guilty" in his entire career.

Eddie O'Brien was going to adult court. There was no longer any doubt about that.

Eddie's lawyers filed a motion to recuse Gailey, based on his predilection for transferring juveniles charged with murder to adult court. Gailey denied that motion on April 11, 1997.

34 Donn, Jeff, "Gangbanger's Reform," Associated Press, St. Augustine Record, February 20, 2005

# CHAPTER 12

## THE SECOND TRANSFER HEARING

On March 12, 1997, Judge Timothy Gailey's first official act had been to order Dr. Richard Barnum to update his clinical evaluation report. Dr. Barnum submitted a fifty-three page "update" to his original forty-one page report on April 21, 1997.

Eddie had now been in custody for twenty-one months and was seventeen years old. He had grown three inches and gained 115 pounds. He was six-foot-six and weighed 385 pounds. He had matured physically from a prepubescent boy to a shaving, towering, hefty teenager.

In December 1995, Eddie had been granted a $500,000/ surety $50,000 cash bail by Superior Court Judge Regina Quinlan. But before he could be fitted with his ankle bracelet and released, DA Reilly appealed Quinlan's decision to the Supreme Judicial Court, and the bail order was revoked.

Eddie's emotional growth had been informed by his living situation, a secure lockup for pre- and post-conviction violent juvenile offenders. His parents and family visited several times a week, his only lifeline to the world.

The second hearing spanned five consecutive days. Transcripts of the prior testimony of many witnesses were substituted for live testimony. Reilly got his FBI crime-scene specialist/profiler to the witness stand. Gailey issued his Findings and Order on May 9, 1997, which is notable for the clarity with which the judge described the contradictory evidence.

"In short, as of July 22, 1995, there was nothing in Mr. O'Brien's history to suggest to anyone that he could possibly be a danger to anyone, that he could possibly do the things that were done the next day. . . . The available psychiatric data . . . do not suggest the presence of any discrete, explicit psychiatric disorder or diagnosis that would explain Mr. O'Brien's actions on July 23, 1995. At this point, he remains a psychological enigma."[35]

Yet Gailey credited "reports" (by persons unnamed in the findings) that during the months before the killing, "Mr. O'Brien had exhibited an interest in Janet Downing . . . was unusually conscious of her activities . . . and had acted at one time in a way which a close observer (also unnamed) interpreted as his having a youthful crush on her," and thus concluded that "Janet Downing was the focus of Mr. O'Brien's special attention, and that may be something of a first step in understanding his incomprehensible actions on July 23."[36]

Those "reports"? They were a handful of remarks that Ryan Downing alleged Eddie had made about his mother. Ryan said Eddie told him he saw his mother once undressing in front of an open window in her house. (Eddie denies ever seeing Downing undress or telling Ryan that he saw this. What he'd told Ryan was that he and Marco Abreu had watched another neighborhood woman undress in front of her window as they sat on the O'Brien porch.)

Ryan also said that Eddie asked him why his mother sat in her car and smoked cigarettes instead of going into the house when she arrived home. Ryan said that he'd explained this was her "transition time" and that Eddie's inquiries had started two years before the murder and occurred as recently

35 Transfer Hearing Findings and Order, May 9, 1997, Timothy H. Gailey, Justice, p. 17

36 Id., p. 12

as the spring before the murder.

Finally, Ryan said that the summer before the murder, Eddie told him that his mother had been in the twins' bedroom with a flashlight while they were away in New Hampshire.

Based on these isolated and innocuous statements Eddie allegedly made, Judge Gailey formulated what in reality is a psychological profile, one that mental health professionals all apparently had missed in their hours of interviews and testing: that Eddie was obsessed with Downing and had a crush on her.

Even a youthful crush on Downing hardly explains why Eddie would want to murder her. It is ludicrous. These incidents were wrested from Ryan and his twin, Paul, two teenage boys whose mother had just been brutally murdered and who, before they ever met DA Reilly, didn't think twice about the remarks. That was all the DA had as "evidence" to transform altar boy Eddie O'Brien into a sexually sadistic murderer.

Judge Gailey apparently didn't mind the lack of real evidence, lack of real motive, or the way the theory was developed by the DA.

This murder theory evolved because there was no motive for the suspect they'd precipitously arrested. It was because there was no motive that Reilly had hired crime-scene analyst McCrary, who looked at the crime-scene photos and said that whoever had done it was a sexually sadistic killer who had no other motive but the murder itself. No one disputes that description of the actual killer.

The district attorney's problem was that they had taken a fifteen-year-old altar boy into custody, an emotional adolescent with no history of violence or antisocial behavior and who didn't fit the profile of the perpetrator that his expert, McCrary, was describing.

Reilly had only two choices: admit he had the wrong

suspect or fit the suspect to the profile.

Regarding Eddie's amenability to rehabilitation, Gailey he had to weigh the "suggestion" of Eddie's hidden potential for acting with extreme violence of a sexual nature.[37] He actually used that word, "suggestion," a suggestion created by Reilly and articulated by his witnesses in support of his sexually sadistic perpetrator theory of the crime. On that scale, the mere suggestion that Eddie had a hidden potential for violence outweighed his actual history of prosocial, nonviolent, nondelinquent behavior, his supportive and intact family, his independent psychological testing results, and the findings of two psychiatric evaluations.

Eddie was ordered bound over for trial as an adult in the Superior Court.

The only real shocker of the second transfer hearing was Dr. Barnum's report. It was hardly an update. Rather, it was a total revision and shift in opinion to the Commonwealth's perspective of the case. Eddie was no longer amenable to rehabilitation, in Barnum's revised opinion. Even though Eddie's psychological profile and psychiatric status remained unchanged from his first evaluation, in his summary Barnum wrote that Eddie's "characteristic avoidance makes it relatively unlikely that treatment in (the Plymouth Correctional Facility) setting would provide the combination of staff, peer, and program support . . . that would likely be necessary to engage Edward successfully in rehabilitative treatment."[38] This is a psychiatrically verbose way of saying that the only rehabilitative treatment available to Eddie was at Plymouth, that the program was voluntary, and that it stank.

I watched Barnum's testimony in its entirety at that

---

37 Id., p. 19

38 Richard Barnum, M.D., Summary of Clinical Opinion, April 21, 1997, pp. iv, v.

second transfer hearing. He was on the witness stand for one whole day. He looked like he was in physical pain. He kept rubbing his forehead and shifting his weight.

I encountered him in the hallway during a break in the testimony. "Your feet must be killing you up there," I said, "you've been standing all day." He rubbed his forehead and said, "No, my feet aren't killing me, it's my conscience."

Apparently Reilly had gotten to him.

Was I surprised? No. Was I disappointed? Terribly. I had a lot of respect for Barnum. I'd worked with him on some very difficult cases in the Boston Juvenile Court over the years. I never saw him falter like this and question his own clinical impressions.

I would have intuited that he was subjected to the DA's pressure if I had read the report itself, which was not provided either to me or Eddie's parents. In it Barnum states that he interviewed Ryan Downing, Paul Downing, Erin Downing, Paul Downing Sr., and Carol Ortiz conjointly at the District Attorney's Office. Why there? Why together?

Perhaps Reilly had a purpose and need to personally tend to these particular witnesses and control access to them. To make matters even worse, Barnum somehow allowed Dr. Donald Condie to be present and participate in the interview. Condie was Reilly's expert witness hired to dispute Barnum's report.

Every lawyer is taught (or learns the hard way) that witnesses should never be interviewed together and that one witness should never be told how another witness will testify. It taints the testimony. You can never be sure if the witness really remembered or was mirroring another witness's testimony. It is bad lawyering. Even on television, lawyers and judges always admonish witnesses not to discuss their testimony with one another. Reilly didn't seem to have any problem with it, and it's unlikely that this joint interview was

Barnum's idea.

If Eddie's lawyer had read the report more closely, he could have used this information to discredit not only Barnum's testimony but the Downing twins' as well.

Every other person interviewed in the report was interviewed in his or her home or place of business, not at the DA's office, certainly not together, and not with the prosecution expert participating.

In April 2015, I discussed the report with Dr. Barnum. After several emails back and forth, he reluctantly agreed to speak with me. He called me at an appointed time and explained that the O'Brien case was a "traumatic memory" for him. "That's why I don't want to revisit it or talk about it," he explained.

I told him about my continued involvement in the case, and the fact that it was traumatic for me to talk about my role back then, too. I felt I had failed Eddie completely as GAL, but didn't know how I could have done it differently at the time. I couldn't protect Eddie. We were both just holding on and trying not to drown.

"But I'm still trying to make up for it," I told him. "I owe him that much. I'll do anything I can to help Eddie. I'll never give up."

I asked him some questions about his change of opinion in his second report. Barnum pointed to four different factors that led him to change his opinion. The first was that Eddie was two years older by the time he wrote the second report. Secondly, he had been in a facility without any opportunity for normal emotional development. The third reason was that the Plymouth program was not the right program for Eddie, yet it was the only program that the Department of Youth Services would classify him to if he were found guilty. Lastly, Eddie's was the first case of this magnitude under the new split-sentencing system and he couldn't predict what treatment would be available to Eddie when he transferred to the Department of Corrections when he was twenty-one years old.

I added, "As if that wasn't enough, there was the ridiculously political atmosphere surrounding this case."

"I certainly wasn't immune to the political pressure," Barnum said. He said he felt like the political chaos surrounding the case put him in a position of adjudicating the facts in the case, in addition to evaluating Eddie psychiatrically.

"Is that why you changed your opinion?" I asked.

"Look, I changed my opinion because Eddie was no longer the fifteen-year-old I met two years before. He was seventeen now. He had aged out of the DYS system, and there wasn't sufficient time for any rehabilitation."

"So why did you write a new report at all?" I asked. "Why not just tell the judge, look, he's too old now for the DYS system. There is not enough time to address rehabilitation."

"What do you mean?" he asked.

"I mean you didn't have to go down that whole primrose path to address whether Eddie was a violent sexual offender. What did it matter how and why he allegedly committed this murder? If he was too old for rehabilitation within the system, then nothing could have made him amenable to rehabilitation. That's what you were just saying, weren't you? He aged out? He was too old?"

"That's a very good point," Barnum said, pausing for at least twenty seconds of complete silence. I didn't know if he was agreeing with me, or would simply end the conversation after that. Was he thinking about what I said or was angry at my bluntness? Finally he said, "You're absolutely right. It was all pointless. It was all a monumental waste of time."

"It was a shit show," I said, "from beginning to end. I didn't have a problem with you changing your opinion, Dr.

Barnum, I only had a problem with the way in which you did it. But I didn't understand until just now."

We both sat in silence for a few minutes.

Then Barnum told me about seeing Eddie in prison about ten years earlier when he was there on another case. "I couldn't believe how well he was doing. I was simply amazed!"

"He is indeed doing well," I said. "He's one remarkable young man." I told him a little about my most recent visit with Eddie. He has grey hair now. He's accepted the fact that he is where he is and still has to find a way to live. He's really well-read and self-taught. He has a tremendous amount of confidence in his own thoughts and opinions. He's also a very spiritual man, not just religious, although he is a "proud Roman Catholic," as he says. He's very spiritual in his view of the world.

I told Dr. Barnum that I did have some good news to share with him. "The Innocence Program accepted Eddie's case for review. For the first time in twenty years Eddie has some hope that his future might change, that he may not spend the rest of his life in prison."

"That's awesome!" he exclaimed. "Thank you for making me talk about this, Margo. You made me feel better. Please tell Eddie I send my regards."

# CHAPTER 13

## PAUL DOWNING JR.

Sixteen-year-old Paul Downing had a different set of friends than did his twin brother. Paul was also one grade ahead of Ryan, who had been kept back in the third grade. Paul's best friend was Eddie O'Brien's older sister, Jeannie O'Brien.

Paul is—and was then—openly gay. It appears that Paul's family, friends, and neighbors were all accepting of Paul's sexuality. Gina Mahoney told me she felt it was Paul himself who wasn't as comfortable with who he was.

On the night his mother was murdered, Paul was with his friends Jeannie O'Brien, Michelle Cameron, and Raquel Vega. Paul was the last person known to have seen his mother alive. Ryan and his friends left the house about 7:50. Paul came home sometime around 8:00. Neither the DA nor the defense counsel ever asked Paul if the front door was locked or unlocked when he entered. If it was unlocked, then it's possible that anyone could have entered the house in the ten minutes between when Ryan and the boys left and when Paul returned home.

Paul said he was inside the house "three minutes."[39] Paul claimed that he then spent the next fifteen minutes at the O'Brien house. However, this was contradicted by the five adult witnesses who saw Paul go directly from his house to the back seat of Michelle Cameron's waiting car. In fact, Jeannie O'Brien remembers that Paul was taking so long

39 TR. SIXTH DAY OF TRIAL, Vol. VIII, September 22, 1997, p. 143

that she actually went to his house, knocked on the front window, and yelled for him to hurry up. According to his own testimony later in the trial, he left his house sometime between 8:20 and 8:30, at which time he, Jeannie, Michelle, and Raquel all went back to Revere Beach.

Something happened on the stairs in the Downing house at 8:15. Paul would have been present when this occurred. He testified that his mother was asleep when he was there and that he never went nearer the stairs than to pass by them on his way into and out of the house.

A good part of the struggle took place on the stairway, specifically on the last five steps. A piece of metal, which the DA alleged was part of the murder weapon, was found on the third step. There was blood on the wall and baseboard going down the last four steps, as well as on the carpet covering the stairs.

*Close up of Downing stairs*

Even though the police knew Paul was in the house at 8:15 and that a sound like someone falling down the stairs was heard at 8:15, the police never investigated that further. At least there are no reports indicating that they investigated further.

Paul, Jeannie, Michelle, and Raquel eventually left Revere Beach to come home at the end of the night. They reached Somerville around 11:15. Janet Downing's body had already been removed from the scene. There was still a large police and fire/rescue presence in the neighborhood when they returned. Michelle and Jeannie reported that they first saw the flashing police lights about a block away from the Downing and O'Brien houses. Paul yelled out, "Oh my God, it's my mother! Something's happened to my mother!"

The girls weren't even sure yet that the problem was at the Downing house. When they got to the front of the houses, Paul jumped out of the car. His father told him what had happened. Mahoney saw him sobbing and grabbed him. She sat with him on the curb as he continued to cry. He told Mahoney he couldn't breathe; Paul's stepmother took him to her car and, along with Joseph Cameron (Michelle's brother), drove him to the hospital. According to Joseph Cameron, while they were driving, Paul said, "Ma, I'm sorry for fighting with you." Then he said, "I don't think I locked the front door."

When he was released from the hospital, Paul went to his father and stepmother's home in Wakefield, another suburb of Boston.

If the police ever inquired about Paul leaving the crime scene before being interviewed, it doesn't appear in any investigative report. In fact, Paul Downing Jr. was the *last* witness interviewed by the police in the days following the murder. Five witnesses (including Ryan Downing and Paul

Downing Sr.) were interviewed at the scene that night; sixteen witnesses (including Ryan Downing and Paul Downing Sr.) were interviewed between 10:00 a.m. and 8:00 p.m. the following day (Monday) at the Somerville police station; seven more witnesses were interviewed on Tuesday, the second day after the murder; five final witnesses (including Ryan Downing, Paul Downing, and Paul Downing Sr.) were interviewed the third day after the murder, on Wednesday. Ryan was interviewed a total of three different times.

Paul Jr. was interviewed only once, according to the police reports produced by the prosecution.

It's highly irregular that the last person to see the murder victim alive, and the only person in the house at the exact time that the neighbors heard a disturbance on the stairs, would be the last person interviewed in a thorough and professional homicide investigation.

Paul's interview with investigators started at one o'clock and ended ten minutes later. Trooper Richard Mahoney, Lieutenant Frank Kelly, and Paul's father were present. The report, in its entirety reads as follows:

*Paul stated that he left the house after Ryan left and he specifically remembers closing the outside door. This door locks automatically upon being closed. Mr. Paul Downing confirms this.*

Paul made a one-sentence statement. There were no follow-up questions. The interview ended at 1:10. What happened during the other nine and a half minutes of the interview? Did they sit in silence? Or did they just not write the conversation down so as to keep those parts of the interview from the defense team?

By the time Paul was interviewed, Eddie was already in custody. He'd been arrested the night before.

By Wednesday, the police knew from Carol Ortiz, Janet Downing's sister, that the front door was usually closed but was never locked. The police never investigated to see if the door automatically locked, as Paul stated.

If Paul was involved in an altercation with his mother or in hurting his mother, or if he was protecting someone who was involved, this sensational murder would be reduced to yet another domestic tragedy. Reilly was already fully committed to his story of the altar-boy-next-door, grandson of a Somerville police chief, murderer of his best friend's mother. He had just announced that he personally would be prosecuting the case. There were TV cameras and newspaper reporters everywhere. There was no going back now.

Since it was clearly established by the first officers on the scene that there had been no forced entry to the house, how the perpetrator(s) gained entry was a critical question. If the front door was unlocked, anyone could have walked into the house. If it *was* locked, then the person who committed this crime either had a key or was let into the house.

Paul left the house two different times: once, shortly after 6:30 when he and Jeannie initially went to Revere Beach, and again at 8:30 when he and Jeannie, Michelle, and Raquel again left to return to Revere Beach.

At trial, Paul testified that he was in his room when his mother returned from grocery shopping at 6:30 and asked him to bring in the groceries. He didn't want to help her, so she had to ask twice. When he finally went downstairs to tend to the groceries, he saw his brother Ryan and Joey Dion outside, rollerblading. He told them to get the groceries from the trunk and bring them in the house. Paul leaned against his mother's car and waited for Jeannie O'Brien to call him about the trip to Revere Beach.

Ryan testified that after bringing in the groceries, he and Joey went up to the top of the hill to meet Chris Ford, after which all three came back to the Downing house. That's when Eddie came from across the street and joined them in the kitchen. At that point, Paul was already gone, Ryan believed, because he did not see him again.

Why was it so important for Paul to insist in his only statement to the police that he'd locked the front door?

It would certainly have been much simpler if Paul said he'd left the door open and unlocked, as usual. Reilly wouldn't have needed to provide a way for Eddie to have gotten in the house to kill his best friend's mother. Everyone knew that Eddie didn't have a key to the Downing home. Reilly knew that the doorknob on the back door from the kitchen to the deck was broken. He also knew that Eddie had just learned this the day of the murder. In their haste to create a scenario that fit with Paul's statement that the door was locked, the prosecution (in the first clear example of creating a story to fit the crime scene) decided that Eddie gained access to the house through the broken kitchen door.

In this rush to explain how Eddie could have gotten into the house, they didn't realize how flawed that theory was.

Earlier that evening when Ryan, Joey, Chris, and Eddie were hanging out in the Downings' kitchen, Eddie went out the back door onto the deck. He tried to get back in, found he couldn't, knocked, and was let in by Ryan. Ryan explained that the doorknob had been broken for a long time: it would turn 360 degrees but wouldn't open the door. Ryan claimed he then told Eddie that the family used the deadbolt at night to secure the door while they slept.

At the transfer hearings, Reilly had each of the boys tell this story, suggesting that Eddie had a specific interest in understanding how the deadbolt on the inside of the door worked. I remember hearing the story over and over again as each witness testified. The sheer repetition of it distracted the listener from the faulty logic of the theory. Even if the deadbolt were off, the door would not open from the outside, as Eddie had learned by locking himself out. If the deadbolt were on, Eddie would have needed a key. So, locked or not locked, this door could not have been used as a means of access into the house because the doorknob didn't work.

Ryan, questioned at trial by DA Reilly, described the conversation he had with Eddie about the kitchen back door:

*A: He—ah—was at my back door. He was on the–he was in–on the outside of my back door. . . . I went over, opened the door. And, ah, he was questioning me about the doorknob, ah, on my back door. And I knew it was broke. But, ah, I was explaining to him that it was–it was broken. . . . But we—we lock the, ah, we locked it with the deadbolt, ah, at night, to sleep. Ah, it's not a night bolt all the time so nobody can come in the house. Ah, and that was it. That was the conversation.*

*Q: Did you show him where that deadbolt was?*

*A: Excuse me?*

*Q: Did you explain the deadbolt to him?*

*A: Yes. I didn't*[40]*—I shut it. And I said, "See. We shut it. And we lock it at night." And I turned it. And I turned it back in. And he–he touched it. He goes, "Like this?" And I said, "Yeah, that." And so I showed him.*[41]

Clearly Ryan is confused about how to answer these questions. The doorknob is not operational. Eddie could not get back in after closing the door even though the deadbolt was off at the time. Ryan doesn't understand what the DA wants him to say about the deadbolt and how it works.

This jumble of misstatements about the back door was too confusing for the jury to understand anything except that Eddie knew something about how to operate the deadbolt on

40 This could be a mistake in transcription for "I did it."

41 TR. SIXTH DAY OF TRIAL, September 22, 1995, pp. 295,296

the back door. But that's all the prosecution needed the jury to know.

Eddie's lawyer didn't ask any questions about the door on cross-examination. He didn't seem to understand that the DA's theory was fundamentally flawed. Access to the house should have been a major question of fact for the jury to decide.

So how and when did the killer get in?

Eddie found the front door open and ajar at approximately 9:15 when he found Janet Downing mortally wounded on the dining room floor. Paul said he'd locked the door. If it was locked, the person who opened it had to have a key. But why would they leave the door ajar, instead of closing it, if they were about to murder Downing? Was it because Downing opened the door to her killer? Did Downing open the door for the perpetrator(s) and then get pushed inside as the murderous rampage began? Or were the perpetrator(s) already in the house when Paul came home at 8:00? Did Paul know who he/they were? Was he protecting someone?

Each of these scenarios is plausible. The fact that the cellar door was open pointed to Artie Ortiz, who, according to Gina Mahoney, kept drugs he sold to the neighborhood in a small refrigerator in the basement. Was Ortiz in the basement when Paul came home at 8:00? Did he wait for Paul to leave, then go upstairs and assault his sister-in-law when she became frightened?

Ortiz had keys to the house. Ortiz apparently had been going in and out of the house without Downing's knowledge for four months since Downing had thrown him and his family out. If Ortiz was involved, he entered the house when Downing's car was clearly visible outside. If the house lights were off, as Paul testified they were when he left at 8:30, then Ortiz could have assumed the house was empty and Downing was visiting a neighbor.

Since Paul would have been in the house at the time the disturbance on the stairs was heard, and because he was the last person alleged to have seen his mother alive, the fact that he was not interviewed further has always been a gaping hole in the investigation.

The Downing family and several neighbors knew that Paul and his mother had been having difficulties. Paul had begun to act out sexually in the prior year, causing his mother concern for his safety. He'd had a few relationships with older men; Downing had confronted one and told him to stay away from her son. Downing talked to both "Big Ed" O'Brien and her friend Gina Mahoney about these episodes and her worries about Paul's safety.

The police interviewed Father Henry Jennings, the pastor of St. Joseph's Church, who told Trooper Martin Conley and Sergeant Robert Fahey that there were problems in the Downing family. He advised them to talk with the neighbors about what was going on in the family, and specifically referred them to Ann Bradbury, a longtime resident who'd lived next to the Downings for years.[42] When the police called Bradbury (no face-to-face interview was ever conducted), she told them that "Janet had trouble with her husband, Paul, her son Paul, and her daughter Kerriann. That's all I can tell you."[43]

The police didn't ask more and she didn't offer more, at least according to the written police reports. Once again, no further investigation was done into what kind of trouble Ann Bradbury was referring to. Attorney Bob George's failure to fully investigate Paul and his relationship with his mother deprived Eddie's defense of offering an alternate theory of the murder, and raising the possibility that Paul may have

42 Somerville Police Detective Report, Sergeant Robert E. Fahey, interview, July 31, 1995, at 1:40 p.m., p. 1

43 Id., p.1

been involved.

Motive and opportunity are the two questions that direct all homicide investigations.

Eddie had neither. Paul Downing had both. And Artie Ortiz had both.

# CHAPTER 14

## THE SEARCH

On Tuesday, about forty hours after the murder, the CPAC Unit prepared the paperwork for a warrant to search the home of Edward and Patricia O'Brien, believing that evidence of the murder would be found.

The basis for their belief was "a bloody fingerprint determined to be that of Edward S. O'Brien was lifted from a post in the cellar of the Downing home. . . . On the night of the murder, Edward O'Brien had lacerations to his hand and scratches on his arm and leg. . . . When interviewed, he denied having any involvement in the Downing murder. . . . Marco Abreu, a friend of O'Brien's, reported he was at the Downing residence at 9:20 that night and observed the cellar door to be open and in addition observed a person he believed at the time to be Edward O'Brien jump from the bushes behind the Downing home."[44]

Authorization to search the house was granted at 5:45 that afternoon.

At about the same time the judge was signing the search warrant, Eddie O'Brien's house was under surveillance by Trooper Martin Conley and Sergeant Robert Fahey. When Eddie and his father returned from buying Eddie new sneakers, Conley pulled them over and told them to go directly to the Somerville police station; when they arrived, Eddie was arrested. It had not yet been forty-eight hours since

44 Report of Trooper Joseph Duggan, interview of Edward S. O'Brien, July 24, 1995, p. 2

Janet Downing was found stabbed to death in her home.

The search of the O'Brien house commenced. Neither Eddie nor his parents were present to read the warrant, call counsel, or oversee the search. While this is legally permissible, the fact that the search commenced once the family had been secured at the station raises suspicion that they wanted no one observing them while they searched.

Nine people from law enforcement participated in the search. From the district attorney's CPAC Unit were Troopers Thomas Sullivan, Martin Conley, David Otte, Richard Mahoney, Mary Ritchie, Thomas Joyce, and Laurie Bender. Daniel Ryan was there from the Somerville Police Department and Robert Pino from the State Police Crime Laboratory. Eddie's room was searched, and a dagger and a bayonet were found in the file cabinet in his room. An open black pocketknife was allegedly found lying on the floor of the room. All of these items belonged to Eddie's grandfather.

Officers came into and went out of the rooms without any log being kept as to who was searching what room at what time. A photographer went into Eddie's room to photograph it. Because there was no log, it was impossible to determine if she went in before or after any officers searched. The O'Briens' marital bedroom and other areas were also searched.

Trooper Otte eventually went to the backyard of the residence to look through the trash. He found a small red penknife wrapped in a paper towel.

The penknife became the centerpiece of the prosecution's otherwise circumstantial case against Eddie. This knife was part of a set of two Eddie had retrieved from his grandfather's attic belongings. It had a three-inch single-edged blade and a four-inch decorative red carved handle. The matching knife had a green handle.

The knife was found in Eddie's own trash can. Would

anybody be stupid enough to throw a knife away in his own backyard trash can? If he wanted to get rid of the knife, wouldn't he have done so already? He'd known since early Monday morning that he was a suspect in the case. There was something wrong about one knife being left on the floor of his bedroom in plain sight, and another being disposed of in the trash behind his house, especially since no one yet knew of the hilt found on the stairs at the Downing home.

Eddie didn't know that the police had found part of a knife at the murder scene. Only weeks later did it became known that a "piece of metal" was found on the third step of the Downing residence's stairwell.

I studied all the police reports and search warrant materials again and again. Something was missing, I didn't know what or why, but I knew the answer had to be in this file somewhere.

I finally found the reason why this knife and the lucky trash can find weren't right. The answer was buried in an addendum to a prior police report summarizing an interview with Walter Golden, the owner of Mid-Nite Convenient. At 8:45 on the night of the search of Eddie's house, Walter Golden was asked to come into police headquarters to be interviewed. Lieutenant Kelly and Sergeant Fahey of the Somerville police interviewed him. He made and signed a statement about knives that Eddie had used at the store and a particular knife, a green penknife, that Eddie had shown to another employee. The report was typed up, and Golden signed it. It is dated July 25, 1995. Fahey witnessed his signature.[45]

Fahey wrote a second one-paragraph report regarding Walter Golden. It was misfiled with reports of the prior day because it was misdated July 24, 1995. It stated, "After interviewing Walter Golden with Lt. Kelly of the Somerville

45 Statement of Walter Golden dated July 25, 1995, p.1

Police Dept. (report filed by Lt. Kelly), myself and Trooper Joseph Duggan Mass. State Police, showed him a red-handled knife found in Ed O'Brien's room."[46]

Those words jumped off the page: *found in Ed O'Brien's room.* In his *room*?

The knife apparently had been found in Eddie's room and intentionally moved to the backyard trash can so that another member of the search team could discover it.

When found in Eddie's bedroom with the sword, the dagger, and the black penknife, the red-handled knife was just part of his grandfather's collection; if found in Eddie's household trash, it became evidence of enormous importance.

46 Somerville Police Detective Report, Sergeant Robert E. Fahey, dated July 24, 1995, p.1

# CHAPTER 15

## THE KNIFE HILT

Finding that piece of metal, the alleged hilt of Eddie's green penknife, on Janet Downing's carpeted stairs the night of the murder was a coup for the prosecution. It was the single most incriminating piece of evidence they had at that time.

Every part of Eddie's own story, which he told before he knew about the Commonwealth's evidence, was consistent with the prosecution's circumstantial evidence. He did kneel down and touch Downing, he did turn her over, he did get her blood on his hands, he did close the front door, he did go down the cellar stairs, he did hit the cellar post, he did run through the clothes hanging on the line and out the cellar door, and he did get scratched up in the thickets behind the Downing home.

Eddie has no idea how this metal hilt got on the Downing stairs. He didn't then, when he learned that the metal piece referred to the hilt of a knife, and he doesn't now, twenty-one years later. He doesn't remember whether he even used the green penknife that Sunday morning to cut the straps on the newspapers that he put together at Mid-Nite Convenient. He generally used whatever knife or box cutter was over by the newspapers. He has no memory of retrieving it from where Jack Arnold had placed it the night before, or putting the knife in his pocket or bringing it back home that day. He had the same shorts on from early Sunday morning until he gave his clothes to the police at 2:30 a.m. Monday. There was no evidence that the knife was or had been in his pocket when his clothes were taken as evidence.

This metal piece, the hilt of a knife that seemed to conclusively tie Eddie to the crime, incredibly was not forensically tested by the District Attorney's Office until July 1997, two years after it was discovered at the scene.

The "metal piece" or "Item 21" (as it was identified in the various forensic laboratory documents) was initially sent for analysis to the State Police Crime Lab in Sudbury on July 24, 1995. In January 1996, the hilt, along with seventeen other pieces of evidence, was sent to the FBI lab in Quantico, Virginia. Everything was returned to the State Police Crime Lab six months later without being tested. The following September the metal piece was sent to Cellmark Diagnostics in Germantown, Maryland, because the Massachusetts lab wasn't certified to do DNA testing at that time. In November 1996, polymerase chain reaction (PCR) testing was performed on it. (Polymerase chain reaction is a technique used to amplify trace amounts of DNA.) No trace of Eddie's DNA was found during the PCR test. Further DNA testing on this item was discontinued after the initial test—at Reilly's request. [47]

In November 1996, Reilly was awaiting the Supreme Judicial Court's ruling on his appeal of the first transfer hearing. He certainly didn't want the defense getting its hands on any evidence that potentially excluded Eddie from DNA on the alleged murder weapon.

In June 1997, with Eddie's trial now pending for September, Reilly ordered the DNA testing on the hilt to be completed. The chemist's report, dated July 25, 1997, excluded Eddie O'Brien as the primary source of the DNA on the hilt. The primary source of the DNA was female. Janet Downing could not be excluded as the primary source of the

47 Correspondence from Cellmark Diagnostics dated November 27, 1996

DNA. No conclusion could be reached as to the secondary source of DNA. The secondary source was male.[48]

Reilly would have known this would be the result when he halted further testing a year earlier. Now, just weeks until trial, it was too late for the defense to do independent DNA testing to determine whose DNA was on the hilt.

Reilly didn't request further testing of the DNA recovered from the hilt, or compare it with any other DNA samples besides Eddie O'Brien. The lab had samples from Paul Downing Sr., Paul Downing Jr., Ryan Downing, and Artie Ortiz. None were compared. The DNA was not run through the national database to see if a match could be found. Unknown crime scene DNA is usually run through CODIS (the FBI's online Combined DNA Index System), to determine whether the contributor was a suspect that the police had never considered or didn't even know about.

And, in what was becoming a pattern of serious omissions and poor decisions, Eddie's lawyer failed to retain a DNA expert or a lab to do independent testing on any of the items found at the crime scene. The state lab reserved a portion of each sample of all the evidence taken for defense counsel to do his own testing.

Despite two years of telling Eddie that he was getting the best forensic people on the case (Michael Baden, medical coroner from TV forensic shows, to challenge the wounds described at the autopsy; Barry Scheck, leading DNA expert and founder of the Innocence Project; and the best labs to do the DNA analysis), Bob George never had anything tested independently.

Eddie needed a DNA specialist to explain to the jury that he could not have used the knife with the broken hilt to stab Downing and cut himself on the blade as the hilt gave way—

48 Report of laboratory examination, Cellmark Diagnostics, July 25, 1997, signed by Charlotte A. Word and Melissa A. Weber

which was the DA's theory of the murder weapon—without leaving DNA behind. Without expert testimony, all the jury heard was "this is part of the murder weapon, it belonged to Eddie O'Brien, his DNA isn't on it because it might have gotten contaminated somehow, but it was definitely Eddie's knife."

There was also no defense expert to question whether a blade three inches long could inflict wounds that severed a rib and penetrated a lung into the back cavity, as Dr. Atkins testified at the transfer hearings. The coroner testified that the penknife could have inflicted Downing's wounds, but he never measured the matching red penknife against the actual wounds. By the time the police seized the red penknife from Eddie's room, and apparently moved it to the trash can, Downing's remains were at the funeral home. Atkins' expert opinion, which he shared with the jury, was that the three-inch penknife could have been the murder weapon.

Atkins' opinion was an educated guess, not a scientifically based conclusion. At least some of those wounds measured to a depth of over four inches. That is inconsistent with a three-inch blade. After the doctor said it could have been the weapon, it's unlikely the jury even realized this discrepancy.

The actual green penknife was never found. The prosecution's theory that the green penknife was the murder weapon was never challenged by the defense.

This single piece of evidence, the alleged hilt of the missing green penknife, provided the defense with a multitude of ways to challenge both the theory that the penknife was the murder weapon and that Eddie was the perpetrator of this senseless, brutal crime. The evidence did not support the DA's theory that he cut himself on the blade of the penknife while stabbing Downing. If it were true, his blood and DNA would have been all over the hilt. In addition, the knife had a second hilt secured by a second pin, which presumably remained on the penknife. That hilt would certainly have prevented Eddie's hand from slipping down onto the blade. Finally, only a double-edged knife could have inflicted the wounds seen on Eddie's hands, not a single-edged knife like the green penknife.

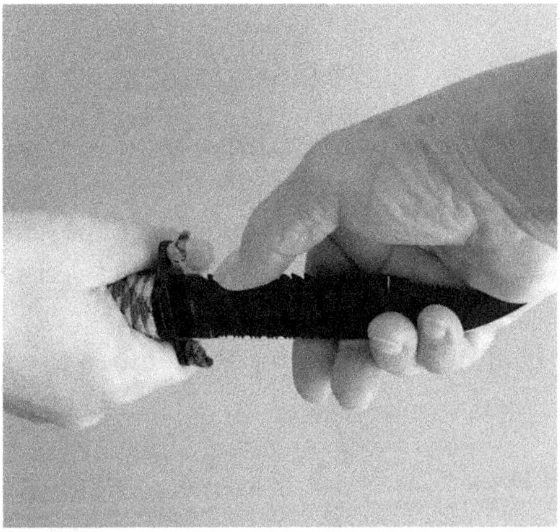

*Illustration of Double Edged Knife*

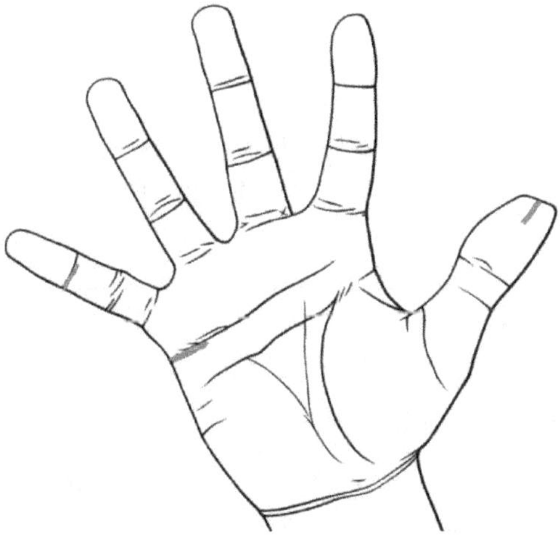

*Illustration of Eddie's Hand Wounds*

# CHAPTER 16

## PRETRIAL SUMMER OF 1997

After Judge Timothy Gailey's decision of May 9, 1997, sent Eddie O'Brien to Superior Court to be tried as an adult, he appeared for his arraignment there. Murder cases in Superior Court in Middlesex County can take up to two or three years to come to trial; the average time is two years.[49]

Eddie's trial date was set for September 19, 1997—just four months away.

Eddie's lawyer, Bob George, filed two motions at arraignment. The first was for a stay of the proceedings so that he could appeal Gailey's transfer decision. That was denied on the grounds that such a request needed to be filed in the Supreme Judicial Court along with the appeal of Gailey's decision. George had not filed any notice of appeal, appeal or request for a stay in the higher court. He also did not do so after Eddie's arraignment.

The second motion requested a continuance of the trial date, because four months would be insufficient time to prepare for a murder trial of this magnitude. George said he just could not be ready by then. (He was right.) Reilly, however, had no time to waste. If he was going to run for attorney general in the 1998 elections, he had to announce and begin campaigning in the fall of 1997. Time was of the

---

49 In 2002, only 20 percent of cases in Middlesex Superior Court were resolved within one year; 68 percent of cases were still pending thirteen to twenty-four months after arraignment; 15 percent were still pending after two years.

essence. He was pushing for an immediate trial.

George's request for more time to prepare was denied. The judge said that the case had been "pending" for two years. Technically that was untrue: a case doesn't start "pending" until the defendant is arraigned in Superior Court, which had only happened that day.

So began a series of pretrial hearings and motions, some procedural and some substantive. The purpose of pretrial hearings is to determine whether the parties have exchanged discovery information appropriately, whether there are any agreed-upon exhibits that will be entered into evidence at trial, and to settle any disputes about the required exchange of information and documents. It is also the time to request that certain evidence be excluded at trial, or to argue for the inclusion of disputed evidence.

George was a well-known defense lawyer in Boston. He had his own two-person firm and hired other attorneys when needed for trial. When he came onto Eddie's case in November 1995, he required a fee of $65,000 to litigate the case; that price soon went up to $85,000. Over the course of the next two years the O'Briens paid him a total of $150,000. After two protracted transfer hearings and four appeals in the Supreme Judicial Court, George told Eddie's parents he was out of money in the summer of 1997, and asked for an additional $150,000.

They didn't have any more money.

Eddie's mother was caring for four kids at home, the youngest of whom was two years old, and working in food service for Tufts University part-time. Ed worked as the manager of Mail and Receiving Services at Harvard University. Their incomes were modest. They had already mortgaged the family home. There was just no more money to be had.

No doubt George's original fee was long gone by this

time. The case had consumed almost two years of constant work.

Estimating what a criminal case will cost to defend is very difficult. These cases are not done on an hourly fee basis, where the client pays for the time expended. Rather, they're done on a flat-fee basis, a sum that will sometimes, but not often, include the cost of expert witnesses and independent testing of the evidence. George's quoted fee included all experts and testing. In this particular case, not even a more seasoned defense counsel could have predicted that he or she would spend two years litigating the case in the Juvenile Court alone, and make four separate trips to the Supreme Judicial Court before even getting to the murder trial.

It is unfortunately not uncommon in the legal business for an attorney to underestimate a fee and be working for free by the end of the case. Rank-and-file defense counsel are rarely wealthy. It is possible to lose hundreds of thousands of dollars on a case you have not priced out right. Big law firms have the ability to absorb such losses. Smaller practitioners like Bob George do not.

Lack of money may be the reason why none of the experts that George discussed with Eddie over the prior two years had been contacted, let alone hired. Or perhaps George had believed that the case would remain in Juvenile Court and that Eddie would, even if found guilty, be freed after serving his twenty-one year sentence. Whatever the reason for not having expert witnesses on board, there was no way he was going to hire them now with no money, and prepare them for trial with no time.

Forensic experts of the necessary notoriety would have required a financial retainer months before their expected appearance. They would have required access to the documents and evidence they would be rendering opinions on months before. If they were to do independent testing, specimens would need to have been sent weeks or months in advance. Nevertheless, when reporter Ann Donlan of the *Boston Herald* asked Bob George how he would explain the forensic evidence at trial, he told her: "We have not yet tested the blood. We have our own experts that will take a look at the blood."[50]

During the many pretrial hearings conducted that summer, the judges (there were several) ruled to exclude certain evidence. Eddie's sodium amytal test was out. Profiler Gregg McCrary's testimony was also out.

Blood evidence would be critical. The science of DNA was in its infancy in 1997. In Massachusetts, DNA evidence was not automatically admissible into evidence. A lengthy foundation which met exact criteria had to first be established in order for an expert to testify as to DNA findings. But just three weeks before Eddie's trial began, the Supreme Judicial Court issued a ruling making DNA evidence admissible at trial without this tedious foundation being established first.[51] The court found that Cellmark Diagnostic's specific tests and the population calculations that were used to compare results were scientifically reliable. Any future DNA evidence using these tests and this calculation would automatically be admissible into evidence.

Eddie's DNA had been tested at Cellmark Diagnostics. The tests and calculations used were identical to the ones in the new ruling. His DNA evidence would now come into evidence as a matter of law.

Eddie's DNA had been identified in four places at the Downing home: the inside of the foyer or inner front door, the dining room door jamb, the cellar post, and a dress hanging on a clothesline in the basement.

---

50 Donlan, Ann E., "O'Brien Faces the Music," The Boston Herald, May 21, 1997

51 Commonwealth vs. Adam Rosier, 425 Mass. 807, August 25, 1997

Prior to this development in case law, Eddie's lawyer could have challenged the introduction of the DNA evidence as scientifically unreliable. Had he been successful, the only evidence the DA would have had to rely on would be the fingerprints and the hilt of a knife that the DA alleged was the murder weapon. That may not have been sufficient for a conviction, especially where motive and opportunity presented such enormous problems.

Because the DNA was now clearly coming into evidence, Eddie's statement about finding Downing and confronting her attacker would absolutely be required to explain his presence at the scene to the jury.

Some of the evidence in dispute included the alleged statements that Eddie made (primarily to his best friend, Ryan Downing) which, according to the DA, showed his motive to murder Janet Downing.

Reilly argued to allow these otherwise inadmissible hearsay statements: "Although the Commonwealth in the course of its presentation of evidence will be able to offer physical and other evidence which directly connects the defendant to this crime, what the Commonwealth will not be able to do with that evidence is explain why this happened; why the defendant killed his neighbor; questions of motive, questions of intent; questions of, or issues of state of mind. . . . [T]he Commonwealth's theory of this case . . . is that this is not a case that is without a context. It is not a case where there is . . . a totally unexplained act of violence. . . . Our theory of the case, Your Honor, is that there was an escalating pattern of behavior on the part of the defendant, Edward O'Brien."[52]

If the DA had been hoping for a sweeping order allowing all these allegedly incriminating statements to be heard by the jury, he was resoundingly defeated. The court ruled

52 TR. September 3, 1997, pp. 54-56

that each and every one of the acts or statements that the Commonwealth sought to introduce into evidence would require a separate and distinct inquiry as to why it was being offered and whether it was admissible under an exception to the hearsay rule, and, if admissible, whether it was actually relevant. This is the proper standard by which such evidence is evaluated by the court. Reilly would have to fight to get each one of these statements into evidence, and he had already lost some of those fights during the transfer hearings.

In another hearing in July, George asked that any unidentified fingerprints lifted at the crime scene be provided to him for comparison. Assistant DA Tom O'Reilly, who was filling in while DA Tom Reilly was on medical leave, stated that no other fingerprints except those belonging to Eddie O'Brien were lifted from the scene.

That assertion was untrue. A report from the state crime lab, dated and received after this hearing, listed seven additional latent prints lifted from the scene, three of which were "identifiable" but were not Eddie O'Brien's. The other four had insufficient detail for an identification to be made.[53]

The denial that any other prints existed and subsequent failure of the DA to hand over these prints for defense analysis are serious breaches of court discovery rules as the prints were potentially exculpatory. (Exculpatory evidence is evidence favorable to the defendant that exonerates or tends to exonerate the defendant of guilt.) Bob George either failed to see the breach or ignored it. He didn't inform the court that other prints existed or file a motion to compel the DA to turn over that evidence.

Those fingerprints remain unidentified. One of them was lifted from the hallway bathroom where the killer washed up and left the water running. That would have been a very

53 Report of Trooper Wayne H. Riley, Crime Scene Services Section of the State Police dated August 7, 1997, pp. 2, 3

important print to run through the Integrated Automated Fingerprint Identification System (IAFIS) to see if a match came up.

Assistant DA O'Reilly further informed the court on July 27, 1995, that evidence "had been sent out" on July 15, 1997, for DNA testing and that the results were not expected back for another four to five weeks—yet another false statement. The only DNA testing not complete at that time was on "the metal piece" (Item #21, the hilt of the knife) and Janet Downing's bloody fingernail clippings. The fingernail clippings had already been sent out for testing, a month earlier, but testing had been ordered suspended until further notice. The letter of transmittal dated June 27, 1997, accompanying the fingernail clippings, said, "Please hold the enclosed blood stained fingernail clippings from Janet Downing until you receive authorization from DA Tom Reilly. . . . Upon authorization, please conduct PCR (STR) testing on these specimens."[54]

The knife hilt had been sent to Cellmark Diagnostics in Maryland a year earlier. Initial PCR testing on that showed no trace of Eddie's DNA. Why would the prosecution try to obfuscate the fact that this evidence was not "sent out" [55] on July 15, 1997? Laboratory reports would eventually reveal the truth. It didn't make any sense unless the prosecution assumed that their "hold" and "discontinue testing" orders would not be included in the letters between the state lab and Cellmark Diagnostics or the final reports from Cellmark Diagnostics.

Studying these letters and reports took a considerable amount of time, especially to connect the dots and clearly

54 Letter from State Police Crime Laboratory to Cellmark Diagnostics dated June 25, 1997, p. 1

55 Report of Melissa Weber, Cellmark Diagnostics, dated November 27, 1996

see the misrepresentations made to the court. When you receive complicated DNA and scientific reports right before a trial, the chances that you are noticing the dates that specimens are submitted and dates that they are tested, and cross-referencing that information with the correspondence file, are slim to none.

Unless, of course, you suspect something unusual has occurred with the evidence.

In Eddie's case, all the evidence was highly unusual and questionable, and required the kind of in-depth effort that has now brought these irregularities into full view.

The pretrial hearings took place on eight separate days over the course of the summer, ending on September 8, 1997, just seven days before jury selection would begin.

Bob George didn't have months to spend scrutinizing discovery material. He barely had time to draft an opening statement.

# CHAPTER 17

## JURY IMPANELMENT

The trial began at 9:00 a.m. on Monday, September 15, 1997.

Jury impanelment took most of the first three days. Several hundred jurors were summoned to court, divided into panels of eighteen. After the judge posed preliminary questions to the entire jury pool, the panels were brought into the courtroom one at a time. Each person in that panel was then asked specific questions about the case they would hear if chosen as jurors. If the judge found that the juror harbored no bias and could serve for the duration of the trial without imposing undue hardship, he declared that the juror "stood indifferent." The Commonwealth and defense attorneys then express that they are "content" with that juror, or they "challenge" the juror, and seek removal of that person from the jury.

In a jury where sixteen jurors are seated (twelve jurors and four alternate jurors), each side can challenge up to sixteen potential jurors who have been found to stand indifferent without stating the reason for their challenge. Those jurors so challenged are immediately excused from service. These are called peremptory challenges.

In addition, either side can challenge jurors "for cause," but must disclose what that reason or cause is. Jurors challenged "for cause" are not necessarily excused from serving. They usually do feel resentment toward the lawyer who challenged them, so "cause" challenges are often argued at side bar, outside the hearing of the juror.

At the conclusion of jury impanelment in this case, 226 potential jurors were questioned, 208 were excused, and sixteen were seated. Bob George used fifteen of his peremptory challenges. DA Tom Reilly used thirteen.

Of the 208 excused jurors, seventy-six were excused because they said they had already formed an opinion that Eddie O'Brien was guilty based on media coverage. Only one person said she had seen no media coverage of the case at all, and just one person said she believed that Eddie was innocent after reading and hearing about the case.

Eddie's case was sensational and its coverage was exacerbated by the nonstop political posturing surrounding it. Every single change in the juvenile justice law occurring in the 1990s in Massachusetts was the result of a specific and horrific murder. It was legislation by fiat, not thoughtful discussion.

Commencing in 1994, an entirely new Juvenile Court system was created, separate and apart from the existing trial courts, and a score of new judges were appointed to preside over those courts. Whereas Heffernan and Gailey were District Court judges who presided over juvenile sessions periodically, the new Juvenile Court judges did nothing but hear juvenile cases. All this reorganization and expansion was in anticipation of the feared wave of juvenile superpredators that never materialized as pundits predicted.

There is little doubt that all the media exposure that was generated had tainted the jury. Over one-third of the randomly selected residents of the largest county in Massachusetts called to jury duty that September had already formed an unfavorable opinion about the case without hearing a shred of evidence. All of the seated jurors admitted they had some knowledge of the case due to newspaper and television coverage of prior proceedings.

Should Eddie's lawyer have renewed his motion for

change of venue after one in three jurors had to be dismissed due to pretrial publicity? It is highly unlikely that, once sixteen jurors were found to "stand indifferent," the judge would have granted such a motion. However, in order to preserve an issue for a later appeal, a lawyer must make the motion and the judge must deny the motion. George never did, and the O'Brien jury was sworn in and seated shortly after noontime on Wednesday, September 17, 1995.

The district attorney took one more run at getting the judge to allow him to reference the statements Eddie allegedly made to Ryan Downing so he could use them in his opening. Reilly reiterated to the judge during a lobby conference (a meeting taking place in the judge's private office) that the statements gave a "context" to the crime. George pointed out that they gave "motive" to the crime, not context, and that the prosecution was not required to prove motive.

Judge James McDaniel relented and allowed the district attorney to refer to four statements in his opening. The judge said he would give the usual admonition given to all juries that opening statements are not evidence: they are what the prosecution or the defendant hope to prove at trial. The only proper evidence that the jury may consider is what is actually said by a witness under oath.

The jury admonition is a powerful instruction, but opening statements can be very persuasive. It is very hard for a juror to "disregard" a statement that made an impression or had the ring of truth to it.

The jury was escorted to a bus at 12:30 p.m. and taken to Boston Street to see the scene of the crime, the Downing home at No. 71. They would also view the Reckley house at No. 73, Eddie O'Brien's house at No. 74, and the Mid-Nite Convenient store. This process is referred to as taking the jury on "a view."

During a view, the lawyers point out certain areas or

features and tell the jurors to take note of them because these places or things will come up during the trial. The judge rarely speaks. The lawyers are not permitted to say how or why these areas, places or things are important, just that they want the jury to remember where the windows are, for example. The jurors are escorted by two jury bailiffs who carry large staffs to indicate that this is a working jury. No one except the lawyers is permitted to speak with the jury while they are working.

The view took most of the afternoon, and the jurors returned at 3:00 to cold pizza that had been awaiting them since the 1:00 lunch hour.

At 4:00, the judge assembled everyone in the courtroom to announce that opening statements would be deferred to the following day, Thursday, at 9:00 a.m.

# CHAPTER 18

## THE RULES OF THE GAME

How do twelve people who have little or no knowledge of a complicated legal proceeding make sense of all these new words and expressions they are hearing for the first time? How do they know what it means when a judge says "sustained" or "overruled"? The truth is that, often, they don't understand. It is daunting and stressful to be a juror.

Judge McDaniel always spent the first part of a jury trial instructing the jurors on what to expect in the coming days and weeks. He defined some of the jargon and formalities required of a trial so that the jurors might feel better equipped to listen to the evidence in an impartial way.

"The only evidence in this trial," he told the O'Brien jury, "will be the sworn testimony of the witnesses who testify and any exhibits that are marked into evidence during the course of the trial—and, of course, any inferences that can be drawn from the evidence. And on that basis, and that basis alone, you determine whether the defendant is guilty or not guilty. It is strictly your memory that governs as to what the evidence and testimony in the case is.

"When an objection is made, then it is incumbent upon me to rule on the objection. If I say the objection is sustained, that means the witness may not answer the question. And you are not to consider that question at all. It is as if the question were never asked. You are not to speculate as to what the answer to the question might have been.

"Of course, if I say the objection is overruled, that means

the witness may answer the question. And then the answer and the question go to you for your consideration.

"Now, sometimes during the question and answer process, lawyers are permitted–especially on cross-examination–to ask what are called leading questions. And a leading question is simply a question that is couched or phrased in such a way that it may suggest the answer to the witness that the lawyer is looking for. . . . A 'no' answer to a leading question is not evidence for your consideration. It is only if the answer is yes, or affirmed in some way [that you may consider it evidence].

"Any words from my mouth indicating to you that you are not to consider that evidence, you are to do exactly that. You are not to consider that evidence thereafter. You may say to yourself, 'Well, I have heard the question; I have heard the answer. And I like it. I'm going to use that later.' . . . You are not permitted to do that."[56]

In fact, the jurors were not permitted to take notes, and the chances that they'd remember everything the judge had just said over the next eleven days were slender.

After his remarks, the judge told the jury that at the end of all of the testimony and taking of the evidence, their names would be put into a basket and four names would be extracted. Those four people would become alternate jurors and the other twelve would become the deliberating jury. He instructed jurors to listen to all the evidence, because no one knew who the alternates would be until the end.

And thc trial began.

56 FOURTH DAY OF TRIAL, September 18, 1997, Vol. VII, pp. 15-24

# CHAPTER 19

## OPENING STATEMENTS

District Attorney Tom Reilly got up and faced the jury. A soft-spoken and somewhat diminutive man in his early fifties, he continually used his hands to express himself and to tell the Commonwealth's story of the crime.

He was well-prepared, and, knowing that what he would say in his opening statement was not evidence, he took substantial liberties with the facts, the motive, and the theory of the case. His narrative went well beyond what he was going to be able to produce in hard evidence. One of the more glaring distortions in his remarks was his slow, deliberate and vivid description the "investigation" that was undertaken on the night of the murder. Shortly after the body was discovered, he said, both Somerville police and State Police officers began to fan out. "Their job was to find and locate, interview people. Someone who may have seen or heard something. Someone who could provide some information that would help them track down Janet Downing's killer. You will find that in the course of this case, they interviewed scores of people."[57]

He went on to tell the jury that the police "listened and listened" to everything that Eddie O'Brien had to say about his mugging, about how he was in the Downing house earlier that day but did not return to kill Downing. "The evidence in this case will show that for two straight days everyone was willing to listen to Edward O'Brien as he told his story. And

57 Id., p. 42

they all came to grips with the unthinkable. But the evidence kept piling up."[58]

This was designed to make the jury believe that Eddie was the last person the investigators suspected. Reilly knew that Eddie was actually the first one suspected. Reilly knew that was the prosecution's weak point, and he made sure he refuted it before George had a chance to accuse him of a rush to judgment and an incomplete and sloppy investigation. It was a good strategy—and it ignored the truth. Eddie was interviewed once—on the night of the murder, not for "two straight days." Neither of the "two straight days" included interviews with the most important witnesses who did see and hear things and who could have helped track down the killer.

There is no record of any police interview with Gina Mahoney, with whom Downing spent the last ten hours of her life. What about Downing's best friend, Jean McGeary? No record of any interview with her, either. And Artie Ortiz, of whom Downing was so afraid? No record of any interview with Ortiz. Reilly initially didn't even know that he'd lived in the Downing home. Police didn't interview Barry and Virginia Reckley, who shared a common wall with Downing and had heard a commotion on the victim's stairway where at least some of the bloodshed took place.

The four statements that Eddie allegedly made to Ryan Downing grew to six statements. They were dramatically woven into Reilly's opening: "Edward O'Brien was developing an interest in Janet Downing. An interest that the evidence will show is unusual for a fifteen-year-old young man and a forty-three-year-old mother of his best friend. It started out rather innocently. More curiosity than anything else. 'Why is your mother always sitting out in the driveway when she comes home from work?' . . . 'Why is your mother

---

58 Id., p. 38

always going next door to Jean's house?'. . . 'What's going on in your mother's bedroom? I see a light flickering. Is she okay?'. . . But it went on and on. And it didn't stop. And, at some point, the tone of it, the context of it changed. 'Your mother's gay. Your mother's a lesbian.'. . . And comments about her cooking. 'Don't ever eat over her house. Her cooking is bad.' And the evidence in this case will show that within hours of her murder on the night of July 23rd, Edward O'Brien was in the den area of her house, watching Janet Downing as she lay sleeping on her couch."[59]

Reilly paused and looked at each of the jurors. "Later that Saturday night," he continued, "within twenty-four hours of her murder, Edward O'Brien, just out of the blue, made the following comment to her son Ryan: 'Ryan, have you ever hurt—felt like hurting someone?" And his fists were clenched. And Ryan didn't know what to make of the comment but said: 'No. No, I haven't," and just passed it off."[60]

The district attorney went on to describe Eddie and Ryan's friends returning to the Downing house after 9:00 that night and seeing someone who could have been Eddie coming from the bushes behind the house. He outlined the physical evidence eventually recovered from the Downing home and crime scene, noting that Downing had type AB blood, a very rare blood type shared by only 4 percent of the population. (And also shared by her ex-husband, her children and Ortiz; that blood type was not so rare in that house.)

He talked about specimens collected that were "consistent" with Eddie's blood, type O, the most common in the population. He emphasized those specimens that actually *were* Eddie's blood, as proven through DNA testing.

Finally, Reilly said in conclusion, this evidence would

---

59 Id., pp. 44-45

60 Id., p. 48

prove, beyond a reasonable doubt, that "Edward O'Brien is responsible for what happened to Janet Downing." It was strangely anticlimactic.

Bob George, a short and solidly built man of Greek descent in his mid-forties, immediately jumped up to address the jury. He had dark hair that was beginning to show a bit of grey at the temples. He had a deep and resonating voice and was known for his adroit oral arguments, honed over a career of fifteen years, first as an assistant district attorney in Norfolk County, then as a criminal defense attorney. George liked to walk back and forth in front of the jury box. He was a master at making eye contact with jurors and speaking to them, not at them.

He liked to lean on, and sometimes pound, the railing in front of the jurors.

He started off strong, telling the jury that what the DA had just said was not evidence, it was a promise. A promise to prove to them, through the evidence he was now bound to produce at trial, that Eddie had committed this crime in the manner in which Reilly said he did. He asked the jury to make sure they held him to his promise.

Then, as if he hadn't prepared, his statement became unfocused and rambling. "Now Mr. Reilly would have you believe, from the evidence which will be coming from that witness stand, that at some time on July 23rd, 1995, after 9:00, that a ninth-grader from Don Bosco, who had never been in trouble his entire life, the evidence will show, suddenly decided, after handing out popsicles on his front porch to the neighborhood kids, and putting 'Sleeping Beauty' into the videotape machine for his little sister, his baby sister, in the room you were in yesterday, just got up, walked twenty-five yards across the street and stabbed his best friend's mother ninety-eight times. It's ridiculous. It's ridiculous. The evidence will show there is no evidence, whatsoever, to indicate that there was anything in his mind, let alone murder."

Hardly an illuminating argument for innocence: The evidence will show there is no evidence that there was anything in his mind?

Then, to make this even more confusing, he adds: "Mr. Reilly will present evidence in this courtroom which he says will show you that he was a developing psychosexual killer, at fifteen. With no evidence, whatsoever, in his past."

Why on earth did George introduce the word "psychosexual" to the jurors when Reilly had not characterized Eddie that way? George had argued to keep all of that "profile" testimony out of evidence. Now he was the one bringing the profile in! This made absolutely no sense.

Now would have been the prudent time to tell the jurors exactly what evidence would show, that Eddie *wasn't* obsessed with Downing. But he didn't do that. George went immediately into a long discourse about how Eddie's mugging was never investigated by the police, how Eddie was a suspect in the murder from the moment he called 911 from the Mid-Nite Convenient store, and how the police at the murder scene and the police at the hospital with Eddie were talking back and forth, deciding that Eddie was the suspect in the murder.

"At that point, Eddie O'Brien was gone. His life was over. Fifteen-year-old under arrest, right then, as far as the evidence went. Anything that happened after that is colored by that. And that's what the evidence will show."[61]

While this is admittedly a very important point, it wasn't presented within the context of a coherent argument for why this rush to judgment was wrong, how the police got it wrong from the very beginning, and how this led to the systematic ignoring of any evidence to the contrary, or the consideration

61 Id., p. 72

of any other person with a possible motive to kill Downing.

George's failure to talk about evidence that may have excluded Eddie O'Brien as a suspect is indefensible under any standard of legal practice. When he finally did comment on the blood evidence, he said, "The evidence will be that some type of metal piece was found in that house that they want you to believe is the murder weapon. You will hear all about that in this case. It was tested. And you will hear all about it."[62]

And he stopped there. *You will hear all about it.*

What he should have said was, "You will hear that Eddie was excluded as the primary source of the DNA is on this murder weapon. The Commonwealth's own tests exclude Eddie O'Brien as the primary source of DNA on the metal piece. You will hear that the DNA collected from underneath Downing's fingernails, the fingernails she used to fight for her life, indicated that DNA from more than one individual was obtained. Eddie O'Brien was excluded as the source of that DNA. The Commonwealth's own tests exclude Eddie O'Brien as the primary source of the DNA under her fingernails."

But he didn't.

His opening statement failed on every level. It didn't tell the jurors what George would be able to prove to them; it didn't tell the jurors why the Commonwealth's theory of the case was not consistent with the evidence that the defense would present. It reinforced Reilly's thirty-minute opening statement without providing any alternative path for the jurors to take.

But the worst was still to come. In his conclusion, George made a promise to the jurors. He promised he would prove that Eddie did not commit the crime because "he is not the type. He doesn't have the background. He doesn't have

62 Id., p. 73

the character. He had no motive. He didn't commit the crime because he is innocent."

One can only conclude by this pathetic ending–"he didn't commit the crime because he's innocent"–that Bob George truly did not understand what powerful evidence of Eddie's innocence he actually did have.

# CHAPTER 20
## THE TESTIMONY BEGINS

The Commonwealth's first witness was John (Jack) Arnold, Walter Golden's son-in-law. He worked one evening a week at the Mid-Nite Convenient. Arnold, coincidentally, was also a court officer in the Somerville District Court.

On Saturday night, July 22, 1995, Eddie brought a green penknife down to the Mid-Nite to show Arnold, who was a knife collector. Eddie wanted to know if the knife, or the pair of knives (it was a set), was collectible or worth any money, and, if so, whether Arnold was interested in buying it. Eddie already had told him about the knives the week before that. Arnold told Eddie to bring them in and he'd take a look at them. There was no dispute about those facts.

The point of Jack Arnold's testimony was simply to identify the piece of metal found on Downing's stairway. Reilly asserted that the green penknife was the murder weapon, but that penknife was never found. All he had was the hilt of a knife. He questioned Arnold about it.

*Q: At some point did he give you that green knife?*
*A: Yeah. He handed it to me. I looked at it.*
*Q: What did you do with it?*
*A: I just opened it up and looked at it.*
*Q: And did you notice something?*
*A: I noticed the hilt on the knife was loose.*
*Q:And what is the hilt?*
*A: Ah, you open a knife, the hilt opens up with the knife.*

*There's two hilts on either side of the blade.*

*Q: Did you touch that hilt?*

*A: Yes, I did.*

*Q: What did you notice about that hilt?*

*A: It was real loose.*

*Q: What happened next?*

*A: Ah, I told him I didn't want it. I thought it was a piece of junk. And that's when I handed it back to him. And he handed it—*

*Q: What did he say?*

*A: He said—asked me to leave it under the counter until tomorrow morning.*

Jack identified a number of photographs of the store and the counter under which he placed Eddie O'Brien's knife that night.

Then Reilly showed him the photograph of the red knife.

*Q: Do you recognize that knife?*

*A: Ah, similar.*

*Q: Similar to what, sir?*

*A: Similar to the knife that Mr. O'Brien showed me on the 22nd.*

*Q: Similar in what respect, sir?*

*A: Everything but the color of the knife. It was green, instead of red.*

*Q: Direct your attention to the hilt area.*

*A: Looks like the same hilt that was on the green knife.*

*Q: Mr. Arnold, I would ask you to look at the object that's in that bag, and ask you whether that object is similar to the green knife you saw on Edward O'Brien on the night of July 22nd?*

*A: It is.*

*Q: In what way?*

*A: Ah, the scrolls, on both sides of the knife.*

*Q: I ask you to examine the piece of metal contained in that bag. And ask if you recognize that piece of metal?*

*A: It looks like the hilt of a knife.*

*Q: Is that similar to the hilt that you saw? Edward O'Brien's green knife?"*

*A: Similar. Yes.*

*Q: July the 22nd, 1995?*

*A: Yes, sir.*

*Q: What was its condition on that night? Was it firm or was it loose?*

*A: It was loose on the knife.*

*Q: How loose?*

*A: You could move it with your hands.*[63]

Reilly ended with the witness. He had gotten exactly what he needed from Jack Arnold. He'd implanted in the mind of the jurors that the piece of metal found at the murder scene belonged to Eddie O'Brien.

George cross-examined him. After establishing that Arnold had known Eddie for a few years, even before Eddie began to do the Sunday morning papers, he turned to the actual knife he'd seen that Saturday night. Arnold couldn't say that the piece of metal in the evidence bag that Reilly had just shown him was the same one from the knife that he'd seen; it was similar.

On redirect, Reilly had Arnold testify that police first interviewed him on the Tuesday after the murder (the day Eddie was arrested). This seemed an odd and isolated fact with no bearing on his testimony. Besides, the police report indicated he was first interviewed on Wednesday, July 26,

63 TR. Fourth Day of Trial, Vol. VII, p. 92

1997.[64]

It acquired importance and context when the next witness testified. The next witness was another son-in-law of Walter Golden, Frank Kling. Kling worked with Eddie on the morning of July 23, 1995.

Reilly questioned him:

*Q: In the course of the morning of Sunday, July 23rd, 1995, did Edward O'Brien show you something?*

*A: Yes. He did.*

*Q: What did he show you?*

*A: He showed me a small knife.*

*Q: What color was it?*

*A: A greenish, pale green.*

*Q: What did he say to you?*

*A: He showed me the knife that he had. And I took it from him and opened it up.*

*Q: And did you notice something about that knife?*

*A: Well, when I opened it up, I noticed it was, ah, cheap. A cheap knife. And the hilts on the side were loose. I just closed it back up and gave it back to him.*

*Q: And what did you do with that green knife with the loose hilt?*

*A: I handed it back to him.*

*Q: And did he take it?*

*A: Yes. He did.*

*Q: Did you ever see that green knife with the loose hilt again?*

*A: No. I did not.*

*Q: At what time Sunday morning was that?*

*A: It was like 10:00, 10:00 in the morning.*[65]

---

64 Somerville Police Investigative Report, July 26, 1997, Statement of Jack Arnold, Lieutenant Francis Kelly

65 Id., p. 121

Reilly had Kling compare the metal piece in the evidence bag with what he'd seen that day. He said that it looked similar to the one he saw.

On cross-examination, George established that Kling had never mentioned that he noticed the hilt was loose on the knife. George asked Kling to review the entire transcript of his testimony at the grand jury hearing in August 1995. Kling admitted that he saw no place in his recorded testimony where he talked about the hilt being loose.

George tried to establish when Kling first told Reilly about the loose hilt. Kling faltered, and said it was when Reilly came to his house with detectives two days before the grand jury testimony in August 1995. He then said Reilly maybe wasn't there, that he told the detectives about the loose hilt at his house two days before he testified at the grand jury. He couldn't explain why, if he'd told them the hilt was loose, in his grand jury testimony two days later and in answer to Reilly's direct question to him he said he'd never examined the hilt. It immediately became clear that the prosecution had revised Kling's testimony during his preparation, a huge score for George.

A lot of skill goes into the questions a lawyer *doesn't* ask. For example, George didn't ask whether Kling had talked to Jack Arnold, his brother-in-law, about the case over the past two years. That could have changed his testimony without implicating the district attorney. And it would make perfect sense that the two of them compared their testimonies and that Kling's memory could have been tainted by Jack Arnold's clear memory of the hilt.

Kling was far from the last witness whose testimony had transformed over the course of the last two years, after multiple interviews by the district attorney and investigators from his office.

A larger question is why Eddie would have showed yet another person a knife that he intended to use in a murder later that night—a cheap piece-of-junk knife with a loose hilt.

These two little decorative knives were a boxed set, with Chinese carvings on them and, to this fifteen-year-old boy, they seemed more collectible, more valuable than an ordinary penknife. He had larger, far more effective knives lying on the floor of his bedroom if he was looking for a weapon to hurt someone.

# CHAPTER 21
## THE CRIME SCENE

The "murder weapon" having been introduced, the Commonwealth turned its attention to the crime scene and the first responders.

Officer Joseph Blair of the Somerville Police Department was the first to testify. He'd been first on the scene, at approximately 9:56 p.m. He encountered Ryan Downing sitting on the curb removing his rollerblades and crying. With him were Barry Reckley and Ed O'Brien Sr.

In fact, Virginia Reckley had been sitting next to Ryan and comforting him. Apparently Blair did not note or remember this, and it was not raised on cross-examination. A minor point, perhaps, but it can remind the jury that in the chaos of a murder scene, the obvious can often be overlooked, even by a police officer.

Ed O'Brien told Blair not to touch anything. Blair stopped, turned and asked him to repeat his statement. Ed said, "You'll know what I mean when you see it."[66]

Blair went in the front door, then the foyer and stood in the hallway. He observed the stairway in front of him and midway up he saw blood on the carpet and right-hand wall. He saw the hallway bathroom beyond the stairs and noted the water was running. He looked to the right and saw Downing lying face up on the dining room floor with a golden retriever beside her. He testified that the dog got up, came to him, grabbed his left hand, led him over to Downing's body,

66 Id. p.152

and lay back down beside her. Blair reached down to check her carotid artery for a pulse and felt none. There was no movement and no reaction to his touch. Downing was cold to the touch and appeared deceased to him. When he pressed on the carotid artery, a gaping wound opened up.

This was Blair's first homicide scene in his eight years as a police officer.

Emergency medical technicians from the City of Somerville soon arrived, and he ordered them out and declared the area a crime scene. Shortly thereafter, paramedics arrived from Cataldo Ambulance. They wanted to make efforts at resuscitation, and Blair allowed them to come in (odd in light of his refusal to allow the city ambulance personnel in). They intubated Downing, inserted intravenous lines, began cardiac stimulation, and defibrillated her. During this process, all of her clothing was cut off with scissors. Blair noticed that her bra was lying loosely across her breasts. The paramedics cut it between the two cups. When they turned her body over, Blair saw the bra was unhooked in the back. He subsequently examined the bra and saw that it had many stab marks on it, yet there were no stab wounds to her breasts, just above and below them.

Blair introduced most of the crime scene photographs into evidence. Since there were no photographs of the victim (the body had been removed before the forensic photographer arrived), he identified what was at the scene when the victim was still there, and what the medical personnel left behind. There was a substantial amount of medical debris (wipes, medical gloves, and paper on the dining room floor) that had to be explained to the jury.

*Dining room in Downing house*

While the paramedics worked, Blair ordered his partner, Officer Steven Johnson, to secure the premises outside. He also passed the dog to Johnson to remove it from the house. Firefighters arrived but remained outside. The paramedics put Downing on a stretcher and moved her out of the house. As they transported her, blood dripped from the stretcher onto the hallway floor, the foyer floor, the front stairs and halfway down the front walk, until Downing was transferred to a rigid stretcher and put in the ambulance.

Sergeants Charles Femino and James Stanford from the Somerville Police Department arrived and took charge of the scene. Blair remained on the scene approximately two hours, until about midnight.

There was not much George could or would do on cross-examination with Blair. The gist of his questioning went to what was not in Blair's written report that he testified to at trial, but these were very minor points. The takeaway that George aimed to leave with the jury was that the integrity of the crime scene was completely compromised by the number of people going in and out of it. He showed through Blair's testimony that there were some fourteen individuals who came into and left the house before any perimeter was set up to isolate the crime scene from further contamination.

George continued through his questioning of all of the first responders to show that the civilians, medical personnel, and police had hopelessly contaminated the scene as they tromped about the house unrestricted. He wanted the jury to deduce that the evidence found at the scene, therefore, was equally unreliable.

This strategy was a double-edged sword. He wanted the jury to understand how blood got transferred from one place to another by stepping in it and carrying it into another room, or by an EMT throwing medical debris containing blood on a chair or against a wall. But if George knew there was blood evidence favorable to Eddie, then he certainly would not want the jury to question that evidence.

Given the opening statement he'd made just that morning, it is unclear whether George understood the narrow line he was asking the jury to walk. How was the jury to decide what was and what wasn't contaminated? How would he establish that the DNA on the hilt of the knife and the DNA under Downing's fingernails was not contaminated, while other blood evidence may have been contaminated?

Sergeant Femino had been with the Somerville police for fourteen years. He arrived at the scene at approximately 10:30 that night—according to his testimony. However, Janet Downing was removed at 10:22, so his memory was clearly incorrect. He observed Edward O'Brien Sr., Barry Reckley, and Officer Johnson inside the Downing house. Femino ordered the two civilians out of the crime scene. The EMTs and paramedics were still working on Downing and preparing her for transport. He walked past the medics and the victim and into the kitchen. He said he wanted to use the telephone in there.

After Downing was removed from the dining room, Femino conducted a protective sweep of the house to look for additional suspects or additional injured victims, assisted by Officer Michael Brown and Sergeant James Stanford. With no one else in the home, crime scene tape was put up outside the perimeter of the house and Brown was stationed at the cellar door to prevent anyone from entering or exiting. Johnson remained at the front door.

In the den area, Femino observed a pair of women's slippers, a package of cigarettes, and an ashtray. On the couch was a pillow. In the living room closest to the dining room, he observed an ottoman tipped over, with a woman's earring next to it. In the hallway he saw blood on the hallway floor, door casings, baseboards, stairs, and rugs.

On the carpeted stairway, Femino testified that he saw what appeared to be the hilt of a knife on the third step.

*Stairway in Downing house*

Femino noted a bloody fingerprint above the doorknob of the inside of the inner front door.

*Inside foyer door*

In the kitchen there was a small drop of blood on the kitchen floor, one on the refrigerator, and much more blood on the door and doorknob to the cellar stairs next to the refrigerator.

In the cellar stairwell, there were bloodstains and smears on both sides of the walls. At the bottom of the stairs he noted a bloody fingerprint on the wooden beam. He followed the trail of blood over to the left side of the cellar, past a clothesline with bloodstained clothes hanging on it, to the cellar door. There he observed a door and bolt with blood smears on them.

*Cellar door to backyard*

The following day, in the daylight, Femino saw what appeared to be small drops of blood on the sidewalk on

Hamlet Street, crossing the street and then stopping on the opposite side, about halfway down the street at No. 20 or 22.

DA Reilly had Femino identify thirty-five photographs of the Downing house and various parts of the rooms on the first floor and cellar. There were additional photographs of the outside of the house, front and back, as well as aerial photographs of the neighborhood. All were marked into evidence.

The tape of Eddie O'Brien's 911 call to the Somerville police about his mugging in Union Square was played for the jury. A photograph of Eddie at the police station that night in his white T-shirt, green shorts, and black sneakers was also introduced. Then the first of the photographs of Downing's body at the autopsy was shown to the jury on monitors through an overhead projector. George objected to the photograph, but the objection was overruled.

Autopsy photographs are almost always permitted into evidence, even though they are highly prejudicial because they are so gruesome. But the objection must be made to be preserved on appeal. Only the jury was permitted to view this photograph, not the audience.

The court day came to a close, the worst time to end from the defense's perspective.

The entire day had been taken up with details of the discovery of Janet Downing's body by her sixteen-year-old son Ryan, the attempts to resuscitate her, and photographs of a bloody, horrible murder scene. Eddie O'Brien then was introduced into the trial for the first time, and a photograph of him taken the night of the murder was shown to the jury.

The day ended with a photograph on the two monitors facing the jury. It showed the deceased woman's battered face and neck with twenty-two slashing wounds across it, ear to ear. Reilly showed the jury the blood and gore of the horrific murder and then successfully connected Eddie

O'Brien to it in the jurors' minds by the simple introduction of the tape of his 911 call and photograph in the middle of the testimony. That would be all they thought about for the next seventeen hours, until they returned.

# CHAPTER 22

## DAY OF DISASTERS

Sergeant James Stanford was the officer who did the protective sweep of the top two floors at the Downing crime scene. Subsequently, at approximately 12:05 that night, he was ordered to Somerville Hospital to interview Eddie O'Brien regarding his mugging in Union Square. Trooper Joseph P. Duggan of the DA's CPAC Unit arrived shortly thereafter as well. Stanford was called to the witness stand to testify about that and the interrogation of Eddie at the Somerville police station after Eddie was treated at the hospital.

While at the hospital, Stanford testified that Eddie, after conferring for a minute or two with his "Uncle Doc" (Richard Daley, who was married to Eddie's maternal aunt Mary) and father, agreed to talk to Stanford and Duggan. Stanford requested that blood swabs be taken from each of Eddie's shins, and was permitted to do so. Both Ed and Eddie believed this to be in furtherance of the investigation of the mugging in Union Square. A dried drop of blood on Eddie's right shin would much later be identified as type AB, consistent with Downing's blood type. Otherwise, nothing else collected from Eddie that night, including his sneakers, his shorts, his underwear, and his T-shirt provided any blood evidence.

Eddie was wearing an "Above the Rim" white T-shirt, inside-out. This is the same T-shirt that Michelle Cameron had described him wearing at 8:30 when she, Paul, Jeannie, and Raquel left for Revere Beach. He had been wearing the

T-shirt inside-out all day long.

After they photographed his legs and his hands, front and back, Eddie was questioned in a detective conference room. Present in the room were his father, Stanford, Duggan, and police Captain Robert Bradley.

Neither the captain nor the DA's CPAC Unit had ever been involved in questioning a mugging victim before. Any doubt that Eddie was a murder suspect disappeared when prior to questioning they presented him with a juvenile Miranda waiver form outlining the constitutional rights of a person over fourteen but under seventeen years of age.

Victims of crimes aren't asked to sign Miranda waivers, only suspects are.

Next Duggan, from the DA's office, presented a consent form to the O'Briens that permitted the collection of "clothes, photographs, fingerprints, and blood" from Eddie. Stanford testified that Eddie signed this form voluntarily after his father, Edward O'Brien, filled it in. Eddie's clothes were collected, he was fingerprinted and photographed, and the "interview" began at 2:40 a.m. The blood had already been removed from his shin; the consent was signed two hours later. At this point, Eddie's father was removed to a separate room to be interviewed, and his mother and Uncle Doc came in to be with Eddie during the questioning.

Stanford testified that Eddie recounted his day, estimating times as best he could. Eddie arrived at Ryan's house. The groceries were already in the house; he hadn't helped bring them in. He and Joey Dion went into the den at Ryan's house to play a video game, but they saw Ryan's mom sleeping on the couch and left. He went into the kitchen with the other boys, just hanging out. They all left at the same time. Eddie went home.

Eddie told police he was on his porch when he saw Paul go into the Downing house for ten to fifteen minutes, after which Paul left with Jeannie O'Brien and two other girls for Revere Beach. Eddie said he went down Boston Street to Burger King. It was busy and the food upset his stomach, so he left to go to Jimmy's, another food establishment in Union Square. He told them about the mugging that happened on his way down Somerville Avenue.

Eddie said he never returned to the Downing home after he'd left with everyone else earlier that night. When asked if he'd been in the thickets behind the Downing home, he said, "I don't go back there anymore." He explained that after he'd left the house he had not seen Ryan Downing, Joey Dion, or Chris Ford again.

On cross-examination, it was clear that Stanford had never seen the hilt of a knife as he went up and down the stairs doing his protective sweep of the home's second floor and attic. Nor was he told there was a piece of metal or a hilt on the stairs to be cautious about. He was directed to the left side of the stairs because there was blood on the right side.

George questioned Stanford in the same incredulous tone he would use with all the police officers about their failure to put on protective gloves, shoe coverings, or other gear at the crime scene. In addition, Stanford had placed the two vials containing Eddie's shin swabs into his upper uniform pocket instead of an evidence envelope. He bagged Eddie's clothes and shoes with his bare hands and brought all of these items back to the crime scene to turn over to Robert Pino, the forensic chemist who would test everything at the State Police Crime Lab. The possibility of contamination was repeatedly suggested to the jury. However, George lacked any evidence of contamination to support this theory. Nor was he able to point to any specific questionable piece of evidence. As a mere possibility, it carried little weight with the jurors.

Diane Roberto, the nurse who cared for Eddie at the

hospital and swabbed his shins, described Eddie as calm during the entire procedure, including when the police were in the room with him. She observed no one in the room behaving in an emotional way. She saw Eddie, his father, and his uncle at 11:35 p.m. on July 23, 1995. When he first came in, she did not notice any injuries to his arms and legs, just the cuts to his right hand. Eddie brought her attention to his other abrasions on his legs. She cleaned his right hand with saline but didn't clean his legs or other areas. "There was not much blood or anything"[67] on his shins.

Before the next witness, Trooper David Otte, took the stand, George was at sidebar to object to the admission of two important pieces of evidence: a *Boston Herald* newspaper and the red penknife allegedly found in the garbage can.

It was Otte who'd found the red-handled knife in the trash behind the O'Brien home. The fact that police Sgt. Fahey's report had said that the red knife was found in Eddie's bedroom and not the trash totally escaped George. Because he was unaware of Fahey's report, he didn't challenge the location the knife was actually found. And that location was the critical issue: it provided the "consciousness of guilt" the prosecution so desperately needed.

So George conceded the red knife, but challenged the admission into evidence of the two bayonets and other black penknife found in Eddie's room, which had no connection to the murder. The judge agreed with him, to which George responded, "Oh, wow." George seemed unaware this was a pyrrhic victory for the defense. The red knife was the problem, not these war relics and black penknife.

Would it have been better to allow those weapons into evidence in order to suggest to the jury that Eddie had far more effective weapons to choose from if he intended to kill someone? This was a strategic decision that another attorney

67 FIFTH DAY OF TRIAL, September 19, 1997 Vol. VIII. p. 295

might have made differently.

The newspaper in question was the *Boston Herald*, dated June 27, 1995, photographed on top of the dresser in Eddie's bedroom. The district attorney wanted to introduce not only the photograph that depicted it, but the front page of the *Boston Herald* itself. The front page had this headline: "We're Natural Born Killers." It was highly inflammatory and prejudicial.

Reilly wanted the jurors to have the actual front page so that they could read the article during deliberations. The photo was too small for them to see it clearly. George wanted it excluded because he said the paper was staged by being propped up on the bureau by another of the search party or the photographer.

What George did *not* argue was that the front page Reilly was offering *wasn't the item depicted in the photograph.* The police never seized the actual newspaper. This violated two rules of evidence allowing for the exclusion of this document.

George didn't argue this, as is soon painfully apparent, because he didn't *know* it wasn't the actual newspaper from the bedroom. Neither the warrant authorizing seizure nor the "return" on the warrant listed a newspaper as being seized from the house. George had had all of these documents for the past two years. His unfamiliarity with them produced a cross-examination that was frustrating and nonsensical. This critical error set off a series of evidentiary explosions which eventually allowed the jury to be exposed to evidence that they never ever should have heard.

David Otte was sworn in very late in the day. He'd been a trooper for ten years at the time of the murder, and was assigned to the Middlesex District Attorney's Office. Otte was sent (with five other officers, some from Somerville PD and some from the State Police) to the O'Brien house to execute a search warrant on July 25, 1995, while Ed and

Trisha O'Brien were with their fifteen-year-old son at the police station as he was being arrested.

What Otte said he first noticed in Eddie's bedroom, which he described as being "in disarray," was the front page of the *Boston Herald* on top of the bureau with the headline "We're Natural Born Killers."[68]

The judge immediately instructed the jury that they could only consider this evidence on the issue of the defendant's state of mind at the time of this particular incident. "And that's the only basis upon which you can consider it. Only on that limited basis." Inexplicably, the judge then added to what is intended to be an instruction limiting the scope of the evidence: "If you, in fact, of course, find that the photograph depicts what actually happened there, that is depicted in the photograph—all right."[69]

Not only is this instruction incomplete and confusing, it contradicts his instruction that it only be considered in terms of Eddie's state of mind.

Reilly offered only Page One of the paper as an exhibit, and it was allowed into evidence over George's objection. The judge had previously instructed Reilly to cut off the last page, which was attached to Page One.

The judge then permitted Otte to read the article into the record: "*As they changed out of their bloody clothes, the men who plunged a knife into an elderly Avon man 27 times bragged that they were natural born killers, Norfolk County prosecutor said yesterday. 'Haven't you ever seen natural born killers before?' suspect Patrick T. Morse allegedly bragged to a girl, after the gruesome slaying of 65-year-old Phillip Miskinnis. The chilling details of the trio's murderous attack and their fascination with the murder spree depicted in the motion picture 'Natural Born Killers,' were revealed*

68 Id., p. 345

69 Id., p. 347

*yesterday, when Morse, 18, and Leonard Stanley, 20 . . . .* That's all the article on the page."[70]

Bob George immediately stood up and asked to present a motion for mistrial at sidebar. It was denied.

Reilly continued his examination, moving to the search of the trash and Otte's discovery of the red knife. Otte testified that he "picked up an object that was wrapped in a paper towel. And it was heavy. And it was kind of hard. So I unrolled it. And there was a knife inside."[71]

When George finally got to cross-examine Otte, it was by happenstance that he discovered that the front page of the newspaper that was offered into evidence was not actually seized by the police from Eddie's room during the search. He had Otte identify another photograph appearing to show the whole newspaper on Eddie's dresser. Otte agreed: The whole newspaper appeared to be there. During his questioning Otte told George twice that he'd never recovered or seized the actual newspaper itself—whether it was the first page or the whole newspaper. Nevertheless, George pressed on as if Otte had never spoken.

*Q: Well, could you tell this jury where the rest of that newspaper is?*

*A: We didn't—we didn't take any of the newspaper.*

*Q: You only brought the front page in?*

*A: We didn't even take that. We just took photographs.*

*Q: Well, you have read the Boston Herald before, haven't you?*[72]

The jurors had to wonder what was going on here. Otte kept telling him the exhibit was not from Eddie's bedroom

70 Id., pp. 349, 350

71 Id., p. 358

72 Id., pp. 376-377

and George just ignored him and continued to question him about what might have been in the paper that day–what other stories might have been covered: sports stories, weather, human interest stories, etc. He seemed to not understand that he should move to exclude the exhibit because it had nothing to do with Eddie's room or the search. George moved two more photographs into evidence before the judge again interrupted, and asked to see counsel at sidebar.

*GEORGE: I move to strike that exhibit, Your Honor.*

*JUDGE McDANIEL: Well, I mean, I thought that was a—I thought that was something seized from the home. That's the only reason I allowed it to be offered into evidence.*

*GEORGE: So did I, Your Honor.*

*REILLY: He never said that, Your Honor. He said that—he never took it. He never took anything from that room. The warrant didn't authorize it. It was the same front page, different edition.*

*McDANIEL: I didn't hear that—I understood it to be the, he took that page, that page was propped up there, like that—And that's why I allowed it in. I never got that understanding.*[73]

George asked the judge to strike the exhibit right away, and give the jury a strong instruction about it, before the jury left for the weekend.

"No," Judge McDaniel responded. "I will do it on Monday. It will come out the same way."[74]

The testimony here was so confusing, and it was so obvious that George did not understand the evidence and was not listening to the witness' answers, that the jury must have been left with a "Who's on First? What's on Second?"

73 Id., p. 380

74 Id., p. 385

reaction to this testimony. It was essential that the judge clarify his own misunderstanding to the jury, but George didn't insist it be done.

The reading of the "We're Natural Born Killers" article, from an exhibit that was now excluded, should have been remedied before the jury adjourned for the weekend. It was the second time that the jurors were left with an overwhelmingly negative view of Eddie O'Brien with lots of time to think about it before it was corrected or mitigated.

# CHAPTER 23

## FUBAR

The sixth day of trial started off with a long lobby conference between the judge and the attorneys. Judge McDaniel had read in the newspaper that he was about to exclude the newspaper page that morning. "I don't like doing that. I don't like reading in the paper what I'm going to do."[75] George first denied then admitted to talking to the *Herald*'s Ann Donlan and apologized.[76] McDaniel then said that since George had told him Eddie would be testifying on his own behalf, that it really didn't matter whether the exhibit was excluded or not.

George backpedaled, saying they weren't yet sure whether or not Eddie would testify. Peter Stelzer,[77] an attorney working with George, gave an eloquent argument about how the issue had become so much larger than just the admission of the newspaper now that McDaniel had allowed the article to be read to the jury. He asked that the court not only strike the exhibit but strike all of David Otte's testimony about the exhibit as well.

McDaniel agreed that if he struck the exhibit, he would

---

75 TR. SIXTH DAY OF TRIAL, Vol. IX, September 22, 1997, p.6

76 Ann Donlan later became Tom Reilly's communications director and press secretary at the Attorney General's Office immediately following his election after the O'Brien trial.

77 Peter J. Stelzer no longer practices law in Massachusetts. He moved to Beijing to become the legal director for International Bridges to Justice, a human and legal rights advocacy organization.

strike all the testimony. He then requested a magnifying glass to see if he could read the article from the photograph itself. He determined that he could, with difficulty, read some of it. He told the attorneys that if the jury asked for a magnifying glass that he would provide them with one. He believed they would be able to read the article from the photograph, and the argument to exclude the newspaper page itself was becoming less compelling to him.

Reilly had already filed a motion to preserve Exhibit 73 (the newspaper front page) with an accompanying memorandum of law, citing cases and reasons why the front page should come into evidence. He argued in the alternative, that the entire newspaper, which George offered at the beginning of Otte's testimony, be substituted for the single page.

George should have explained that he only proposed to admit the entire newspaper when he believed the front page that was going in came from Eddie's room. He should have renewed his motion for a mistrial. He did neither. All he said was that he wasn't able to read the article in the photograph with the magnifying glass.

Ultimately the judge decided to reserve his ruling regarding the newspaper, in order to review Reilly's motion and memorandum first.[78]

He ordered the trial to proceed.

Otte continued to testify under George's cross-examination about the search on July 25, 1995, noting that Eddie's room was searched at approximately 7:30 that evening. There were approximately five others with him, but only two or three with him in the bedroom. He couldn't recall if the photographer went in before or after him.

---

78 This ruling was never to come. The jury was never instructed that this piece of evidence did not come from Eddie's room, or that the judge had made a mistake in thinking that it had come from Eddie's room.

George asked him to testify about the many sports trading cards found in the room on the floor and in other places. Didn't that show that collecting and trading sports cards was on Eddie's mind during this time period?

He returned to the newspaper, and Otte testified that the two photographs George showed him indicated that the entire newspaper, not just the front page, was on top of the bureau. The disaster of the prior day's testimony was somewhat minimized as George went through all of the other things in Eddie's room that reflected Eddie's state of mind on July 25, 1995: an astronomy book and telescope, sports trading cards, photographs of friends and family, a Celtics jersey hung on the wall, barbells, a baseball glove, religious photographs, and even more newspapers under Eddie's bed.

Each time he asked Otte whether or not these things also reflected what was on Eddie's mind on July 25, 1995. Each time he made the point that the newspaper wasn't the only thing on Eddie's mind. It mitigated some of the damage.

George picked up his copy of the entire newspaper and walked to the sidebar. He told the judge that he wanted to offer the paper, but he didn't want to lose his rights to his previous objections and arguments about excluding Reilly's Exhibit 73. McDaniel assured George he would mark it for identification only, and not as an exhibit. (When something is marked for identification only, the jury will not be able to take it back into the deliberation room with them. It is not yet "evidence" in the trial. It is marked for identification so that the attorney can refer to it and have the witness testify about it. The witness cannot read from it or quote from it because it is not yet in evidence.) George didn't want it marked into evidence because he was objecting to Reilly admitting it into evidence.

George handed Otte the newspaper and asked if he could identify it. Otte testified that it appeared to be a copy of the same paper he saw in Eddie's room. George said: "I offer this, Your Honor." The judge responded, "Exhibit 84." George had apparently forgotten that he was supposed to ask that it be marked for identification only. Instead, he'd just had the exhibit he was seeking to exclude from evidence marked into evidence. He did nothing to correct the record. He continued with his examination of the trooper. Then he caught himself, and partially fixed the problem by asked that the newspaper be a "chalk"—something used to illustrate testimony—instead. The newspaper was clearly not a "chalk" as defined legally. It's not a chart or a drawing or a model of the newspaper, it's the actual newspaper. Nothing in the record explains why George didn't just mark it for identification as they'd agreed to do.

The larger question is why George continued to inquire about the newspaper with this witness. When McDaniel decided the trial would continue notwithstanding the fact that he hadn't ruled on Exhibit 73, George could have asked for permission to continue his cross-examination after the judge made his ruling. If the exhibit was excluded, then there would be no need to refer to it further. If it was kept in evidence, he could have asked the questions he thought were necessary later. Why didn't he do this? It made no practical or legal sense for George to question the witness further about an exhibit that he had moved to be stricken from the record. There was nothing to gain from this questioning. Technically he couldn't ask Otte to read from a "chalk" newspaper. But that was precisely what he did.

George was focused on letting the jury know that Eddie had the newspaper in his room because it contained notices for sports card shows in the area. Eddie went to these shows frequently to buy or trade cards or to have cards autographed. George directed Otte to the classified section in the back of the paper. But there was nothing Otte could read that would untangle the knot that this witness had caused by reading the "Natural Born Killers" article. The jury was never going to forget those words about the thrill of stabbing someone. They were never going to forget that Otte kept trying to tell George that he never seized any newspaper from the bedroom while George seemingly ignored his testimony and grilled him about throwing the paper away.

George continued to compound his problems with this exhibit at every possible turn: forgetting to mark it for identification only, marking it as a chalk. All of these are classic rookie mistakes, an inexplicable embarrassment for an experienced defense attorney.

George needed to cut his losses and try to regroup, reserving the right to recall Otte after the court ruled on the newspaper's admissibility. This witness and this evidence had become what military personnel call FUBAR: fucked up beyond all recognition.

# CHAPTER 24

## EDDIE O'BRIEN'S FRIENDS

It was only 10:30 a.m. when David Otte left the witness stand; Day Six of the trial would be long and arduous.

The next four witnesses took up the remainder of the day: Eddie's childhood friends Paul Downing, Joey Dion, Ryan Downing, and Chris Ford. Through these witnesses, Reilly intended to show that Eddie was obsessed with Downing in some sexual way that motivated him to murder her.

Reilly called Paul Downing to the stand. Paul had been the last to see his mother alive, had been taken from the crime scene to the hospital because he couldn't breathe, and, then, according to the police reports produced, gave his one and only statement, a single sentence, at 1:00 p.m. on Wednesday, July 26, 1995, the day after Eddie's arrest.[79]

Paul was now nineteen years old and a sophomore at Suffolk University, studying clinical psychology. He testified that his brother Ryan's friends, specifically, John Fitzpatrick, Marco Abreu, Eddie O'Brien, Garvey Salomon, Joey Dion, and Seth Dion were at the Downing house on an almost daily basis. All the boys were "very respectful" toward his mother, and she was cordial to them.

Paul said that in the summer of 1994 Eddie O'Brien had called him to say that he saw Paul's mother up in Paul's room with a flashlight. Paul explained that his lights go out periodically up there. After that, "continually over the

79 cf. chapter 13

years" Eddie commented about his mother. He said that Eddie asked why his mother sat in her car in the driveway smoking cigarettes.[80]

In the winter of 1995 Paul remembered that he was changing a light bulb in his mother's room and the light flickered for several seconds. He said Eddie called and asked why the light was flickering in his mother's bedroom. Paul told him he was changing the light bulb and that it was 10:30 p.m. and Eddie should be in bed.

Reilly asked him if he'd had any other conversation with Eddie about other neighbors.

*A: Uhm, it was the day after. I went over to get Jeannie and ah—*

*Q: I'm sorry, Your Honor. The day after what?*

*A: The day after the story. You know. Uhm we were—the week before, on a Saturday, I came to get her on a Sunday.*

*Q: In relation to the—July the 23rd, when did you have this conversation with him?*

*A: I said—*

*Q: When?*

*A: When?*

*Q: Yes.*

*A: Ah, prior to my mom's murder. Ah—*

*Q: How soon prior?*

*A: Prior? A week.*

*Q: Okay.*

*A: It was that Sunday.*

*Q: The Sunday before your mother died?*

*A: Yes.*

*Q: Would you tell us what Edward O'Brien said?*

*A: Uhm, he said to me that one night he was, ah, in his bedroom window. And he saw the neighbor across the street,*

80 TR. SIXTH DAY OF TRIAL, Vol. IX, September 22, 1997, p. 119

*a black woman, changing. And he described her. Ah, what he could see, the chest area. And she was wearing no—he described that she was wearing no clothes, except for a bra. And he just pretty much gave me the details of what he saw.*

*Q:What were the details of what he saw?*

*A:Exactly?*

*Q:Yes.*

*A:Uhm, he said that, ah, he could see her chest and her bra?*

*Q:And he said her chest?*

*A:He said, he said to me, "Oh, you should have seen it. I could—you could see her tits. She was wearing a red bra. You should have seen it."*[81]

Eddie had never told Paul about this event. Paul either heard it from one of the other boys and forgot that fact or altered the story, because Eddie was not in his bedroom when this occurred, and he was not alone. Eddie saw this woman undressing while sitting on his front porch with Marco Abreu. Marco and Eddie both saw the woman undress, as Marco confirmed in his own testimony on cross-examination.

However, Reilly was actively trying to create the impression that Eddie sat in his bedroom looking out his window at the neighbors' houses.

Paul testified about a conversation he said he had with Eddie at 6:30 on the night of his mother's murder. This was the first time this story had been told, even though Paul had testified at the prior transfer hearing. Paul said that he was leaning against his mother's car after Ryan and Joey brought the groceries in, waiting for Jeannie O'Brien to come out so they could leave for Revere Beach. He said that Eddie came up to him and asked if his mother was okay. Paul said she was and asked why. Eddie told him he'd just seen her

81 Id., pp. 128 - 131

sleeping on the den couch, and wondered if she was okay. Reilly continued:

*Q:Where did that conversation take place?*

*A:Ah, I was sitting on my mother's car, when I was waiting for Jean to come. He walked over to me. And he said: "What's wrong with your mom?" I said to him: "What do you mean?" He said: "Well, I walked in the house and I looked to my left, and I saw your mom lying down. I could see her head." I said: "She's tired." And he said: "Oh."*

*Q:Now who was in the house at that time?*

*A:Uhm, nobody. Just my mom.*

Bob George tried but failed to catch Paul in several inconsistencies in this new story about this conversation on cross-examination:

*Q:When was it [the conversation]?*

*A:It was when I—when—it was—when they brought in the groceries, I went back in the house to bring in the perishables.*

*Q:Okay.*

*A:Jeannie called. That's about like five minutes later. I went back outside. Ryan and them were already gone. Went over to get Jeannie. Went over back to my car. Ed approached me. He asked about my mom.*[82]

Thc story, if taken in the context of all the testimony, could not have occurred; but not all of that testimony had yet been heard. This is a challenge that vexes attorneys and jurors alike. It's not possible to tell the whole story of an event in a linear way. Each witness supplies a piece of the puzzle.

82 Id., pp. 140, 141

It was impossible for this conversation to have taken place. Why? Ryan Downing and Joey Dion soon testified that after they put the groceries inside the house, they got a call from Chris Ford and agreed to meet him at the corner of Munroe and Bigelow Streets, 351 feet from the Downing house. Ryan was on rollerblades. They met Chris, who was on a bike, and immediately came back to 71 Boston St. Paul was not there. He'd already left for Revere Beach.

For Paul's story to be true, the following would all have had to have transpired in the time it took Ryan and Joey to skate one block (351 feet) up the street, meet Chris (who is on a bike) and skate/bike back again:

Paul would have had to leave his mother's car and go back into the house and put away the perishables. About five minutes later, Paul would have answered a call from Jeannie O'Brien and arranged to go to Revere Beach. Paul would then have gone back outside and leaned against the car to wait for Jeannie. After a while, when she didn't come out of her house, Paul would have walked across the street, knocked on Jeannie's door, told her to hurry up, and returned to lean on the car again to wait for Jeannie. At this point, Eddie would have had to walk past Paul, without Paul seeing him, walk into the house, observe Janet asleep in the den, walk back out, and have the conversation with Paul that he described. Eddie would then have had to vanish so that Jeannie could come out of her house without seeing her brother, and start her car. Paul would have then crossed the street and gotten into Jeannie's car, and driven off for Revere Beach.

Because this was the first time that Paul mentioned this conversation, after two years and all of his prior testimony, George knew that it was probably fabricated. It couldn't have happened this way in the time frame Paul said it did. But George was not able to tell the jurors what they were about to hear from other witnesses. He couldn't "impeach" or show the inconsistency of this statement as compared to the other boys' statements, because they hadn't testified yet.

Reilly had to know this story was at the very least embellished, and at worst entirely fabricated. He was eliciting it; the testimony did not come as a surprise to him. He was encouraging Paul to tell this unlikely story.

Reilly very well understood that a story about Eddie seeing Janet Downing asleep on the couch while he was with all of his friends did not support his theory. During his opening statement Reilly had told the jurors they would hear about Eddie "watching" Downing as she was sleeping. Reilly needed the jury to think that Eddie was the kind of kid who would walk into the house when Downing was home alone and watch her sleep. That's what he told them at the start of the trial. Paul's story fit his theory and made Eddie O'Brien a creepy and voyeuristic kid.

It also suggested that this is precisely what Eddie O'Brien did just three hours later in order to commit an unspeakable and horrific crime. Bob George never asked Paul what direction Eddie had come from when he approached him at the car. He never asked Paul if he saw Eddie pass by him to walk into the house. He never pushed far enough to expose the impossibility of this conversation ever taking place.

According to Eddie, Paul was already off to Revere Beach with Jeannie when he walked back from Union Square. Eddie left the Mid-Nite Convenient at about 6:30. He stopped at Prospect Hill Park to talk to some girls who were not from the neighborhood. After that, he walked up to Bigalow Street and down to Boston Street, where he saw his friends Ryan, Joey, and Chris walking in the Downing front door. He crossed Boston Street and joined them in the house. Eddie insists that this conversation, as described by Paul, simply never took place: he wasn't there.

Much of Paul's testimony was either exaggerated or

untruthful. George was able to show numerous inconsistencies in his testimony on cross-examination, including his saying that Eddie had never been inside his house or played video games in his house. George asked him if this was the way he wanted to leave it with the jury, that Eddie was the only boy in the entire group of Ryan's friends who he never saw inside his house. He responded "Believe it or not, yeah."[83]

What? Did he mean believe it or not, I do want to leave it this way with the jury? Or did he mean, believe it or not, Eddie O'Brien never went in my house even though he and my brother were friends since they were toddlers?

Paul seemed to be challenging George to call him a liar. He was flippant, almost defiant in his misrepresentations. Why was he lying? What was the purpose? What did he gain? Was he being so blatant about it because he was uncomfortable with the lies, or because he didn't care about them?

George moved on to Paul's statement that Eddie asked him every single Sunday about why his mother sat in the driveway smoking cigarettes in her car.

*Q:And why is Sunday locked in your mind as the day of the week that he was asking you about it?*

*A:Because that was the day I would go—come over to Jeannie and get her for—we had CCD classes in the morning. And he'd usually answer the door.*

*Q:And that's when he would say that to you?*

*A:Yeah.*

*Q:And CCD, was, and is, Catholic education?*

*A:Yeah.*

*Q:And that would be about nine o'clock in the morning?*

*A:Yeah. About ten o'clock.*

*Q:Well, you know that Eddie O'Brien worked at the Mid-*

83 Id., p. 172

*Nite Convenient store from seven o'clock to noon?*

*A:No. He'd get off early. The papers had to be done by, I think, like seven o'clock in the morning.*[84]

Again, what Paul said was simply not true. It could be proven false, and he didn't care.

The final confabulated testimony came when George questioned Paul about the previous Sunday, the week before his mother's murder. Paul testified that this was the day Eddie told him about seeing the woman undress in her window.

*Q:And the comments he made to you on that day, the Sunday before your mother's death, which would be the 16th of July, 1995—is that the day he told you that he saw a woman undressing across the street?*

*A:Yes.*

*Q:And you remember that day specifically for what reason?*

*A:Because that—that was like one of the first times I heard—heard him ever, talk about looking into someone else's window and describing what, you know, what he saw.*

*Q:And the reason you remember it was that Sunday is because that's the first time, in the entire time you knew him, that he said something like that?*

*A:Uhm, that vividly. Yes.*

*Q:Okay. And that's why you remember that Sunday?*

*A:Yes.*

*Q:And what time was that?*

*A:That was, uhm, in the afternoon.*

*Q:Okay. And do you recall today—and I know it's hard to focus from before—but do you remember whether it was late afternoon or early afternoon?*

*A:Ah, I think it was probably like around three o'clock.*

---

84 Id., p. 183

*Q:And where was that said to you?*
*A:Ah—*
*Q:Where were you two located?*
*A:Ah, I was up on his porch.*
*Q:Was anyone else there?*
*A:No.*
*Q:Was anyone else present in the house that day?*
*A:Other than Jeannie, yeah. Jeannie was there.*
*Q:Well, if I told you that Edward O'Brien's grandfather's birthday party was that day, and there were almost thirty or forty people there, would that refresh your memory?*
*REILLY: Objection.*
*JUDGE McDANIEL: Sustained.*

This question is objectionable because the birthday party occurring on July 16 was not yet in evidence. No one had testified about it yet, and therefore the question "assumes facts not in evidence."

*Q:Did you see Edward O'Brien's grandfather there that day?*
*A:No.*
*Q:Did you see any guests at a birthday party that day?*
*A:Do I remember any guests? No.*
*Q:Okay, so nothing was going on at the house the time you were there, at about three o'clock that Sunday?*
*A:Not that I recall.*[85]

By this time, Paul's credibility about anything he'd asserted during his testimony was seriously questionable. In his zeal to shore up his assertions in the face of contradictory evidence, he became even more entrenched in his stories. He said that Eddie was "just like a family member," one who

85 Id., p. 188

apparently had never been in his house.

George returned to the time during which the conversation with Eddie outside of his house supposedly took place. He asked Paul to tell the jury again what he did, step by step, after the boys put the groceries in the house.

Paul started by restating that he went back into his house to put away the perishables. He stopped and thought for a minute, then said, "And then we went—okay. Wait. Okay. Uhm, I went—Jeannie—after I put the perishables away, Ed's already been dropped off to the—Ed had already been dropped off—because this is around six o'clock. . . . Around 6:00, 6:45. And Jeannie called me. We went out. After that we went directly out."[86]

Paul failed to remember his alleged conversation with Eddie. In this version, he seemed to be trying to remember where Eddie was, and determined that Eddie had been dropped off in Union Square. In this version Paul went "directly" out from his house with Jeannie. There was no waiting against the car for Jeannie or knocking on her door.

Paul's testimony continued on cross-examination with what happened when he returned from Revere Beach that evening. He said he and Jeannie returned home at 8:00 in order for Jeannie to switch cars with Michelle Cameron. The only reason he entered his house, he said, was because he was hungry. He got a saltine to eat and maybe a lollipop. He said he came right back out after about three minutes. When asked on direct examination, Paul said he came out between 8:20 and 8:30.

That was the first contradiction.

On direct examination, not even an hour before, Paul testified that he'd come out of his house and gone "across the street to Ed's house." He said he stayed on the porch there "for about fifteen minutes."

86 Id., p. 208

On cross-examination Paul testified that when he came out he saw Ed Sr., Ed Jr., and John Roberts on the O'Brien front porch but didn't talk with them. He said that after leaving his house, he got in the back of Michelle Cameron's car and they left again for Revere Beach.

That was the second contradiction.

In fact, Paul, in addition to getting a saltine, emerged with a backpack when he left his house at 8:20 or 8:30. He threw the backpack in Michelle's trunk before they left. After the murder, the police had seemed to be well aware of the backpack. They had questioned Jeannie O'Brien about it extensively, wanting to know where it was and if he had towels in it. (Jeannie didn't know the answer to either of these questions.) The police went to Michelle Cameron's house to retrieve it from her vehicle. It was later sent for forensic testing, along with Paul's sneakers, an Orlando Magic T-shirt and a knife.

What follows is a drawing made by Robert Pino, the crime scene chemist from the State Police lab who collected and numbered all the evidence related to Downing's fatal stabbing.

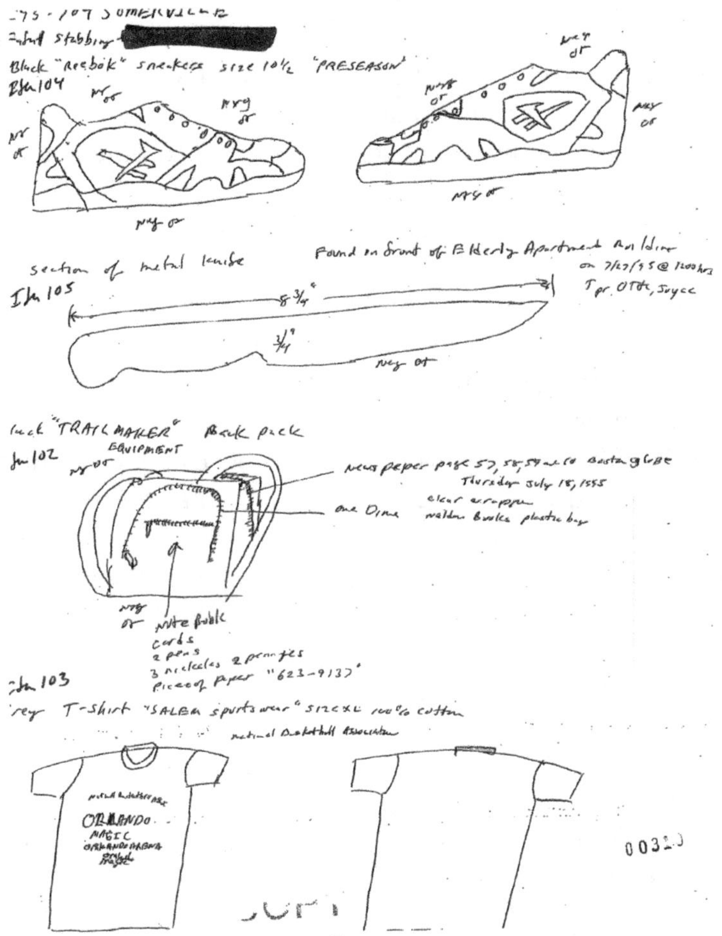


*Pino drawing of contents of Paul's backpack*

What is most curious about this forensic drawing is that the only item on it that contains notations about where, when, and by whom it was found is the knife. The notations suggest that the knife was found three days after the backpack was seized. If this knife was not found with the backpack and other items of Paul's, why was it delivered to the lab with Paul's backpack? Why is it included in this drawing with his items that were to be tested? Why don't the sneakers, shirt, and backpack contain notations about where and when they were found, and who confiscated them? According to the lab report, no blood was found on any of the items.

For the first time at the trial, during George's cross-examination of Paul, the family dog was mentioned. The Downings had a golden retriever that barked at everything, according to Virginia Reckley, the neighbor who shared a common wall with the Downings. Virginia noted that she did not hear the dog bark at all on the night of Downing's murder. Yet the dog was found beside Downing's lifeless body when the first police officer arrived at the scene.

George asked Paul where the dog was when he went in the house at 8:00. He said that the dog was on the main floor where the living room, kitchen, and den were located. Paul insisted he never went near the stairs between 8:00 and 8:20 or 8:30 and that everything in the house, at that point, was normal.

*Q: Where was your mother?*

*A: She was, uhm, she was still alive, on the couch, sleeping.*[87]

Interesting answer to the question, "Where was your mother?" – "*She was still alive.*" Paul nevertheless said he didn't talk with his mother or interact with the dog. So how did he know she was "still alive"? He said the lights were off in the downstairs rooms, and it was just becoming dark out.

Would Paul's inconsistent, exaggerated, and fabricated testimony affect how the jury considered him and his actions on the night of the murder? Would they wonder if he had

87 Transcript, Supra, p. 144

also not told the truth about what happened in that house at 8:15 when Virginia Reckley heard that loud noise? Would they wonder where the dog was while Downing was being attacked? Would they wonder why no one heard the dog barking, even with all the windows open on that hot night? Would they consider that possibility that the dog may not have barked if Downing's attacker was not a stranger?

# CHAPTER 25

## DAY SIX, CONTINUED

Joey Dion was one of the Ryan Downing/Eddie O'Brien group. He'd met Eddie when he was ten years old. He was sixteen in 1995, about a year older than Eddie. Joey was by the time of the trial a student at the Boston School of Art.

He told the jury that *all* the boys wondered why Janet Downing had the habit of sitting in her car; it wasn't only Eddie who commented on this.

He could remember only one comment Eddie made about Janet Downing's relationship with her best friend, Jean McGeary, "but it was like joking around."[88] The comment was made "quite some time before" the murder. [89] Joey testified that on July 23, 1995, the day of the murder, Joey was at Ryan's house playing Sega Genesis in the den during the afternoon. At some point Downing came home with groceries. Joey and Ryan helped bring the bags of groceries into the kitchen. Eddie was not there at the time. They left to meet Chris Ford at "the Tower," a park at the end of Bigalow Street where the kids hung out, and the three returned to 71 Boston St., about a hundred yards away.

They stayed outside for a few minutes, then entered the Downing house, and, while they were going in, Eddie came from across the street into the house with them. The boys hung out in the kitchen for a while, discussing possible plans for the evening. Joey said this group of boys had been in

88 TR. SIXTH DAY OF TRIAL, Vol. IX, p. 224

89 Id., p. 253

the Downing home countless times together. Joey and Eddie went into the den to play Sega Genesis. As Joey followed him in, Eddie came back out.

Someone (he couldn't remember who) asked where Ryan's mom was and Eddie told them that Ryan's mother was sleeping on the couch in the den; it was why he and Joey couldn't play video games. The boys stayed in the kitchen, then decided to go swimming at a friend's house; they all left. Eddie went home. Joey said it was not unusual for Eddie not to go swimming with them: "Because usually, when we went swimming to a pool, you know, a public pool or anywhere else, he wouldn't go. I don't—I don't know why. But it was—it wasn't like surprising, you know."[90]

Reilly's theory was that Eddie didn't go with them because he was already planning to murder Ryan's mother while the others were swimming.

When asked what Eddie was wearing that night at 7:50, Joey said he had on a striped polo shirt with a collar and dark green shorts. (Each of the boys remembered a different kind of shirt. Only one remembered it was the white Nike "Over the Rim" shirt. This is not uncommon with eyewitness testimony, which is notoriously unreliable.)

On cross-examination, George questioned Joey about the house where a woman named Mrs. Kenney lived. Mrs. Kenney was an elderly neighbor with a huge run-down Victorian house. The kids and the adults in the neighborhood all called it the "Boo Radley" house, after the reclusive neighborhood character in *To Kill a Mockingbird*, and wondered what it looked like inside. Oddly enough, George had gotten Paul's testimony regarding Mrs. Kenney's house stricken from the record, yet he continued to reintroduce the subject with subsequent witnesses.

Ryan Downing followed Joey Dion on the witness stand.

90 Id., p. 257

Ryan had been the family member most often interviewed by police, and he testified at three proceedings: the grand jury, the first transfer hearing, and at the trial. Ryan was now nineteen and a freshman at Bunker Hill Community College, living with his father and stepmother.

Ryan named the same group of friends–Marco Abreu, Joey Dion, Chris Ford, and Garvey Salomon—as being "very good friends." He added that as for Eddie, "we're, like, best friends." His mother and his friends had a mutually respectful relationship, he said.

Eddie "occasionally" asked him questions like why his mother parked in the driveway a lot when she came home from work, and had commented on her cooking. He testified that Eddie said Ryan's mom's cooking tasted bad and said they shouldn't eat at her house. This made Ryan angry. He asked Eddie if he didn't like his mom, but Eddie said he did like Ryan's mom.

So far, the evidence was not painting a picture of a boy so clearly obsessed with his friend's mother that he was compelled to murder her. These single comments Eddie made about Downing's friend and her cooking sounded like nothing more than what two fifteen-year-old kids might say to one other. Even adding more questions—about why Downing sat in her car in the driveway so much—didn't make this any more than adolescent banter.

Reilly knew he was in trouble. Paul's testimony had been so over the top as to raise serious credibility questions, and Ryan wasn't giving Reilly the answers he was looking for.

After the lunch break, Ryan's testimony changed. Reilly began to elicit testimony about a conversation that Ryan and Eddie allegedly had on the night before the murder. Ryan had never mentioned this conversation in his testimony to the grand jury in August 1995. It wasn't mentioned in any of his three interviews with the police. Five months later, at the first transfer hearing in January 1996, Ryan testified about it for the first time:

*A: We were just making plans for the next day and—and then he asked me—before I left, he asked me, he said that he'd never seen me angry, ready to hurt somebody. And I told him that I'm not like that. I—I don't get mad very easily. Then, he said, there's only one time I—I recall you being angry, and that was when we were little when he said something to me, and you [sic] chased me. And he said, but since then he never seen me like hurt—really hurt somebody. And I told him that I'm—I'm not like that—*

*Q: Did he ask you if you ever felt like hurting—someone?*

*A: Yes. He said did I feel like hurting somebody. And I said I'm not like that.*[91]

"Did he ask you if you ever felt like hurting someone?" is a question that suggests the answer Reilly wants Ryan to give him. It's a leading question, and not permissible. He is literally putting words in Ryan's mouth because the only possible answers are either yes or no. George should have but did not object to the question.

*A: And we just started talking . . . Uhm, we—we were just talking about, ah, what to do the next day. And he asked me if I wanted to play basketball. And, ah, after he gets out of work. And I said: "Yeah. Sure. I'll do that." And, uhm, then he asked, uhm, he asked me a question, if I—if like, I ever—like I wanted to hurt somebody? And I said, no. I—really didn't. And he said: "Well I remember one time you did." Uhm, it was when I was little. And—and he made—he made a comment about me staying—me being kept back. And I chased him around, uhm, a car. And he said: "That was the*

91 Transfer Hearing, Vol. VII, January 18, 1996, pp. 25, 26

*only time I really, ah, felt like—that was the only really time I ever saw you really want to hurt somebody like—a person when they hurt somebody, like this." And, ah—then I said: "I'm not like that. I don't get angry." And—and he—that was it.*

*Q:Can you describe for the jury, what he said about hurting someone. How he was acting.*

*A:Like conscious, just, and sort of like wanting to hurt somebody.*[92]

It was obvious that Ryan had been well prepped about what he was to tell the jury. He was having a great deal of trouble doing it, however. His tentative wording ("sort of," "like") showed that he was either uncomfortable with what he was expected to say or he couldn't remember what he was supposed to say. He did not know how to imply that Eddie was saying that *Eddie* was thinking about hurting someone.

Reilly asked how Eddie "acted," and Ryan said he acted "like conscious and sort of like wanting to hurt somebody." "Sort of like wanting to hurt somebody," is vague, nondescriptive, and contrived.

Reilly moved on to the night of July 23. Ryan said Paul wasn't home when he and Joey came back from the Tower with Chris Ford. Ryan, Chris, Joey and Eddie all went into the Downing kitchen and were hanging out. "Joey and Ed kind of drifted off" into the TV room and then came back. Chris Ford asked where Ryan's mom was, and that's when Eddie responded she was asleep in the den. It was at this point that Eddie went out onto the back deck and got locked out of the house.

George was successful on cross-examination in clarifying that Eddie only made one comment about Ryan's mother and Jean McGeary, and that he never mentioned it again.

92 Transcript SIXTH DAY OF TRIAL, Supra, pp. 286, 287

He made only one comment about Ryan's mother's cooking, and never made fun of her cooking again. Ryan testified that Eddie was not angry during any of these exchanges. Since Ryan first knew Eddie when he was a toddler, he said, Eddie was always respectful and never angry toward Ryan's mother.

George questioned him about the conversation on the night before his mother died.

*Q: I mean, how did the conversation turn [from basketball] to the time that he chased you around the car, for—*

*A: Oh, uhm—*

*Q: Teasing you. How did it turn in that direction?*

*A: It—he just stated, he—he brought up the question, that will do it. And, uhm, I—I was kind of—I was trying to understand what he was talking about. Then, he, he—he, uhm, specified with, uhm, the story.*

*Q: And is it fair for me to say that that incident he's talking about was a result of Eddie teasing you, at the time, for you staying back in the first grade?*

*A: Yes.*

*Q: Did he say anything after that?*

*A: No. I don't think so.*[93]

This account is much clearer than the one he gave on direct examination, yet Ryan said that the topic came up when Eddie "brought up the question." He doesn't say what the question was. Ryan was struggling with this new version of events. Instead of saying "he asked me," he said, "he brought up the question."

That was the best George could do with Ryan's statement. Even though Ryan couldn't articulate how Eddie brought up the question "out of the blue" as Reilly had said in his

93 Id., pp. 363-365

opening statement, he had successfully suggested that the night before the murder Eddie O'Brien was thinking about wanting to hurt someone.

The final witness for this long day of patchwork testimony was Chris Ford. Chris was now eighteen and attending art school in Boston. He testified that Janet Downing treated all of Ryan's friends equally and with respect. They, in return, liked and respected her. Reilly asked if Chris was present when Eddie asked Ryan if his mother was a lesbian. He testified that he was and that he never heard Eddie mention it again.

Chris said he'd met Joey Dion and Ryan Downing at Bigalow Street sometime after 6:30 on July 23 and they rollerbladed (Ryan), biked (Joey), and walked (Chris) to the Downing home down Bigalow Street. Chris also did not see Paul Downing either inside or outside the house when they returned from the park. As they were walking up Ryan's pathway to the house, Eddie came from across Boston Street and joined them. They all went into the kitchen. Eddie and Joey wandered away for a minute. Chris asked Ryan where his mother was because he wanted to tell a story with a swear word, and didn't want to swear in front of her. Eddie responded that she was in the den sleeping on the couch. He and Joey Dion had gone in there to play Sega Genesis, and he noticed she was sleeping and returned to the kitchen. They left the house to go swimming. He next saw Eddie at Mid-Nite Convenient at about 10:15.

Chris stated that Ed was wearing "a dark-striped polo style shirt, three buttons, a collar, dark shorts and black sneakers" at the Downing home earlier. In Union Square he was wearing an inside-out white Nike "Over the Rim" T-shirt. But, Chris testified, his shorts and sneakers were the same as appeared in the police photograph of Eddie that Reilly showed the witness.

There would be four more of Eddie O'Brien's friends testifying the following day. So far, with the exception of Paul and Ryan Downing, Eddie's friends were proving to be kids who were trying to tell the jury the truth about him. Ryan appeared to be struggling between his own memories and how the district attorney wanted him to present his recollection to the jury. Paul, on the other hand, was a wild card, prepared and going beyond what was expected or needed. His young age and inexperience betrayed him in the end, and he couldn't remember what he'd said before, resulting in totally contradictory testimony.

# CHAPTER 26

## LOBBY CONFERENCE RULINGS

The morning of Day Seven started with a lobby conference in the judge's chambers that Bob George had requested. George announced that he wanted to alert the judge that his associate, Peter Stelzer, was going to move for a mistrial. "I just wanted to protect the record. That's all," he said, almost apologetically. "The reason I'm moving for a mistrial is for the following—and the 'Natural Born Killers.'"[94]

He referenced Eddie's statements about Downing that Reilly said proved motive and context for the murder but were in fact innocuous, immature, inconsiderate, childish statements made among a group of boys—yet that wasn't what the jury was hearing.

The cumulative nature of having these boys testify to the same statements made it appear that Eddie repeatedly made the statements, and this was all he talked about. Of course that was precisely what Reilly wanted the jury to think: Ryan's mother is a bad cook, over and over and over again. Why does your mother sit in the driveway, over and over and over again. Is your mother a lesbian, over and over and over again. It no longer mattered that Eddie asked the questions only once and stopped after the first time. That wasn't what the jury would take away from the testimony.

The judge responded "of course, this kind of evidence, in some respects, is not necessarily the kind of evidence the defendant wants to hear in this case. But if it's relevant–and

94 SEVENTH DAY OF TRIAL, Vol. X, September 23, 1997, p. 6

I think it is relevant–it's relevant to his state of mind at or around the time. And the way it's coming in, it's coming in as if this was something he was dwelling on, for some reason. And it would explain, it would tend to explain what his state of mind is and why he may or may not have committed this particular act. And so, I am going to allow it. And I am going to note your objection to my ruling. And your motion is denied. Your objection is noted. Your rights are saved on the record as to this particular issue."[95]

The *Herald* headline, and the reading of the "Natural Born Killers" story to the jury was now lost in this sweeping ruling in which George only mentioned the newspaper in passing. No specific ruling as to Exhibit 73, the newspaper page, would ever be made.

Stelzer never got his chance to present his motion for a mistrial based on the "Natural Born Killers" article. George had rolled it into his argument about the statements Eddie allegedly made, and McDaniel made his all-inclusive ruling. The newspaper was squarely in evidence.

Bob George failed to argue that the newspaper violated the Best Evidence Rule, that the original copy of a document is superior evidence. In fact, he barely mentioned the newspaper. This was a huge mistake and one from which the defense couldn't recover.

---

95 Id., pp. 15-16

# CHAPTER 27

## MORE FRIENDS

Reilly called Garvey Salomon to the stand. Garvey was now eighteen and attending Johnson & Wales University in Providence, Rhode Island. In 1995 he'd worked at the Meadow Glen Mall in Medford, Massachusetts, during the summer months. Garvey was Haitian-American and the only person of color in the group of boys. The group hung out most of the time at Garvey's house, but their second hangout was the Downing house. Garvey testified that he never once heard Eddie O'Brien say a bad word about Janet Downing.

Garvey testified that on the 23rd of July, the day of the murder, he worked until about 7:00 p.m. When he got home he talked with Eddie on the telephone and Eddie was at Ryan's house at the time. It wasn't unusual for Eddie to answer the phone at Ryan's house. They talked about Eddie possibly coming over to Garvey's because the other boys were going swimming. Garvey next saw Eddie at Mid-Nite Convenient that night. Reilly questioned him:

*Q: Could you tell us what he looked like?*

*A: Uhm, his, ah, shorts were wet. And he was just really, like—not really speechless, just like this shock. He, like, you know, he wasn't much for words at that time.*

*Q: Was there any conversation with respect to Janet Downing?*

*A: Uhm, yes.*

*Q: What was said? And what did he say?*

*A:I asked him if he knew what happened up at Ryan's house. And he's, he was not really shocked, but I—he didn't, like he didn't know about it. . . . He said "Wow," like "What happened?" And I said that—and I told him something happened at Ryan's house. And, ah, Marco said something about it, too. And he goes like—like he was in shock that it happened. Like, not shock, but he, at that time, yeah.*[96]

Garvey's memory was that Eddie had on a dark shirt at the Mid-Nite Convenient store that night. When shown a photograph of Eddie in the white "Over the Rim" shirt, he recognized the shirt as one that Eddie wore, but he "was pretty sure he was wearing a dark shirt when he saw him" in the store that night.

Seth Dion was next on the stand. He had been sixteen in 1995. He'd known Eddie since the first grade. Seth never heard Eddie say an unkind word about Janet Downing in all the years he'd known him. On the night of July 23, he, Marco Abreu and John Fitzpatrick walked up to Ryan Downing's house to see if he was home yet from the pool. They went up the walkway to the front door, and Seth noticed that the screen door was closed but that the outer front door was open. Seth said he knocked on the living room window for Ryan. He didn't hear the dog, and when there was no answer, John opened the screen door and went into the vestibule area. Seth shut the front door on him, fooling around. John tried to get back out, and Seth let him out.

None of them heard any noises coming from inside the house. They left the front steps and walked down the side lawn toward the deck stairs. Seth went up the deck stairs to the back door. Marco and John stayed on the side lawn. Seth opened the screen door and knocked on the closed kitchen

96 TR. SEVENTH DAY OF TRIAL, Vol. X, September 23, 1997, pp. 70-72

door. Again, he didn't hear anything. The dog didn't bark. The kitchen light was on. He also noticed the light in Ryan and Paul's bedroom was on upstairs on the third floor.

Seth was coming back down the deck stairs when he heard a rustling in the bushes behind the house. When he came down off the deck, he said saw Marco on Hamlet Street and noticed that the cellar door was open. They all went over to the O'Brien house to tell Eddie's father, Ed O'Brien, that all the lights were on in the Downing house and the door was open but no one was answering the door.

O'Brien told them that was normal but suggested they try to call the house. Marco called on the O'Briens' phone. There was no answer. It was about 9:15 as best as he could remember. The boys left the O'Brien house. Seth and Marco went back to Ryan's house later and saw the emergency vehicles. They also learned about Eddie being hurt, and went down to Mid-Nite Convenient to see him. Seth had no memory of what Eddie was wearing. He described his demeanor as "regular." Seth didn't participate in any conversation with Eddie at the store.

John Fitzpatrick was fifteen during the summer of 1995. He had known Eddie since the first grade. They went to the same grade school. John considered Eddie one of his best friends.

John thought that it was about 9:00 when he, Seth Dion, and Marco Abreu left Marco's house and walked to Ryan's house, which he estimated was about ten minutes away. John went in the front screen door. The inside front door into the house was closed, so he knocked on the inside door three times. He heard no sounds coming from inside the house, and the dog didn't bark. They all walked down the side lawn toward the back of Ryan's house. Seth went up onto the deck.

John noticed that the cellar door was open. Then he heard rustling in the bushes behind the house. He couldn't see anyone there. He moved to the corner of Hamlet and Boston Streets toward the front of the house. There he saw someone he believed was Eddie O'Brien crouched on the retaining wall along the sidewalk, preparing to jump down. The figure jumped down onto the sidewalk and started to walk down Hamlet Street toward Highland Avenue. John said "Nice hiding spot, Ed." There was no response.

The first question Bob George asked John on cross-examination was whether or not he had given several statements to the police since that night. John agreed that he'd talked to the police several times. George continued.

*Q:And each time you talked to the police, were there different police officers there? Or were you giving them over and over again to the same police?*

*A:Ah, sometimes different police. But mostly, ah, Mr. Reilly.*[97]

When George asked if he was sure it was Edward O'Brien that he saw jump off that wall, John said:

*A:No, I am not. I never said that.*

*Q:What did you say in your written statement on July 24, 1995, at 10:17 a.m.?*

*A:I said that I didn't think it was Ed O'Brien because—ah, he didn't answer to his name.*

*Q:There's another reason that you didn't think it was Edward O'Brien, because he didn't turn around? You couldn't see his face?*

*A:Yes, that's true.*[98]

He said that between him and the figure, there were no

97 Id., p. 165

98 Id., pp. 186,187

streetlights. John remembered the kitchen light, the dining room light, and Ryan's bedroom light being on.

Marco Abreu was the last witness who'd been at the front door of the Downing home at about 9:20 with Seth Dion and John Fitzpatrick. His testimony differed only in that he remembered leaning against the railing at the front steps when he heard a crashing noise coming from the bushes in back of the house. Then Seth went up on the back deck. He saw the cellar door was open. He got "like a little scared, but not scared, scared, like."[99] Marco backed off to about three feet away from Hamlet Street. He said he saw Eddie O'Brien walk out of the bushes with his hands clenched and walk down the sidewalk on Hamlet Street toward Highland Avenue. Marco testified that Ed "looked over his right shoulder at me and smiled." [100]

At some point, Marco said, Eddie turned around and faced him. Eddie's eyes were as "wide open as he can get it." Eddie was "smiling. Chuckled. He laughed." Marco said Eddie had a black T-shirt on and black shorts.

Marco left and went over to the O'Brien house and made the call to the Downing house. None of the boys mentioned to "Big Ed" O'Brien that they might have seen Eddie jumping out of the bushes.

A little after 10:00, Marco Abreu said, he and Seth Dion went back to the Downing house. He saw fire engines, police cars, and ambulances. Ryan was in the driveway. He was crying and could hardly talk. Then Marco heard Eddie's sister Jessica say that Eddie had been hurt in Union Square, and he went to the Mid-Nite Convenient store. He saw Eddie standing on the sidewalk outside the store. Eddie had on "tan shorts and a white T-shirt." He appeared "pretty calm."[101]

99 Id., p. 230

100 Id., p. 237

101 Id., p. 255

Reilly asked Marco if Eddie had a different shirt on at 10:00 than the one Marco saw him wearing earlier that day. Marco responded that Eddie had on a white "Over the Rim" shirt when he saw him at Mid-Nite Convenient.

Reilly was trying to establish his theory that Eddie had somehow changed his clothing between the Downing home and Mid-Nite Convenient. Marco Abreu was the guy who would propose that theory to the jury. The theory was just as ludicrous as the broken kitchen doorknob theory.

There were just too many witnesses who saw Eddie wearing that same shirt and shorts at 9:00 that he'd worn all day. These were the same shorts and shirt he was in at 10:00 at Mid-Nite Convenient. In order to change his clothing, Eddie would have had to take off his sweaty clothes (which he'd worn all day), put on a new outfit, sneak away from his house without his father or sister noticing, hide the clothes he'd taken off somewhere between his house and Union Square, return to his house to tell them he was going to Burger King, and then go to the Downing home and murder Janet Downing. He would have had a total of five to seven minutes to do all of that, including the ninety-eight wounds of the murder.

Afterward, he would have had to run out of the basement, retrieve his clothing, exchange blood-saturated clothes for his old sweaty clothes, all without getting any blood on the white T-shirt and green shorts. And, of course, it was never even suggested that he changed his sneakers, so he would have had to accomplish this murder without getting any blood on them whatsoever.

He would then have had to dispose of the bloody clothes where they would never be recovered and arrive at Mid-Nite Convenient with no blood on his clothes, underwear, face, hands, or body. He would have had to carefully avoid getting even his own blood on the shorts and shirt from his scratched up legs and arms while changing into them. Having achieved all that, he would have had to keep intact the one tiny drop of blood on his right shin that contained AB blood, consistent with Downing's blood. Plausible? Possible? Hardly. Nevertheless, Reilly persisted.

Reilly handed Marco the photo of Eddie taken at the police station, Marco stated that the shirt was different, that Eddie had on a dark shirt on Hamlet Street. Reilly asked, "Pants the same?" to which Marco responded yes. Marco had testified just minutes ago that Eddie's shorts were tan. The shorts in the photo were dark green.

Marco said that at Mid-Nite Convenient he asked Eddie three times if he'd heard what had happened at the Downing house before Eddie finally responded and said that he'd heard. This is completely inconsistent with the testimony of Garvey Salomon, who was standing beside Marco listening to the conversation.

George focused on the varying statements Marco had given to the police. In the first, at 9:12 Monday morning, July 24, Marco did not tell the police he'd seen Eddie's face or eyes, as he had testified in court. Marco told Detective Femino and Trooper Duggan that he "couldn't say it was definitely him, but couldn't—couldn't say it wasn't Ed."[102] In fact, he didn't think it was Eddie because the person didn't respond to Marco calling his name, and he called out three times. The person was walking away, down Hamlet Street. It was when he called out the third time that the person turned around, Marco said, and he realized it was Eddie. By then the figure was most of the way down the dark street.

Marco was interviewed again at 6:30 Monday night, this time by DA Reilly and Femino. At that interview Marco said that he thought the person he saw was Edward O'Brien, but he couldn't be 100 percent sure.

---

102 Id., p. 301

Two days later, on July 26, Marco's mother called the police to come and interview her son again. Femino and Duggan went to the Abreu home. At that time Marco said he was 100 percent sure it was Eddie O'Brien he'd seen.

Marco admitted—on cross-examination—that on Tuesday, July 25, Eddie's father had confronted him and told Marco he wasn't welcome at the O'Brien house anymore.

*Q:And it was the very next day that you told the police that you were a hundred percent sure? The next day?*

*A:Yes, but it wasn't because of that.*[103]

Marco now repeated his earliest testimony, that Eddie was wearing tan shorts when he saw him at the Mid-Nite Convenient store. When George again showed him the photograph of Eddie with the dark green shorts, Marco said that the pants in the photograph were different, that he'd been wearing tan shorts at Mid-Nite, thus contradicting his own testimony that the pants "were the same."

Marco remembered that the kitchen lights and Ryan's bedroom light were on in the Downing house when the three boys approached the door about 9:15.

The final witness Tom Reilly presented on the seventh day was a man who resided at the corner of Hamlet Street and Highland Avenue. Anthony Stamatouras attempted to solidify Reilly's theory about Eddie's change of clothes. The outcome was not what Reilly expected, however.

Stamatouras testified that he'd fallen asleep at 7:00 the night of July 23. His dog was in his backyard. He was asleep on the second floor. At 10:00 a loud noise awakened him. He went to his enclosed back porch, looked through the window, he said, and saw a large person in a black shirt, with a white shirt hanging down from underneath it, jump over his fence

103 Id., p. 311

to the next yard. His dog was barking. Stamatouras said he knew Eddie O'Brien from the neighborhood and said that the person he saw was similar to Eddie in size and height. (Eddie was at Mid-Nite Convenient by 10:00 p.m.)

On cross-examination, Stamatouras said two state troopers from the DA's office interviewed him on July 26, three days after the murder. The interview took place at his house. He was shown a photograph of Eddie O'Brien by the troopers and told them that he didn't recognize the person in the photograph.

Stamatouras testified that he showed the troopers the digital clock he'd looked at when he heard the noise that woke him up. He told them he remembered looking at it and it said 10:15. On cross-examination Bob George established that the troopers noticed immediately that the clock was showing the wrong time. They called for the correct time by telephone to compare it with the digital clock. It was then that Stamatouras learned his clock was nineteen minutes slow. So the large person he'd seen with the black shirt with a white shirt under it, actually jumped over Stamatouras' fence at about 10:35, about thirty-five minutes after Eddie O'Brien called the police from Mid-Nite Convenient to report his mugging.

George did a masterful job with this witness. He showed that the testimony that Reilly elicited was flawed and he knew it was flawed. Reilly knew the truth and obfuscated it in his direct questions to the witness. It was a shameful and embarrassing moment, or at least it *should* have been, for Tom Reilly.

# CHAPTER 28
## THE SCIENCE OF FINGERPRINTS

The scientific or forensic testimony began on Day Eight and took up much of the next two and a half days. Added to the burden of remembering the judge's initial instructions, and the limiting instructions during the testimony, the jury would now listen to complex scientific concepts and language well beyond the knowledge of even the attorneys who routinely presented evidence like this.

They were about to have crash courses in chemistry, genetics, and fingerprint analysis. Their unanimous decision about whether Eddie O'Brien was guilty or innocent would rest on their understanding of this evidence.

This was the most difficult part of the trial intellectually. For the attorneys, this was where you lost jurors overwhelmed by the information or embarrassed by their lack of comprehension. This is where their level of exhaustion met their level of frustration. Jurors inevitably begin to resent the science lessons and start making snap judgments during this phase. Keeping the jurors focused on what was important was a nearly impossible task for the attorneys.

The first witness called by the district attorney was Wayne Riley, a state trooper and part of the crime scene service section. He was a photographer and fingerprint expert. He began with a short explanation of a latent fingerprint versus a patent fingerprint.

*On the palm surface of your hands on your fingertips*

*there are ridges that are furrow shaped, that are like hills and furrows. . . . At the peaks of them, there are very small, minute pores which exude sweat, perspiration. It is that perspiration when a hand touches an object that, left on the object, would be known as a latent print. . . . Most often they are invisible. But they can be visible . . . chemical enhancement or powders . . . bring up the contrast so we can then photograph it, preserve the evidence.*

*A patent print would be a reproduction of those same ridges, but it would be in such a way that if the hand had already had a substance on it, like blood or again, the perspiration or oils, that matter would then be transferred to a surface by the touch . . . leaving the impression of the ridged details. That would be a patent print. It's a visible print.*[104]

Riley was deemed by the court, based on his experience and education, to be an "expert" in fingerprint analysis. This is important, because an expert's testimony is not limited to what he saw and what he did; he's permitted to give the court his opinion about what he saw and did and what it *means*.

Expert witnesses are required when the ordinary person needs guidance to determine the meaning of the evidence presented. An ordinary person can't compare a known sample and a fingerprint from a crime scene and determine if they match or don't match.

Trooper Riley said he arrived at the Downing house at approximately midnight on the night of the murder. He was directed to a fingerprint in the basement on a post at the bottom of the stairs. He observed that it was difficult to see, but it appeared to be reddish-brown. At that time he made a decision that it would be fine to leave the print where it was.

---

104 EIGHTH DAY OF TRIAL, Vol. XI, September 24, 1997, pp. 37, 38

"There was no urgency to remove that print, at that time, to make a lift or to do anything to retrieve it at that very moment."[105]

He left the house and went to the Somerville police station to await a search warrant permitting him to remove the print. While at the police station, he was asked to photograph and fingerprint Eddie O'Brien. As witnesses and victims of crimes are not fingerprinted and photographed, this shows that a little after midnight on the night of the murder Eddie was a suspect.

The search warrant was issued, and the trooper returned with other police to the crime scene between 2:30 and 3:00 and started taking photographs. He was directed to the third stair that contained a white marker–"a white piece of paper or a napkin"–beside a metal fragment. He removed the white marker and took the photograph of the metal piece on the third stair.

After photographing the entire crime scene, he began to collect fingerprints. On the inside of the inner front door, Riley observed a set of prints in a substance, a reddish-brown stain. The trooper testified that it was the print of a right hand, touching the door in such a position that would close the door. Riley photographed the door and then removed the entire door in order to treat it chemically back at the lab. Eventually he treated it with a chemical called Amido Black, which adheres to the proteins in blood (the reddish-brown stain) and turns the blood blue. Through this process, he was able to identify three distinct prints.

The prints developed were then compared with Eddie's known prints.

Every fingerprint has approximately 200 points of identification that can be made. In order to conclude that there is a match in the prints, the State Police require that at least eight points match perfectly.

---

105 Id., p. 48

Eddie O'Brien's known prints matched thirty-one points in the prints lifted from the inner front door. Eddie's right index finger, which touched the door twice, and his right middle finger matched the three prints on the door. His fingers were positioned in a way that his back would have been toward the door as he pushed it closed.

On the cellar post Riley observed what appeared to be a thumbprint on the side of the square post at shoulder height. He cut out that piece of the post and took it back to the lab. There Riley used the Amido Black again to enhance two prints above the thumbprint. The test resulted in an "unfavorable response in that it washed away the test area, the pattern I was looking at."[106] He stopped testing and took steps to preserve the thumbprint.

At a later date, he tried a different type of chemical called Hungarian Red, an aqueous solution for staining impressions found in blood. It's much safer than other staining compounds. It has been used in crime scenes to recover nearly invisible latent fingerprints and footprints in blood.

However, all DNA evidence from the crime scene should be collected before using Hungarian Red, because this process interferes with subsequent blood analysis. Hungarian Red, the manufacturer advises, should not be used on physiological fluids that will be subsequently subjected to other forms of forensic examination.[107]

Riley lifted six impressions, but was only able to identify two. One, the left thumb, had sixteen points of identification with Eddie's left thumbprint. He determined that there was initial contact and then a slip of the hand, due to a substance that was on the hand, causing slippage. Contact was initially made higher on the post than the print in question. The

106 Id., p. 94

107 Penyan, Don, "Latent Blood Prints: Methods for Chemical Enhancement," cstechblog.com, March 16, 2011

position of the thumb was sideways on the post.

The second was the area below the left middle finger in the palm portion of the hand. There were fifty points of comparison made with Eddie's finger there. The third was lost through the Amido Black treatment.

It's impossible to tell either from the lab reports or the testimony whether DNA evidence was collected prior to chemical testing. Riley testified that no chemicals were used on the thumbprint. Yet taking the testimony all together, he does leave the impression that one print was lost and the other two were obtained by use of Hungarian Red. It is at best unclear.

This is important because the biological material on the thumbprint was used to identify and match Eddie's DNA.

On cross-examination, George established that Riley had been asked by his superior at the CPAC Unit from the District Attorney's Office to photograph and fingerprint Eddie at the Somerville police station on July 23 as part of his investigation into the crime scene at 71 Hamlet St. This established beyond any doubt that four hours after the murder, Eddie was a suspect. The trooper confirmed that he wasn't assigned to investigate the mugging in Union Square. He was not asked to take any other fingerprints of anyone in connection with the Downing murder until August 1997, when he took palm prints to eliminate a bloody palm print on the doorway at the entrance to the dining room. Prints from the entire Downing family, Artie Ortiz, and Carol Ortiz were compared. None matched the bloody palm print on this surface.

The palm print remains unidentified, yet it is identifiable. It has sufficient points to make a match, and indicates that there was an unidentified person who had Downing's blood on his hand when he grabbed the molding at the entrance to the dining room, the room where Downing bled out and died.

Riley testified that none of the other prints found on the inner front door had sufficient detail to identify them. He said he was never asked to examine the door in the kitchen that went out onto the deck. "That actually was not examined. The door was out of the "curtilage [the immediate surroundings] of the crime scene." This was the door with the broken lock about which DA Reilly questioned Ryan Downing to suggest that Eddie had used it to gain entry to the house and kill Janet Downing. The theory was ridiculous to begin with and was never even considered by the crime scene investigators.

Riley testified that the crime scene technicians determined the scope of the crime scene by following a bloody trail. They examined the hallway, the stairway, the powder room, the dining room, the kitchen, the staircase leading down to the basement, through the basement, and out the door to the basement. The second and third floors were not processed for fingerprints or photographed because they were not part of the crime scene according to the technicians. The inner front door, the kitchen door to the basement, and the cellar door to the outside were all removed.

After the cellar door was processed for fingerprints and blood evidence, it was replaced on the hinges to keep the scene secure. Regarding the fingerprints on it, Trooper Riley testified that "there was insufficient detail to continue with it."[108]

Altogether the crime scene revealed five fingerprints with sufficient detail to make a match to a known print, but didn't match any of the known prints of the Downing family, Ortiz family, or Eddie O'Brien.

Two were on the same basement post where Eddie's thumbprint was found.

One was in the first floor powder room, where the water

108 Transcript, Supra., p. 158

was running in the sink. The fifth was the bloody palm print on the dining room doorway.

Finally George had Riley identify the photos he'd taken of Eddie's hands that night at the police station. He noted there was no blood on either of his hands, front or back, when he took the photos. Each time he was asked, Riley added that Eddie "had gone to the hospital, apparently, to have his hands stitched, or something, sutured. So they would have been clean."[109]

When George asked about his left hand, which hadn't been sutured, Riley responded, "I just said his hands would have been clean, at this point." When asked about the back of his hands and whether there was blood observed there, he said, "Again, he had just come back from having the sutures and stuff. So his hands were clean."[110]

Eddie's injury was to his right hand on his palm, the back of his pinky finger at the first crease, and the tip of his thumb. According to the nurse, those were the areas that were cleaned. His left hand was not treated and not cleaned. If Eddie had committed this murder, blood would have been in every crease and crevice and under the fingernails of both of his hands.

George could have impeached this witness with the nurse's testimony. But he did not. The jury was left with the impression that his hands were medically swiped and cleaned at the hospital.

When Bob George asked Riley if it was possible to lightly brush over a print with blood and not destroy the print, Riley became indignant, asking George what he was trying to insinuate. He felt George was implying he fabricated the bloody print. But Riley was in fact protesting more than was necessary, sounding both defensive and insincere.

---

109 Id., pp. 195, 196

110 Id., p. 197

# CHAPTER 29

## CHEMISTRY BY PINO

Robert Pino was a civilian employee and supervising chemist in the State Police Crime Laboratory in Sudbury. In 1997 he'd been employed there for fourteen years. During his first twelve years he was assigned to the criminalistics section. Criminalistics deals with the recognition, collection, identification, individualization, and interpretation of physical evidence of crimes.

Pino had been supervisor of the night shift for six years. In the prior two years he'd been assigned to the drug unit. He'd worked on over 200 homicide crime scenes in his career. He explained to the jury that blood was collected from a crime scene using a Q-tip-like swab or a cotton swatch. The swab or swatch is moistened with distilled water and applied to the stain in question, and the cotton would turn a red/brown, indicating the presence of blood. The swab is then placed in a glycine paper, a kind of wax paper, allowing it to "breathe" so it could dry. Once dry, swabs are packaged into separate envelopes to prevent cross-contamination. During the collection of blood samples, the chemist wears several layers of rubber gloves and removes the top layer periodically to ensure there is no cross-contamination between swabbings.

Pino used a sequential numbering system as he collected samples. The samples were taken back to the crime laboratory, where they were assigned a case number. Each piece was logged in, steps were taken to make sure specimens were dry, and then they were stored in a climate-controlled cold storage room.

On July 23, Pino arrived at the Somerville Police Department at approximately 11:00 p.m. The first four items he numbered that night were Eddie's black sneakers, green shorts, white T-shirt, and white underwear. Then he numbered the two vials containing the hospital swabs from Eddie's shins. These were the first six of 106 items collected during the investigation.

Pino arrived at 71 Hamlet St. at approximately 3:00 a.m. He waited while Trooper Wayne Riley photographed the scene, after which Pino began to collect bloodstains from various areas of the crime scene. He collected a metal piece from the third stair, and marked it Item #21.

He collected samples from the door leading to the cellar stairs and rubber bands on the doorknob with blood on them. He also collected samples from the smear of blood on the right wall when descending the cellar stairs, and from two smears on the left wall of that stairwell (marked #36). He collected the clothing with bloodstains on the hanging line in the basement and marked the pink dress #38. Samples taken from the deadbolt on the cellar door to the outside yard were marked #42.

On the wooden post in the basement, samples were taken from the area around the bloodstained fingerprints and marked #70: "This (part of the post) was secured at the scene and then cut free and taken back to the laboratory, where it was later resubmitted for a bloodstain analysis,"[111] Pino testified.

It appeared from the testimony that Pino had taken a sample from the post that night and then again later in the laboratory after it was resubmitted. Yet, if the number system is sequential, which he said it was, this sample should have been numbered between #36 (the stairwell sample) and #42

111 Id., p. 233

(the deadbolt sample).

Sample #70, taken from the wooden post, was therefore taken *after* the post had been resubmitted to the lab for bloodstain analysis. The question is, was this done before or after Wayne Riley applied the Hungarian Red dye? There is no way to determine from the reports or testimony.

Pino removed items of Janet Downing's clothing that had been cut off her body by the medical personnel at the crime scene.

When working a crime scene, Pino said he did blood collection first before any fingerprint work was done.

On cross-examination, George established that no forensic testing was done on any items in the den where Downing was supposedly sleeping, or in the adjacent living room that opened up to the foyer hallway. The police were never able to establish whether any of the struggle took place in these rooms, or exactly where the struggle with her assailant(s) began, Pino said.

George next focused on items marked #79, #80, #81, #82, #83, and #84, which Reilly had neglected to bring up on direct examination.

- #79 was three swabs from the top of Downing's head.
- #80 was hairs from the top of Downing's right index finger.
- #81 was fingernail scrapings from Downing's left hand.
- #82 was fingernail scrapings from Downing's right hand.
- #83 was a swabbing from a stain on Downing's right hand.
- #84 was a white fluid substance found in Downing's palm.

Pino testified that the whitish substance found in Downing's palm, marked #84, was tested and determined not to be seminal fluid.

*Q: Were you able to determine what it was?*

*A: No sir, I was not.*

*Q: And was it then packaged and sent to serology?*

*A: No sir, it was not. It was packaged away with the rest of the evidence.*

*Q: Was it ever further tested, after you looked at it?*

*A: No sir, it was not further tested.*

The hairs on the top of her right index finger, Item #80, were determined to be feline hairs, cat hairs. The Downings did not own a cat. Eddie's family did not have a cat, either. In the palm of that same hand were brown Caucasian hair fragments and white cat hairs. No DNA testing was done on the brown Caucasian hair. On her left hand were bloodstained brown and white cat hairs. No tests were done on the blood.

*Q: Was any serology testing done? Was there simple blood testing?*

*A: No sir, not on those bloodstained hairs, no sir.*

*Q: Was any serology testing, simple blood testing, done on anything found on the right hand?*

*A: No, sir, no further testing was done on the substance on the right hand, or the hairs on the right hand.*

*Q: Now, there was further testing that was done on items #81 and #82, isn't that so? Which are the fingernail scrapings?*

*A: I don't recall. There could have been. Yes, sir.*

*Q: But from your report, you can't tell us?*

*A: No, sir, my report just goes to the microscopic examination of the fingernails.*

*Q: But those fingernail scrapings were collected by you?*

*A: Yes, sir.*

*Q: And you packaged them?*

*A: Excuse me?*

*Q: How did you collect them?*

*A: No, they were submitted with the autopsy specimens. And then I looked at them and then packaged them.*

*Q: And where did they go from you?*

*A: They went with the rest of the others.*

*Q: And where did that evidence go?*

*A: The blood evidence and—it was then stored in a minus 80 degree freezer. Minus 80 Centigrade. Approximately [minus] 170 degrees Fahrenheit or less.*[112]

Was it possible Bob George would end this line of questioning here without even asking if Pino now understood that the fingernail scrapings were examined by Cellmark Diagnostics and that Eddie had been excluded as the primary source of DNA from underneath Downing's fingernails?

It was, and he did. A golden opportunity to show the jury that evidence indicating Eddie was not the murderer had just been missed.

Pino admitted that he understood Eddie O'Brien was a suspect in the murder when he received his clothing at the police station sometime after midnight on July 24. He was never told about any mugging in Union Square. He returned to the stand the following morning, and Bob George resumed his questioning about the collection and testing of evidence.

Pino said that Eddie's white T-shirt had some diluted blood on the stomach area, most likely from his hand wound. There was a spot of blood on the right sleeve hem, which tested positive for human blood, but was insufficient to test further. An additional single spot of blood was found on the inside of his right sneaker; again, too small to test. That was all that was found on the boy's clothing.

Pino examined and measured the red penknife seized at

112 Id., pp. 287-289

Eddie's house. It was a single-edged blade measuring three-and-one-eighth inches long and five-eighths of an inch at its widest point. No testing was done on this knife; it was used only to compare it with the hilt or metal piece (Item #21) previously collected from the third step on the Downing stairs. This hilt measured one-and three-eighths inches wide, as did the red penknife hilt. The red knife had two hilts, one on each side of the blade. Each hilt was attached to the knife by a separate pin. Only one hilt was recovered at the crime scene. No pin or any other part of the knife was recovered.

George briefly asked about another knife, listed as Item #105, sent to the lab along with Paul Downing's knapsack, sneakers, and shirt (numbered #102, #103, and #104). George did not attach any significance to the fact that the knife came into the lab at the same time as Paul's knapsack and was numbered sequentially with those items. He did not refer to, and may not have seen, the forensic drawing where Pino drew all these items together.

Another missed opportunity.

Pino said, "105 was a stamp of a metal knife, without the handle, without the wooden handles attached."[113] George asked only if there was blood detected on it, and the answer was no. There was no blood detected. George didn't ask how Pino determined the missing handles were wooden. Couldn't they have been metal, bone, or plastic? In fact, George did not ask him any further questions about the knife itself. And he didn't inquire as to why the knife came in with Paul's belongings.

Pino continued to describe the other areas comprising the criminalistics section of the State Police Crime Lab. Blood testing was done at the serology section. No educational certificate was required to qualify as a chemist in serology at the lab and, in fact, the State Police lab itself was not

113 NINTH DAY OF TRIAL, Vol. XII, September 25, 1997, p. 26

certified; certification by the American Association of Crime Laboratory Directors was voluntary. It was not a requirement at that time.

The lab was trying to gain certification "but there are many things that the laboratory has to do before certification can be allowed,"[114] he said. They needed more space and written procedures for how evidence is handled, for example. (So there were no written procedures on how to handle evidence in 1995? George never asked him.)

DA Reilly re-examined Pino regarding the crime scene and the hairs in Downing's palm. Pino testified that he did a microscopic analysis comparing the hairs to those of Janet Downing and Paul Downing.

*Q:What were the results of your comparison?*

*A:The hairs that were found on the right palm and right side of the index finger were found to—the Caucasian hairs were found to be that of Janet Downing.*

*Q:And did you also find that—another hair, on the fifth stair where you also found bloodstains, two stairs above the hilt (Item #21)?*

*A:Yes, sir.*

*Q:Did you do a microscopic analysis of that hair?*

*A:Yes, sir. It was hair, in blood, on the fifth stair baseboard, that were cut. They were found to be the hairs of Janet Downing.*

But George, who well knew hair could not be identified forensically by microscope, came back at Pino on re-cross-examination to make it clear that Pino was misrepresenting this information to the jury:

*Q:Now, you just testified a few moments ago that the*

114 Id., p. 43

*hairs found on Janet Downing's hand were hers. Do you recall testifying to that?*

*A: Yes, sir, I did.*

*Q: Well, that is not what your report says, does it?*

*A: It says that the hairs could have originated from Janet Downing.*

*Q: Now "could have originated," what did you mean when you wrote "could have originated"? Or when you found—made that finding—back on November 2, 1995?*

*A: The word could have been consistent, I use in hair analysis, because hair analysis is not absolute.*

*Q: I just want the jury to hear that. What do you mean when you say it's not absolute?*

*A: Everyone in this courtroom has, even though there's a different, there's a different microscopic structure in the hair. All your hairs on your head are not exactly the same. They each fall into a range of different items. This would be a thickness. It could be a color; it could be a pigmentation of the hair itself. Since these things fall into a range of hair, you can only say that someone could have and you can't be absolute that the hair actually came from that person. With DNA analysis you could say that these hairs originated from a certain person. But no DNA analysis was done on these hairs.*

*Q: Can you tell whether a hair was male or female when you look at it?*

*A: No, sir, you cannot.*

*Q: So, you can't tell us whether the brown hairs on Janet Downing's hands were male or female?*

*A: I can only say that the hairs, the brown hairs on Janet Downing's hairs and—excuse me—on Janet Downing's hands were consistent in color, microscopic appearance with the hairs from her head.*

*Q: But you are not testifying that they are her hairs?*

*A:I am not testifying that they are her hairs. I am saying they are consistent with her hair, and consistent with that of Paul Downing.*[115]

Pino had in fact said, twice, "the Caucasian hairs were found to be that of Janet Downing." He was caught in the lie, with no way to backtrack. It was equally obvious that this was exactly what Reilly wanted him to say. Reilly didn't even attempt to correct him, or qualify his answer.

Why did Reilly continue to let witnesses perjure themselves? Did he really think that he wouldn't get caught?

In 2007, Robert Pino would be suspended after an investigation revealed that he'd failed to make timely and/or accurate notifications of DNA "hits" or matches in several old but still open cases. As a result, in many of the cases, a suspect was identified prior to the expiration of the statute of limitations, but neither the police nor the district attorney was notified in a timely matter, and the statute of limitations passed before the cases could be filed. In a few cases, Pino made notification to law enforcement officials of DNA "hits" on old cases when, in fact, no match had been made.[116] He responded to his firing by asserting that his superiors should have been fired as well, because they knew about all of these issues.

Reporters in an exclusive interview with a Boston-area investigative team posed the question: Why was Pino taking the brunt of the blame for problems everyone else seemed to know about? "I think all of it's politics," said Pino.[117]

In 2014, Pino's reputation was further impugned due to

---

115 Id., pp. 72-74

116 Commonwealth of Massachusetts, Department of the State Police, Public Affairs Unit Press Release dated January 12, 2007

117 Boston Globe, "Former State Police Crime Lab Administrator Tells Troubling Story," July 6, 2007

his forensic work in another murder case from Somerville. A man named Michael J. Sullivan was convicted of murder in 1986, and Pino was the chemist and crime scene investigator in that case as well. In 2014, Sullivan was granted a new trial by the Supreme Judicial Court based on a re-examination of Pino's forensic work in the case.

Pino's role in Eddie O'Brien's case, especially in light of the testimony he gave under oath, adds one more layer to the growing pile of questionable behavior in this case on the part of the police, the investigators, the district attorney and now the State Police lab.

Maybe Robert Pino was right. Maybe it *is* all politics.[118]

---

118 See Appendix B for full article.

# CHAPTER 30

## LESSONS IN FORENSICS

The second witness of the day, Mary Kate McGillivray, would later succeed Robert Pino at the State Police lab when he was fired. In 1997, however, she was Pino's colleague in the serology unit. She'd been there for ten years.

She was a diplomate, meaning someone certified by the American Board of Criminalistics. Her title was Supervisor Chemist III at the serology unit, a specialty offshoot of the criminalistics unit. McGillivray explained forensic serology to the jurors.

*A:Forensic serology is the application of immunology and biochemistry to the identification and characterization of blood and body fluids. The purpose of conducting these serological characterizations has—is in an effort to generate a genetic profile of a particular individual and also to generate a genetic profile of particular bloodstains or body fluid stains collected on evidence or at a crime scene. And then those genetic profiles are compared to each other to determine if an individual could or could not be a potential source of that blood or body fluid.*[119]

I doubt very much that this explanation enlightened very many people on the jury. The best they might come away with was that she tested blood and body fluids for something to see if she could match it to a person. This lesson would get

119 NINTH DAY OF TRIAL, Vol. XII, Sept. 25, 1997, p. 79

harder as she continued:

*To obtain a genetic profile on a blood sample or on a known blood sample from an individual, I would look for substances in the blood called genetic markers. A genetic marker is something that an individual is born with. He inherits it from his parents. And it remains constant with him throughout his life. So, it never changes. One of the most familiar genetic marker systems is the ABO system, which is your blood type. So, a person could have blood type A, type B, type AB or type O. And that is a genetic marker system. That is, in fact, one of the genetic marker systems that we use in forensics to help characterize bloodstains.*[120]

Usually by this point, a scientific expert witness has lost 50 percent of the jurors. As a reader, you are free to skim over or past all of this, but as a juror you are forced to listen to every difficult concept she is explaining. At least half of them are probably wondering when the judge will let them have their midmorning break, so they can stretch their legs and get some coffee.

The other half are trying to remember what their blood type is or even if they've ever known it.

The important thing for a juror to understand, and which they may miss, is that serology tests do not definitively identify the source of the sample. McGillivray explained that when she said "consistent with" it meant that a person could not be excluded as a possible source of the biological material. It did not mean they were the source. When she said "excluded," it meant that a person could not have been the source of the biological extract she'd tested. These tests are therefore generally referred to as "exclusionary" tests. They are conducted in order to exclude, which they are 100 percent accurate at doing.

120 Id., p. 79

The juror who is already lost to the language of this science is usually just grasping for an easier way to understand what the witness is really saying—okay, just tell me, is he a match or not? How the examiner frames the question is very important; it has an enormous impact on the way the juror hears and processes the response from the expert witness.

With blood serology, the proper question is, "Is the defendant excluded as a potential contributor to that specimen?" because the only 100 percent accurate result from the test is one that excludes the defendant. The improper question, but one that is always used by the prosecution, is "Are the results of that test consistent with the defendant's blood?" If the defendant is not excluded, then the answer is always yes to this question. A juror hears "consistent with" as a potential match to the defendant's blood. The "yes" answer to the "consistent with" question gives the juror a false impression that there is a match.

Reilly continued his direct examination, asking for the genetic profile of Janet Downing's blood. McGillivray said it was type AB. "She has a PGM subtype of 1+, 2+, she had an Esterase D type of one. She had an EAP type B. She had an ABA type of one, and an AK type of one." [121]

McGillivray was reading from a large chart made by the district attorney. It could have been a Times Square billboard. No one in that courtroom understood any of this. Reilly continued his questioning:

*Q: What percentage of the population would have blood type AB? Or how common is type AB?*

*A: Type AB occurs in approximately 4 percent of the population.*

*Q: What percentage of the population shares all of the characteristics that you found in Janet Downing's blood?*

121 Id., p. 88

*A:I can combine the frequencies of all these results to obtain a percentage of the population that would share all those results. And that percentage, in the Caucasian population, is 0.23 percent.* [122]

But what does that mean? How many people are 0.23 percent of the Caucasian (white) population? Do you mean Caucasian population in the United States, or worldwide?

(This illustrates how technical and dense this forensic testimony can be. It went on and on like this for twenty or thirty minutes without further clarification or instruction.)

Following the chart, McGillivray testified that Eddie O'Brien had type O blood, which is found in approximately 45 percent of the population. The share of the population with all of Eddie's subtypes is 0.21 percent.

Now it sounds like they are neck-in-neck with percentages appearing in the Caucasian population. She's 0.23 percent and he's 0.21 percent. But her blood type was rare and his is the most common? This makes no sense.

Reilly moved on to the swab taken from Eddie's right shin at the hospital. McGillivray tested this sample.

*Q:And what were the results of your tests?*

*A:In the ABO system, I detected A and B antigens on this blood sample. That is consistent with having come from a person of AB blood—type AB. I did conduct a series of other tests on this sample, but I was unable to obtain any results. Those results were inconclusive.*[123]

In other words, the sample had none of the subtypes for Janet Downing, even though McGillivray did a series of tests to determine these subtypes. Therefore she could draw no

122 Id., p. 88

123 Id., p. 92

conclusion as to whether or not Downing was a contributor to the blood swab from the boy's shin. Reilly, wisely, didn't ask her to explain what was inconclusive about the tests to the jurors. It was evidence not favorable to him.

It would be up to George to capitalize on this finding. It was enormously important because it was the only blood found on Eddie O'Brien or his clothing that linked him to Downing. Two years later, it was finally revealed that serology tests determined the sample was "inconclusive."

McGillivray tested the blood swipes from the hallway floor between the front door and the bathroom/powder room. Eddie's blood was consistent with only one of the subtypes, not all five of them. This is about as far from a "match" as you can get.

McGillivray was unable to conduct further testing because of the limited size of the sample. She had to preserve half of the sample for testing by the defense.

At least five times after McGillivray testified to the testing of an item, Reilly asked her if she'd preserved half of the sample for independent testing by the defense. Each time Reilly asked, "and where are those samples" she withheld for the defense, McGillivray responded, "They remain at the crime laboratory, frozen in storage."[124]

Reilly certainly made one thing perfectly clear: George could have done his own testing to refute the Commonwealth's findings. He'd either decided not to or failed to do so. Either way, it had to give the jury the impression that the defense didn't believe retesting would produce any different result.

Reilly went through a list of twenty additional samples that McGillivray tested. Each time he asked if she identified genetic markers. Each time she described the various genetic markers she'd identified. Each time she determined whether Eddie or Downing could or could not be excluded from the

124 Id., p. 94

sample. Each time he asked the percentage of the population these characteristics could be found in. It was torture. It seemed endless.

The abbreviated version is that Eddie could not be excluded from six bloodstains tested:

- the inner front door
- the right door jamb of the dining room
- above the second stair
- the back of a picture lying on the hallway floor (perhaps the one that Virginia Reckley stepped on in her bare feet?)
- the pink dress hanging on the line in the cellar
- the cellar post, which held a mixture of blood from which neither Downing nor Eddie could be positively excluded.

Eddie was conclusively excluded from fourteen bloodstains tested: the threshold of the front door, the front of two pictures on the floor, the samples from the third, fourth and fifth stairs and the baseboards of the fourth and fifth stairs, the dimmer switch in the dining room, the left wall going down the cellar stairs, the blue blazer on the clothesline in the cellar, and the deadbolt area on the outer cellar door.

*Q:In addition to the tests that you performed, are there further tests that can be done to profile blood?*

*A:Yes, there are.*

*Q:And what type of, ah—additional testing can be done?*

*A:Ah, the DNA testing is another type of test that can be conducted on blood samples to characterize them.*

*Q:And did you send certain samples to a lab for further testing?*

*A:Yes, I did.*

*Q:And what lab did you send the samples to?*

*A:The samples were tested by Cellmark laboratory in Germantown, Maryland.*

*Q:And what samples did you send them?*[125]

In addition to the known blood samples from Downing and Eddie, she'd sent:

- a sample from the sneakers, #1
- a bloodstain extract from the inside front door, #12
- a bloodstain extract from the inner front door above the doorknob, #13
- a bloodstain extract from the right doorjamb of the dining room, #14
- a bloodstain extract from the metal piece recovered from the stairway, #21
- a bloodstain extract from the wall on the stairway, #22
- a stained portion of the pink dress, #38
- bloodstain extracts from inside the cellar exit door by the deadbolt, #42
- bloodstains recovered from the sidewalk on Hamlet Street, #50, #69 and #66
- bloodstain extracts from the wooden cellar post by the fingerprints, #70
- bloodstained fingernail clippings from Downing, #81 and #82

The state lab wasn't certified to do DNA testing in 1997. McGillivray was not able to give the jurors the DNA test results from Cellmark Diagnostics on the above fourteen items, since she didn't do the tests.

McGillivray concluded that at least two people were bleeding at the scene. At the level of analysis she did, she could not exclude Eddie as a bleeder in addition to the

125 Id., pp. 125-127

victim. A total of two liters (4.2 US pints) of blood had been present at the crime scene.

Finally, the morning recess was announced, and a very weary jury filed out of the courtroom.

# CHAPTER 31

## THICKER THAN BLOOD

The afternoon session was all Bob George's. He had to challenge the blood evidence on cross-examination.

His focus was the blood that was not consistent with Eddie or any of the possible contributors to each tested sample. He started with the blood extracts from the sidewalk on Hamlet Street. They were inconclusive. No blood type could be identified.

The bloodstain from inside the front door above the doorknob "showed weak reaction for both A and B antigens. And I detected a strong reaction from the H antigen,"[126] McGillivray said. She explained this was atypical for a sample from just one individual, and suggested that it could be a mixture of blood from more than one individual.

The cellar support post had additional bloodstains on the side and back. No ABO blood types could be identified when she did her initial report in August 1995. At that time she had samples only from Downing and Eddie O'Brien with which to compare the sample. She eventually obtained blood samples from Paul Downing Sr., Paul Downing Jr., Ryan Downing, and Artie Ortiz. Further comparison in August of 1997 revealed that the stains on the back of the wooden cellar post now had possible single source contributors that included Janet Downing, Paul Downing Sr., and Artie Ortiz.

In December of 1995, McGillivray sent a number of bloodstain samples to the FBI lab "in hopes that they would

126 Id., p. 169

do DNA testing on them." [127]

- Item #1, a stain from a pair of sneakers (Eddie's)
- Item #13, a bloodstain on the front door, above the doorknob
- Item #21, bloodstain extract from a metal piece on the third stair
- Item #30, bloodstain extract from the kitchen floor
- Item #31, bloodstain extract from different portion of kitchen floor
- Item #32, bloodstain extract from cellar doorknob inside kitchen
- Item #34, bloodstain extract, small stair, on right wall inside cellar stairway
- Item #35, bloodstain extract large smear on right wall, inside cellar stairway
- Item #42, bloodstain extract on inside of cellar door exit
- Item #70, bloodstain extract from the wooden post by the fingerprint
- Items # 50, 51, 56, 57, 66, and 69, all sidewalk bloodstains on Hamlet Street
- Items #95 and 107, known blood samples of Janet Downing and Eddie O'Brien.

McGillivray could not determine the date that these materials had been sent because there was no letter of transmittal accompanying them. She said that a state trooper (whose name she could not recall) came and picked up the package at the lab to transport it to FBI headquarters. She personally examined each item, cut it in half for independent testing by the defense, and then packaged the other half for transport. She did not know when they arrived at their destination or who received them. She didn't know which division of the FBI might have received them.

127 Id., p. 181

In June 1996 the samples were returned to her with the packages unopened. No testing had been done on any of the items submitted in the almost seven months they were with the FBI. She did not know why. They were delivered back by a state trooper with no letter of transmittal.

In September 1996, approximately fourteen months after Downing's death, McGillivray sent several of those samples for DNA testing to Cellmark:

- Items #1, 13, 21, 42, 50, 66, 69, and 70 from the original FBI submission; plus four additional items which had remained at the State Police lab during the prior fourteen months
- Item #12, bloodstain extract from inside inner front door
- Item #14, bloodstain extract right doorjamb of dining room entrance
- Item #22, bloodstain extract right wall of second stair
- Item #38, stained section of pink dress on clothesline

Testing on item #21, the extract from the metal piece (the hilt of the knife) was discontinued, she said, because the sample was too small for her to retain half of the sample in the laboratory and still have the analysis done. So "we asked them to hold onto it until, uhm, defendants had the option, or opportunity to come and watch them do the testing and review the results as they were being, uhm, tested."[128]

This explanation is not supported by the evidence Bob George had in his possession. Cellmark's letter to McGillivray dated November 27, 1996, said that "an extraction procedure was performed on the metal piece on third stair (Item #21). Testing on this item was discontinued at the request of Mr. Tom Reilly."[129]

A letter from Cellmark Diagnostics to McGillivray, dated

---

128 Id., pp. 195, 196

129 Cellmark Diagnostics Report of Laboratory Examination November 27, 1996, Melissa Weber, Senior Molecular Biologist, p. 1

July 25, 1997, describes "DNA previously extracted from the thread labeled metal piece on third stair." The DNA was extracted in November 1996, and preliminary testing (PGM testing) excluded Eddie as a possible contributor to the DNA on the hilt of the knife. It was then that Reilly ordered further testing discontinued.[130]

Nothing in the official correspondence indicates that testing was stopped for the reasons McGillivray now asserted under oath.

If the district attorney knew that initial testing excluded Eddie, and he ordered the lab to discontinue further testing after he was so informed, that would constitute prosecutorial misconduct.

Further DNA testing by Cellmark Diagnostics in July 1997 proved that the metal piece, item #21, contained two DNA profiles: that of Downing and that of a male.[131]

However, George never connected the dots for the jury to see how the prosecution may have withheld this exculpatory evidence by not completing the testing. Was he aware of Reilly's order to discontinue testing? Did he even read the report? George certainly never pressured the district attorney to get the testing done. He never arranged with the lab to get his samples to do his own testing. Wasn't he just as guilty as Reilly in allowing these vital pieces of evidence to go untested for two years while his client sat in jail?

McGillivray conducted further serology (not DNA) testing in June 1996. On June, 16, 1997, almost two years after the murder, samples from Paul Downing Jr., Ryan Downing, and Artie Ortiz were submitted for analysis. The results of that testing were reflected in McGillivray's final report of August of 1997.

130 Id., p. 1

131 Cellmark Diagnostics Report of Laboratory Examination July 25, 1997, Melissa Weber, Senior Molecular Biologist, p. 1

The chart Reilly used under direct examination of McGillivray did not reflect how the new samples changed her findings regarding certain important items collected at the crime scene.

Specifically, regarding the blood on Eddie's right shin, Artie Ortiz, Paul Downing Sr., Paul Downing Jr., and Ryan Downing[132] could not be excluded as contributors:

- Paul Downing Jr., could not be excluded from the bloodstain from the hallway floor if the stain was a mixture of more than one individual.
- Paul Downing Sr.'s blood was "virtually indistinguishable" from Janet Downing's in many of the samples, so where McGillivray obtained a result that was consistent with having come from Janet Downing as the single source of the bloodstain, McGillivray could not exclude Paul Downing Sr. either.

Item #36 was a swab taken from the left stairwell wall, going down the cellar stairs. George asked McGillivray:

*Q: Who are the possible single sources of that blood?*

*A: In that sample, I was unable to obtain an EAP result, which is what distinguishes Janet Downing from Mr. Ortiz. So, in that sample, Janet Downing is a possible single source, Paul Downing Sr. is a possible single source, because he's indistinguishable. And, at this level of analysis, Mr. Ortiz cannot be excluded as a single source either.*

*Q: Okay, so let's go to Item #70 (wooden cellar post sample) on the big board that Mr. Reilly showed you on direct examination.*

*A: Yes.*

*Q: Now, who were the possible contributors, according to your report dated August 7, 1997, when you had everyone's blood samples? Paul Downing?*

132 NINTH DAY OF TRIAL, Vol. XII, Sept. 25, 1997, p. 216

*A: Yes. Assuming that they are a mix–*

*Q: Which you do.*

*A: Right.*

*Q: Paul Downing?*

*A: It could be—Paul Downing could have contributed into the mixture.*

*Q: Ryan Downing?*

*A: Ryan.*

*Q: Mr. Ortiz?*

*A: Yes.*

*Q: Paul Downing Sr.?*

*A: Yes.*

*Q: And Edward O'Brien?*

*A: Yes.*

*Q: How come only Edward O'Brien's name is on that exhibit up there for this jury?*

*A: I don't know.*

*Q: Where is everyone else's name?*

*A: They are contained in my report.*[133]

Score one for Bob George. Reilly took a direct hit on this one. It appeared he was trying to hide this new information in order to implicate Eddie O'Brien alone. Over Reilly's objection, the judge allowed McGillivray to add to the chart all the possible contributors to the blood extract from the wooden post (Item #70), the extract from the front door above the handle (Item #13), and the extract from Eddie's right shin (Item #6).

*Q: And is there some reason that you only received the samples of those other persons that we talked about—Mr. Ortiz, the two Downing children—is there any reason you just received them so late?*

133 Id., p. 232

*A:I have no idea.*

*Q:Now, the fingernail scrapings from Mrs. Downing were sent to Cellmark?*

*A:Yes, they were.*

*Q:And eventually the metal piece, Item #21, was sent to Cellmark?*

*A:Yes. That was sent out originally. But it wasn't tested until, uhm, July . . . of '97.*[134]

Once again, George failed to remind her that testing was done on the metal piece in November 1996 but discontinued at Reilly's request. He neglected to ask any follow-up questions about these two pieces of critical evidence that conclusively excluded Eddie O'Brien as the source of DNA on them. Granted, McGillivray could not testify to another person's report, but there were ways in which he could have suggested that she understood that these tests excluded Eddie without raising objections.

For example, he could have asked whether the items required any additional testing to identify the contributors to the fingernail scrapings and the hilt of the knife. She would have had to say they did not.

He could have asked if she knew the identity of both contributors to the material. She would have had to say she did not.

His final question then could be if she knew whether Eddie O'Brien's DNA profile had been provided for comparison. She would have had to say it was.

There were only two sources of DNA on both the fingernails scrapings and the hilt of the knife: Janet Downing and an unknown male.

Instead of asking such questions, George took the witness methodically through every sample she tested to show that

134 Id., pp. 271, 272

Eddie O'Brien could not have been a contributor to each sample and that most, if not all, of the Downing family and Artie Ortiz could have been contributors. The impression he was trying to leave with the jurors was that there was a huge volume of blood in the house, all over the dining room, hallway, stairway to the second floor, kitchen, stairway to the basement, and out through the basement door and that except for a very few small and isolated samples, none of it was Eddie's blood.

That point having been made, a larger, more important question still loomed unanswered: Were any of those other people bleeding at the scene? Yes, they were possible contributors by blood typing, but if they didn't bleed there, then they couldn't have contributed to the blood. George didn't have any evidence that one or more of them bled at the scene that night, and Reilly drove this point home.

*Q: When you are using the word "possible contributor," when is it significant?*

*A: It's significant if, in fact, the stain is a mixture. So, a stain would have to be a mixture of more than one individual for those people to be included as sources of that bloodstain. If the stain is from one person, a single source, then only the individual that I mentioned could be the source of that blood.*[135]

The point was further emphasized using the example of the blood on Eddie O'Brien's right shin. The only way that there could have been contributors other than Downing to that blood would be "if it were a mixture of blood, and Paul and Ryan Downing were both bleeding on Edward O'Brien's shin," said McGillivray. [136]

135 Id., pp. 274, 275

136 Id., p. 277

# CHAPTER 32

## DNA – THE CART BEFORE THE HORSE

Since the State Police lab in Massachusetts wasn't certified to do DNA testing, selected specimens were sent to Cellmark Diagnostics in Maryland for analysis. The specimens were tested by Melissa Weber at Cellmark. Instead of putting Weber on the stand, Reilly called Dr. Jennifer Reynolds, the "reviewer" of Weber's work. The lab required that a second person review the entire contents of the case folder, read all the laboratory reports, and sign the report.[137]

It was not clear at the time why Reilly chose to put the reviewer, and not the chemist, on the stand first.

Normally, the chemist would testify first, describing each test and why it was done. Then they would testify about the results obtained from that test in the questioned sample: how it was matched or failed to match a known sample to which the results were being compared.

Putting the supervisor on first made an impossibly complex subject even more muddled. Why? Because she couldn't testify about the *actual testing* done. She could only testify that she reviewed the work someone else did and approved it.

It is impossible to convey just how impenetrable the testimony about DNA sounds to a nonscientist. Dr. Reynolds went on for at least twenty minutes talking about chromosomes and double helixes and bases and pairing . . . All of it was information that could only be fully understood

137 TENTH DAY OF TRIAL, September 26,1997, p. 9

by a fellow scientist.

The judicial system doesn't take into account the complexity of information the jury is required to comprehend and apply to the facts of a case. It encourages jurors to tune out the actual details of the testimony and rely entirely on the conclusions of the expert witnesses without understanding the process by which they came to that conclusion.

To simplify, here is a short synopsis of DNA technology.

In 1997, there were two tests that could be performed to forensically identify a person's unique and individual DNA:

- RFLP (Restriction Fragment Length Polymorphism) testing, a technology in use in the scientific community for about twenty years that was used routinely for prediagnosis and cancer diagnosis and other types of biomedical research.
- PCR (polymerase chain reaction) testing had been around since about 1985. It was the most widely used test used for medical diagnoses. PCR testing was much more sensitive than RFLP and it did not require a large sample in order to be accurate. PCR testing is used only to *exclude* a possible source, which it does with 100 percent accuracy. Since PCR tests cannot *include* a person with any certainty, the only reliable result is whether or not that person can be excluded as a contributor to the specimen.

Over the past twenty years, far more accurate and sophisticated DNA testing has been developed. The FBI discontinued RFLP analysis in 2000 in favor of STR-13 multiplexing testing. Moreover, mitochondrial DNA (mtDNA) can now identify DNA recovered from damaged, degraded, or very small biological samples.

That development came too late for Eddie, though: RFLP testing was used in his 1997 case. This test compares the banding patterns in the DNA as well as the size of the bands.

If the evidence sample and the known sample bands appear identical and their sizes fall within a strict match criteria, then they are statistical and visual match. Banding matches look like this:

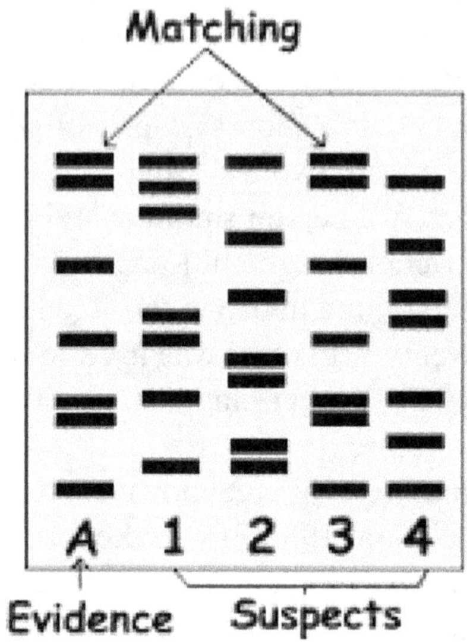


*DNA Banding Pattern Chart*

The matches are compared with five separate regions to determine how frequently in the population this banding pattern with that matching size would occur. Cellmark did RFLP testing on four evidence samples and two known controls (Janet Downing and Eddie O'Brien). The four samples were:

- A swab from inside the inside front door (Item #12): The results showed that the darkest and primary banding pattern on Item#12, inner side of the inside front door, matched exactly the banding patterns of Eddie O'Brien. The frequency of finding another person who matched exactly the banding patterns of Eddie O'Brien in the Caucasian population would be 1 in 180 million individuals. A second banding pattern detected matched Downing.

- A cutting from the pink dress on the clothesline in the basement (Item #38): The banding pattern on the dress (Item #38) matched exactly Eddie O'Brien's banding pattern. The frequency in the Caucasian population would be 1 in 180 million individuals. The second banding pattern detected matched that of Janet Downing.
- A swab from the cellar exit door (Item #42): The cellar exit door swab (Item #42) matched exactly Janet Downing's banding pattern. The frequency of matching her banding pattern to another in the Caucasian population would be 1 in 3.2 billion individuals.
- A swab from the right door jamb of the dining room (Item #14): The swab from the right door jamb of the dining room revealed only one banding pattern that matched Eddie O'Brien's banding pattern. The frequency was 1 in 180 million. It was the only DNA banding pattern detected in the sample.

Cellmark did PCR testing on ten evidence samples and compared them with two known samples (Janet Downing and Eddie O'Brien). Three genetic sites are examined to see how often the base repeats itself. Finally, they look to the gender location to see if the DNA is male or female.

- Cutting labeled "sneakers (suspect)" (Item #1)
- Sidewalk bloodstains group #27 (Item #66)
- Sidewalk bloodstains group #20 (Item #69)
- Bloodstain extract on inner front door (Item #13)

The result for these four samples was virtually identical: Janet Downing could be excluded from all the samples. Although Eddie O'Brien could not be excluded, 1 in every 270 Caucasian males would match all of the types found in these samples.

- Thread from the metal piece on third stair (Item #21)

The "thread" referred to the actual size of the sample tested. It was as small as a thread of clothing. The result for this sample showed a mixture of two people, a male and a female. Janet Downing could not be excluded as the primary donor; Eddie O'Brien was excluded. There was one genetic marker present in the sample that neither the victim's nor Eddie's DNA contained, therefore the other DNA detected on the sample is from an unidentified male person. Reilly asked, "What are the possible sources of that 12 (in the TPOX marker) then?" Dr. Reynolds responded "I have no idea. I don't know."[138]

- Right hand and left hand fingernail scrapings of Janet Downing (no item number): The primary source was consistent with Downing's sample. Eddie was excluded as a contributor to the sample. A secondary source of DNA detected was male. "But besides that, we can't draw any conclusions."[139]
- The wooden post in the cellar (Item #70): "This gave us a mixture where the types observed were consistent with both the types observed from Edward O'Brien's sample and Downing's sample." The primary contributor could not be determined.[140]

In summary, there were four distinct places where Eddie's DNA was detected: the inside of the inner front door, the door jamb of the entryway to the dining room, the wooden post in the cellar, and on one of the pieces of clothing (the pink dress) on the clothesline in the basement.

All of this was consistent with the account that Eddie had given Dr. Spiers in 1995 about what happened at 71 Hamlet St. on the night of the murder. Eddie *did* touch Downing's

138 Id., p. 24

139 Id., p. 31

140 Id., p. 30

body to turn her over to see if she was alive. He *did* close the inner front door when ordered to do so by Downing's attacker, he *did* hit the post at the bottom of the cellar stairway, and he *did* push the clothes away on his way to the backyard. Eddie told Spiers that the outer cellar door was already open when he ran out of it. The lack of any of his blood, fingerprints, or DNA on this door is also consistent with his original story.

The jury had not yet heard any information about Eddie's presence at the crime scene. They didn't hear Spiers or see his videotaped interview. His testimony and the tape were excluded by the judge because the sodium amytal test, like the lie detector test, had not yet been generally accepted as reliable in the scientific community.

Without any information about how Eddie's blood came to be at the scene of the crime, the case against him, at this juncture, appeared quite damning. Would the jurors be able to keep open minds until all the evidence had been heard?

Would they remember the bloody fingerprint in the powder room that didn't belong to Eddie and the bloody palm print on the opposite door jamb to the dining room that didn't belong to either Eddie or Downing? Would they remember that on the hilt of the knife (Item #21) and under Janet Downing's fingernails there was a secondary source of male DNA that could not be identified? Would they remember there were unidentified fingerprints at the scene that the police made no attempt to identify?

The defense was still a day away from presenting any evidence. The jury had been listening to the case for seven full days now. The last several witnesses were all forensic experts. The jurors couldn't take notes, and they couldn't talk to one another about the case at all. How much were they expected to retain before they began to forget some of the evidence?

# CHAPTER 33

## ALL WILL NOT BE REVEALED

Melissa Weber had been at Cellmark eight years by the time she testified at Eddie O'Brien's trial. She was the one who did the actual testing on all evidence submitted. If the jury expected that she was going to describe all of these tests and what the results revealed, they were either sadly disappointed or happily relieved.

All District Attorney Tom Reilly did with this witness was to have her identify large charts and ask if they represented her findings in the case accurately. He then asked that the large charts be admitted into evidence. Bob George correctly objected. At sidebar, Reilly almost pleaded with the judge to allow them into evidence, because the jury was permitted to have chalks in the jury room. These were like chalks, he reasoned.

But chalks are not evidence and could not be considered by the jury as evidence. Judge James McDaniel reminded him they were hearsay, and if George objected, which he did, then he had to rule them inadmissible because they were hearsay. The judge asked why Reilly didn't simply have her testify to the information.

Reilly mumbled an acceptance of the judge's suggestion, but did not elicit any testimony from the witness regarding the actual tests. His reasons weren't immediately apparent. Had he gotten everything he needed from Jennifer Reynolds, Weber's supervisor? Even Judge McDaniel expressed his opinion that Reynolds should have testified after Weber, not before.

Reilly clearly wanted this witness on and off the stand in a hurry. There had to be a reason. Was he worried what Weber might reveal communications she'd had with him directly about aborting the testing of some evidence? (She was, after all, the chemist he instructed to suspend all further DNA analysis on the hilt of the knife for an entire year.) Perhaps he was worried about George uncovering the reason he ordered all further testing halted—because the first extraction showed that Eddie's DNA did not appear on the hilt of the alleged murder weapon.

If that was his thinking, he needn't have worried. Although Bob George had all three written reports, he never asked why all testing had been suspended for an entire year at Reilly's request.

George was clearly poorly prepared. How could he understand such complicated new evidence (the hilt and fingernail scrapings results had come in just before the trial started) without the guidance and advice of his own DNA expert? How could he properly question Reilly's expert, or capitalize on the fact that Eddie had been excluded as the primary source and that the secondary male DNA was not identified on the hilt of the knife–the alleged murder weapon—if he didn't understand what the DNA results actually meant?

George's failure to secure his own expert witnesses to interpret the results and to obtain independent blood and DNA analysis eventually played a huge role in costing Eddie O'Brien his freedom.

The ineffective assistance of counsel is not necessarily better than no counsel at all. It can be worse. Eddie would never be able to get a new trial on appeal with regard to this particular evidence. In order to be granted a new trial, Eddie would have to prove that there was new evidence that did not exist at the time of trial or there was evidence that was not available to him at the time if his trial.

All the DNA evidence was known and available to the defense attorney, Bob George. The only time Eddie had the opportunity to challenge this evidence was at trial. George failed to do what was minimally necessary in order to interpret and properly address the Commonwealth's DNA evidence. He failed to get any independent DNA analysis of his own, even though one-half of all the samples were reserved for him to do just that.

# CHAPTER 34

## MEDICAL EXAMINER AND AUTOPSY

Dr. Leonard Atkins, the medical examiner, previously testified at the first transfer hearing. Much of what he testified to at trial has been described in that section. He had very little to add two years later.

At trial, it was important to Eddie O'Brien's case to raise a reasonable doubt that the green penknife was the murder weapon, or the only murder weapon. Janet Downing had suffered several wounds that measured inches longer than the green penknife's blade, including seven wounds to her right lung. "These wounds passed toward the back . . . and their total depths measured up to approximately four inches," testified Atkins.[141]

In the lower front part of her right chest area were four wounds. One passed through the last rib, which is made of hard cartilage and perforated the cartilage. Its depth measured four inches. It would have taken severe force to inflict this wound, in the medical examiner's opinion.

The green knife had a blade three-and-one-eighth inches long. George, on cross-examination, began by focusing on the four- to five-inch deep wounds. Atkins agreed that they would have had to have been inflicted by a blade passing four to five inches into the body.

On re-direct examination, Reilly asked Atkins:

*Q:Can a blade that measures three-and-one-eighth*

141 TENTH DAY OF TRIAL, September 26, 1997, p. 137

*inches long—would a knife of that size be capable of inflicting four- to five-inch wounds?*

*A: Yes.*

*Q: Why is that?*

*A: Because of the compressibility of the body tissues. If there's a very strong or powerful force, the body tissues can compress and produce a longer wound than the length of the blade.*

Bob George then re-crossed the witness.

*Q: When a knife, the blade of a knife is pushed so hard into the human body that the wound is longer than the blade . . . does that cause any kind of bruising or contusion?*

*A: It may or it may not.*

*Q: And does that depend on where?*

*A: That may be a factor.*

*Q: Okay. Did you find any bruising or contusions around those particular wounds?*

*A: No.*

*Q: Now it is clear, isn't it, doctor, that there is no disturbance of the skin, other than the wound itself?*

*A: That's correct.*[142]

This was a great re-cross for Bob George, and would have been better if he'd realized that there still would have been one hilt attached to the knife identified as the murder weapon. That knife originally had two hilts, each attached by its own pin. Only one fell off. A hilt attached at the top of the blade would have prevented it from penetrating more than three-and-one-eighth inches. And, certainly, the imprint of the hilt would be clearly visible on the wound.

Had George completely understood the evidence, he

142 Id., p. 190

could have proved to the jury that the green penknife could not have been the weapon used to inflict many of the injuries. Reasonable doubt would have been raised about the green knife being the—or the only—murder weapon.

Atkins also testified that "there was a seven-eighths of an inch wide stab wound in her back . . . below the right shoulder."[143] The green knife's blade was only three-eighths of an inch wide. The blade that inflicted this wound had to have been seven-eighths of an inch wide, almost twice the width of the green penknife.

George never caught that discrepancy, either.

Atkins methodically described all of the ninety-eight knife wounds and various abrasions and bruises. After this testimony, Reilly introduced sixteen gruesome autopsy photographs to the jury.

No matter how shocking and (one might argue) prejudicial they are, autopsy photographs come into evidence in every homicide case. They tend to produce a visceral response from the jury that can overshadow much of the other evidence, which is why defense attorneys always argue to strike them or at least limit the number of photos. The photographs are relevant to prove the "extreme atrocity" of the crime when that has been included in the defendant's charges.

"Extreme atrocity," like "premeditation," is an aggravating factor that changes the severity of a homicide from second-degree murder to first-degree murder. Without premeditation or extreme atrocity, the jury's verdict cannot exceed second-degree murder.

The introduction of the photographs required yet another limiting instruction from the judge: "These photos which are about to be distributed to you, which depict the condition of the body of Janet Downing, with reference to the testimony the doctor has just given concerning certain stab or incised

143 Id., p. 140

wounds are–again, I caution you as I did before–these are to be observed by you in terms of any clinical significance they have, any significance on the theories which I will later describe, or discuss with you when I instruct you. So you are to look at it that way. You are not to be influenced in any way by any pity or sympathy that the gruesomeness of these photos may indicate to you, in other words, sympathy or empathy of any kind. So, please consider these photographs as I just suggested to you, only in that manner."[144]

After all the photographs were marked and shown to the jury, Reilly placed Downing's death certificate into evidence and finished his questioning of Atkins. With his last witness off the stand, Reilly formally rested his case. The Commonwealth had completed presenting its portion of the evidence.

It is almost mandatory that the defense counsel, at the close of the Commonwealth's case, move for a required finding of not guilty. If this motion is not presented, you may not argue that the trial judge erred in this respect in any subsequent appeal. A motion for a required finding requests that the court find, as a matter of law, that the evidence presented by the Commonwealth failed to prove all the elements of the crime. It literally requests that the judge require the jury to enter a finding of not guilty, thereby removing any decision from them.

Such a motion is only granted when the evidence weighs so heavily in favor of one party, and so lightly in favor of the other, that no reasonable jury could find for the party that has no evidence to support its case. These motions are almost never granted, but always made. The Massachusetts Standards of Practice that attorneys follow dictate "unless it is clearly frivolous, counsel should file a motion and move at the close of the prosecution's case for a required finding

144 Id., pp. 148, 149

of not guilty on all charges and/or any aggravating element, where appropriate."[145]

George presented his motion for a required finding outside of the jury's presence, as is done with all legal arguments. McDaniel responded, "Well, I'd like to think it would be difficult for a woman who has ninety stab wounds–whether it was stab wounds or incise wounds which caused her death–for a person, whoever did it, not to have premeditated that particular murder. I find that highly unlikely. I think that this is sufficient, of course, to go to the jury on all issues. The motion is denied."[146]

With that, the defense was instructed to call its first witness.

---

145 Committee for Public Counsel Services, Manual, Chapter IV, Criminal: Performance Standards and Complaint Procedures, p. 53

146 Id., pp. 201-204

# CHAPTER 35

## DEFENSE OR NO DEFENSE

Eddie O'Brien's chance to tell his side of the story was at hand.

I went back to his holding cell behind the courtroom to visit with him. He was ready and anxious to go. It had been hard for him to wait for two whole years, listening through three lengthy hearings about what a cold-blooded murderer he was.

He'd faithfully followed his lawyer's instructions and hadn't spoken to anyone at the jail about his case. Consequently only one "jailhouse snitch" had surfaced to say that one dark and lonely night Eddie decided to pour his heart out to him and confessed. This is a common occurrence in high-profile cases in which another inmate might be trying to buy himself a shorter sentence or gain a little notoriety. Reilly informed George he was going to call this inmate as a witness. As it turned out, the inmate had not been incarcerated in the same facility during the time Eddie had been there. They'd never even crossed paths.

Going into this phase of the trial, Eddie still believed that he was going to sit at that witness stand and tell the truth about what happened. I asked him that day (as I had on many other days during this trial) if his lawyers had been up to the jail to prepare him for his testimony yet. "Not yet," he said, "they said they are coming up tonight."

I knew then that they weren't going to put him on the stand. He could not be properly prepared for such an important event in one night. I didn't have the heart to tell him. He so believed that the whole case was about to turn around once he got his chance to talk. I told him I thought it was unlikely that his lawyers could prepare him in one evening. He shrugged. "Well, they think they can, I guess."

Needless to say, a lawyer cannot prepare a witness in an hour or two in a jailhouse visiting room. This is especially true when the witness is just seventeen years old and has never been subjected to cross-examination before. Such preparation, even with an articulate, mature adult defendant, takes countless hours of going over and over the testimony, peppering him with accusatory, demeaning questions, and then teaching him how to respond without getting upset, defensive, or angry, and especially without answering a question with a question of his own. (It is amazing how many witnesses, when asked a question like "How did it feel when that happened?" respond "How do you think it felt? How would you feel?" Such responses tell the jury that the witness is angry and argumentative.)

So it was clear to me that it wasn't part of the defense plan to put Eddie on the stand. This is not unusual. In fact it's highly unusual for a defense counsel to put his or her client on the stand. For a defendant with prior convictions, getting on the stand means all of those prior convictions will come into evidence. Juries are more likely to believe you committed this crime if you have committed others before.

Even for a defendant with no record like Eddic, there is just too much risk that he will say or do something that triggers a catastrophe. Eddie would certainly be asked why he didn't call the police right away, or go to his house and tell his father what he saw. His answer might have been because he was scared that the killer would hurt him and his family if he told anyone. Reilly would have a field day with such a response: "Well, you weren't scared to lie to the police, were you? You weren't scared to lie to your father, were you? And you weren't even scared to lie to your own attorney, were you?" Eddie most certainly would have heard those questions as accusations that he lied about what he saw and was lying now on the witness stand. He was a kid. We all know what kids do when they are accused of lying. They generally don't respond in a calm and rational manner. Even a hint of anger coming from Eddie would have been a game-changer. He just wasn't mature enough to be in control of his emotional responses. So I agree that Eddie shouldn't have testified on his own behalf, but I do not agree that this was the only way that his story could have gotten into evidence.

George started the defense's case with Michelle Cameron. She established that she had been friends with both the Downing family and the O'Brien family for at least twelve years. Specifically, she was friends with Jeannie O'Brien and Paul Downing Jr.

Michelle testified that she drove up and parked in front of the O'Brien house at about 8:15 on Sunday, July 23, 1995, to meet Jeannie and Paul so they could all return to Revere Beach together in one car. Jeannie pulled up a few minutes later. (Even assuming Michelle's time is correct, and the other witnesses who said it was 8:00 that Paul and Jeannie came home, there is still the problem with what the Reckleys heard at 8:15. If someone was attacked on the stairs at the Downing house at 8:15, surely Paul would have seen the blood on the stairwell when he walked in the house. But most assuredly, his mother was clearly not still sleeping in the den.)

Michelle testified that while Jeannie went into her house and Paul went into his house, she talked with Eddie and his father; they were sitting on the front porch steps with a neighbor and some children. Eddie was playful, taking Michelle's fake ID card and giving it to his father, saying:

"You won't believe what Michelle has, a fake ID!" His father joined in the teasing, put it in his pocket, pretending to confiscate it. They were all laughing and playing around. Then Jeannie came out at about 8:30 or 8:35, Paul came out of his house, and Michelle got her fake ID back. They all got into Michelle's car and left for Revere Beach. She remembered the time they left because she turned her radio on and it said either 8:30 or 8:35.

Michelle testified that Eddie was wearing a white "Above the Rim" T-shirt and it was inside-out. He had on dark shorts. She identified the photo of Eddie taken at the police station and said that the shirt was the same one he had on at 8:35 that night.

Reilly asked her whether Paul had any blood or scratches on him when he got back in the car, and Michelle said hadn't noticed any. (She was driving; Paul was in the back seat.) Michelle testified that they returned at about 11:00 or 11:10 and Paul was "all upset" when he learned about his mother.[147]

The day following the murder, she said, the police came to her house and retrieved Paul's backpack from the trunk of her car.

Gina Mahoney followed Michelle Cameron on the witness stand. She told the jurors that she lived at 70 Boston St. and was friendly with the Downings, the Reckleys, and the O'Briens. She had known Edward O'Brien, Eddie's father, since he was six months old. She was ten years older than Edward. Mahoney testified that Janet Downing had spent the entire day at her house on the day she was murdered.

When asked by George if Downing was in fear of Eddie O'Brien that day, Mahoney answered a clear no. When George asked if Downing was in fear of anyone else, Reilly objected to the question, and the lawyers went to sidebar with the judge. It was at this sidebar conference that George

147 TENTH DAY OF TRIAL, September 26, 1997, Vol. XIII, p. 226

fumbled the facts and his argument for why Mahoney's testimony should be an exception to the hearsay rule.

This error would prevent the jury from hearing about Downing's fear of Artie Ortiz, which was at the heart of the defense's case.

*GEORGE: Your Honor, I'm trying to put it in on state of mind of the victim. She threw him [Artie Ortiz] out because he was drug-dealing. And this is what I believe the witness will say.*

*McDANIEL: Yes.*

*GEORGE: That she threw him out because she thought he was drug-dealing in the house. And there was a very hostile time from his moving out. Threats back and forth. She was in great fear of him.*

*McDANIEL: What do you mean, she was in great fear? Who is going to say that?*

*GEORGE: This witness will say that when Artie Ortiz moved—Artie Ortiz and his family moved out of the house in March 1995, it was as a result of Janet Downing catching him drug-dealing in the house. That when he left. She had to–*

*McDANIEL: Did she see the drug-dealing?*

*GEORGE: No.*

*McDANIEL: Then how does she know?*

*REILLY: It's hearsay, isn't it?*

*McDANIEL: That's my point.*

*GEORGE: State of mind exception to the hearsay rule.*

*McDANIEL: No. Not in these circumstances, it isn't.*

*GEORGE: The state of mind of this—well—she will say that Janet Downing told her that.*

*McDANIEL: Yes?*

*GEORGE: But moving to the next step . . . Janet Downing's fear of Artie Ortiz was expressed at the same time.*

*McDANIEL: But that is totem pole hearsay.*

*GEORGE: It's the victim talking to her.*

*McDANIEL: She is telling me something someone else told her.*

*GEORGE: Are we talking about the drug-dealing or the fear?*

*McDANIEL: Who told her?*

*GEORGE: Janet Downing, the victim, told her that she was in fear of Artie Ortiz.*

*McDANIEL: Yeah.*

*GEORGE: When she put him out of the house, in March. State of mind of the victim. Under Commonwealth vs. Boradine, it's admissible. If she had a fear of Ed O'Brien, if it was admissible in this case as state of mind of the victim.*

*McDANIEL: Okay. But suppose she was—okay, let's assume for the sake of arguing that she was in fear of Ortiz. Okay? What about it? How is it relevant?*

*GEORGE: How is it relevant? It is relevant because Artie Ortiz's blood was consistent with some of the blood at the crime scene. They [the prosecution] can joke and laugh about this all they want, but it's important on third-party culprit, which is part of a defense. It's part of this defense. I mean, I have a right to explore. Only you determine.*

*McDANIEL: I haven't even answered. I haven't said a word. I'm just standing here listening. I am just standing here and I see all this whispering, and so forth, back and forth. That's okay, too. But I have some work to do.*

*GEORGE: I basically said it like it is. The fear of Artie Ortiz is something that came from this victim as being said to her, by the victim herself, on the day of the murder.*

*McDANIEL: Is that what she's going to say?*

*GEORGE: No, she'll say–*

*McDANIEL: On the day of the murder?*

*GEORGE: No, no, no. What I'm saying is, I am now with her on the day of the murder, when she did—no. She did not say it on the day of the murder.*[148]

Downing *did* say it on the day of the murder! Why was George denying it? Did he not *remember* when it was said? McDaniel indicated that if it was not too remote in time, that he would permit the witness to testify about whom Downing was afraid of.

Reilly finally entered the discussion and noted that there were prior cases that held that the victim's state of mind as to whom she was afraid of, or whom she thought might harm her, are not admissible into evidence. He requested a short break in order to retrieve copies of those cases from his office. Bob George said he'd already written a memorandum on it and submitted it to the court. Since the judge had not read the memorandum or the cases, McDaniel decided to delay any decision on whether Mahoney could testify about Downing's fears of Ortiz.

He told George to move on with the testimony.

*GEORGE: I'll bounce back to it, Your Honor. I'll come back to it.*

Suddenly McDaniel called George and Reilly back to the sidebar.

*McDANIEL: As a matter of fact, I do recall a case, just recently. A case of—I think Judge Murphy was the judge on it. It was reversed on that grounds [sic] I'm pretty sure there was such a case. His [Reilly's] position is quite correct. In the meanwhile, I will wait. I know there was a case on it.*

*GEORGE: I need to—I want to clarify something at sidebar. I didn't—the statement made about the fear of Artie*

148 Id., pp. 241-246

*Ortiz was made on the day we are talking about, July 23, 1995.*

*McDANIEL: Even so, I think it is too remote in time, anyway.*

(Obviously the judge was either not listening or did not realize that July 23 was the day Downing was killed.)

*GEORGE: Okay.*

*McDANIEL: Of course, the time element is the basis of the argument.*

*GEORGE: I just want them to know it wasn't in March. It was the day of the incident.* [149]

First George argued vigorously that the statements Downing had made weren't made on the day of her murder. Later he "clarified" that they were made on the day of her murder. There was nothing to "clarify" about what he'd said. He screwed up the facts. And his clarification certainly didn't make it clear to McDaniel that July 23 was the date of the murder.

Mahoney continued to testify that she'd seen Ortiz at the murder scene when she went outside at about 10:00. He asked to use her phone at her house. She permitted him to do so, and when he got off the phone he announced that he'd talked to the hospital and that Downing had been pronounced dead. (In fact, Downing was still in her house at the time, being worked on by the EMTs.)

She then observed Ortiz cross over to Downing's house and try to go past the police tape and walk into the backyard. He had told her he'd lost his keys back there. The police wouldn't allow him past the crime scene tape.

George still had no ruling as to whether or not he'd be

149 Id., pp. 251, 252

allowed to question Mahoney about the conversation with Downing regarding Ortiz that took place earlier on the day of her murder. He had the option of asking the court to allow him to recall her to the stand after the ruling was made.

He did not choose that option.

George went over to the sidebar and told the judge that he wanted to ask Mahoney only whether the women had discussed Ortiz that day.

*GEORGE: I'm asking permission to put questions to this witness as to whether she mentioned Mr. Ortiz to her on the day of her murder, and leave it at that.*

*McDANIEL: What? If she mentioned what? I didn't follow your question.*

*GEORGE: Whether, during the—the last—the, ah, last hours that she was talking—to Janet Downing, whether she mentioned Artie Ortiz to her.*

*McDANIEL: It's irrelevant, it's irrelevant anyway.*

*REILLY: It's hearsay.*

*McDANIEL: Why is it relevant?*

*GEORGE: Are you finding this to be hearsay? Because I suggest to you it's state of mind. It's under the state of mind exception to the hearsay rule.*

*McDANIEL: Well, my point is, what is the point to the question? That's what I'm asking you. "Did you talk to Ortiz on the last day of this incident?" Is that the question you want?*

*GEORGE: No.*

*McDANIEL: Okay, what?*

*GEORGE: Did she discuss Ortiz with you the last day?*

*McDANIEL: Did she talk about Ortiz to her the last day? Yes or no?*

*GEORGE: Yes.*

*McDANIEL: Okay.*

*GEORGE: Okay. Thank you.*[150]

George asked Gina Mahoney whether during the entire day that she'd spent with Downing on July 23, 1995, Downing had mentioned or discussed Artie Ortiz. Mahoney said yes, and George thanked her and passed the questioning to Reilly.

George did not reserve the right to recall her.

Reilly asked several questions about whether or not Mahoney had noticed any blood or scratches on Ortiz the night of the murder, and Mahoney said she hadn't. Riley announced he had no further questions, and Mahoney walked out of the courtroom with a lot of information that would never be shared with the jury.

The jury was discharged until Monday morning. But the day was far from over. Attorneys Reilly, George, and Stelzer went into the judge's lobby to discuss this state of mind of the victim issue yet again.

The judge wanted to know if any of George's other witnesses were going to present this problem of the victim's state of mind when they testified the following week. George went through his whole witness list and told the judge that he was "basically over the issue of Artie Ortiz that I can see. . . . So Gina Mahoney was it. . . . So that, so far as state of mind of the victim, I stay away from state of mind of victim."[151]

*McDANIEL: Yes. We left all that out.*

*GEORGE: Right. So, I am very careful. But I—and they will not discuss it on the stand, because all of them knew it. They knew she [Janet] was concerned about things being moved around. But they are going to stay away from it.*[152]

---

150 Id., pp. 273-275

151 Id., p. 291

152 Id., pp. 291, 292

What was George's reason for staying away from this testimony? Mahoney would have testified that Downing believed it was Ortiz, who still had keys to her house, who was coming in and moving things around, trying to scare her. Mahoney would have testified that she observed Ortiz's cab at the Downing house many weekdays while Downing was at work and the children were in school. She would have testified that she told Downing to get a restraining order against him.

It wasn't hearsay testimony; these were Mahoney's own observations and statements. Moreover, it was consistent with Ortiz possibly having some role in Downing's death.

Why not let Reilly's witnesses testify that things were being moved about in the house in the weeks prior to the murder? That testimony would have helped, not hurt Eddie. Downing had never told anyone she thought it was Eddie who was coming into her house and moving things around. She had said it was Ortiz.

What would Downing's best friend, Jean McGeary, have said? Reilly never called her as a witness. Why? Because she likely would have told the jury that Downing was terrified of Ortiz and thought it was Ortiz coming into her house to scare her. Which raises the obvious question: Why didn't George ever interview McGeary? Why didn't George call Artie Ortiz to the stand and ask him about his keys that night? Why didn't he ask him about his cab being parked at the Downing house before the ambulances arrived? What time he picked his cab up that night? Where he'd been in the hour between 8:00 and 9:00?

None of this speaks to a well-thought-out theory of the defense. Not having a coherent theory of the case, not understanding what evidence was advantageous to Eddie, not thoroughly understanding the scientific and DNA reports and the exculpatory evidence that was available to the defense all pointed clearly to the real problem: an ill-prepared and ineffectively tried case.

# CHAPTER 36

## THE BOSTON STREET NEIGHBORS

Bob George called a series of the neighbors to the witness stand, people who lived in the Prospect Hill neighborhood. Each gave the jury a sense of the community that existed there.

Ann Bradbury had been a lifelong resident of 75 Boston St. in Somerville until she moved to New Hampshire a year before the murder. Her house was directly across the street from the O'Brien house and it abutted Downing's property at her driveway. Bradbury described what a special neighborhood it was, with so many of the residents living in their homes for three generations. Her grandparents had originally bought her house, her mother grew up in it, and she did, too— and raised her children there. The neighbors lived on their porches in the summer and raised their children together. They were constantly in and out of one another's houses to retrieve their children, have coffee, and celebrate holidays.

Bradbury's children were younger than Eddie, but she said he was always calm and patient with them. He taught them how to play video games, played ball with them, and took them to the park. Her relatives used to own the Downing house, and she often babysat there when she was an adolescent. She testified that she was able to hear loud voices and conversations of the neighbors through the common wall.

George directed Bradbury to a specific conversation

she'd had with Eddie's father in the summer of 1994 at her house.

*Q:The conversation that I'm talking to you about, was young Ed in and out of the room while you were having the conversation?*

*A:Actually, he—we were on my front porch, like I said. And, uhm, it wasn't until the conversation was over that I realized he was in the doorway.*

*Q:And what was the conversation you were having with the boy in your doorway?*

*A:Well, Ed and I were just discussing what was kind of odd, some of the behavior that we thought was odd. This conversation was between the two of us, as good friends do together. And, uhm, Janet would occasionally pull into the driveway and—and sit there for a very long period of time. And one of the parts of that conversation was that we thought it was strange, that over the years that she had been separated and divorced from Paul, that we had not seen her with a male companion. And after we had discussed that, I realized—we realized that Ed was there.*

*Q:Do you regret that conversation today?*

*A:Yes. I do.*[153]

On cross-examination, Reilly's questions concerned whether or not Eddie had actually heard this conversation. Bradbury said she didn't know for sure, but she assumed he did, because he had a look on his face "when a child is caught hearing something that he should not have heard. . . . Like, 'whoops.' . . . It was my opinion that he had heard what we said."[154]

153 ELEVENTH DAY OF TRIAL, Vol. XIV, September 29, 1997, pp. 48, 49

154 Id., p. 50

George had offered this testimony to show that Eddie wasn't "obsessed" with

Janet Downing's comings and goings. Everyone in the neighborhood commented on her behavior. He also offered it to corroborate the fact that Eddie heard his father say that Downing might be a lesbian.

Reilly, in making sure that Eddie actually heard the conversation, got an unexpected gift from Bradbury when she likened Eddie to a child who "is caught" overhearing a conversation. He would, in his closing argument, describe Eddie as lurking in the shadows, intentionally eavesdropping on adult conversations, when he was simply had been present without Bradbury realizing it. Reilly was able to make this testimony bolster his creepy-surreptitious-sneaky suspect theory.

John Roberts, the neighbor who was on the O'Briens' porch on the night of Downing's murder, was next. Roberts testified that he got to the O'Briens' at about 8:15; he'd just dropped the babysitter off in Belmont, a town about five miles from Somerville, and he'd left his house at approximately 7:30 to do that. Shortly after he arrived, a young girl drove up (this was Michelle Cameron).

Roberts testified that Eddie was his usual playful, teasing self. They talked about whether or not he would go to football camp this year. They talked about basketball, and set up a time to play the next night together at seven o'clock. Ed Sr. was going to ref the game.

After that, they were all joking with Michelle about her fake ID. Ed was putting it in his pocket. "So we were just playing around with that." Eddie came out with popsicles for the kids; Timothy, Roberts' son, didn't want a green popsicle, so Eddie went back in and got him another color.

Roberts said he kept looking at his watch because his daughter was getting tired and he felt he was being rude. It was 8:40, 8:41, then 8:42. He decided to take the kids home, and told Eddie's father he was leaving. At that point Timothy began to act up because he didn't want to go home. "And—the—so Big Ed asked Little Ed: 'Hey can you give John a hand?' So Eddie went over and he got Timothy and picked him up. And helped him—ah, helped me by bringing him over to the porch . . . [Eddie] dropped Timothy off at [my] porch. And by that time, Timothy was okay and ready to go in."[155]

Reilly established on cross-examination that Eddie had no cuts on his hands or scrapes on his legs when John Roberts last saw him at 8:50. Roberts could not remember exactly what Eddie was wearing that night, although he thought it was a T-shirt and shorts.

As outlined earlier, Virginia Reckley's version of what she knew about the night of Downing's murder raised key questions about the timing of events. George wanted her testimony to show the jury that something had happened in the Downing home at about 8:15, and that the DA and the police did not find it significant enough to further investigate. She was a critical witness for the defense.

Reckley, her husband, and their two children had been Downing's tenants for the five years prior to her death. Reckley testified that she and Downing were close friends and that during those years Downing never said anything negative to her about Eddie O'Brien.

The Reckleys were babysitting their fifteen-month-old granddaughter the day of the murder. They were in and out of the house, taking walks all afternoon because it was so hot inside. Her daughter Christine arrived at 6:00. They visited for a while and then had dinner together. After dinner, they took the baby out to the wading pool in the backyard so she could cool off. It was Barry Reckley's birthday, and

155 Id., pp. 63, 64

they planned to have birthday cake before Christine took their granddaughter home. Virginia had a clock over her basement stairway door in the kitchen and looked at in when they came inside. She said it was shortly after 8:15 or so, certainly between 8:15 and 8:30, that they brought the baby back inside to change her into dry clothing and have birthday cake.

George asked her: "Will you tell the jury what came to your attention about, sometime between 8:15 and 8:30 on July 23rd, 1995?"

*A:Chrissy and I both heard, uhm, a noise from the stair area next door that sounded as though someone had fallen down the stairs.*

*Q:And could you describe those sounds more particularly for the jury?*

*A:I could give an example.*

*Q:Yes.*

*A: Uhm, an example would be when I personally fell down the stairs. I had gone down the stairs, and I'm on the fourth or fifth step. My heel just didn't quite make it. And I went down the stairs, the last four, on my fanny. And it sounded just like that.*[156]

At the time this happened, Reckley was standing at her dining room table, which was pushed up against the common wall shared with Downing's dining room and stairway. Reckley said that her daughter panicked at hearing the sound. She told her daughter that she didn't hear the dog barking, so it probably wasn't important. Those were the only sounds they heard coming from the Downing home that night.

After they got the baby dressed, they had birthday cake at the dining room table. Reckley put the dishes in the sink

156 Id., p. 89

and helped pack up the baby and her things for her daughter. Her daughter left at about 9:00.

Reckley testified that she then went into the kitchen to do the dishes from dinner and the birthday cake. She noticed that the water pressure was so low that it took almost five minutes to fill the big pot that she'd cooked the pasta dinner in.

*Q:What did that mean to you, Mrs. Reckley?*

*A:It meant that there was water being used on the other [Downing] side of the house.*[157]

This was a common problem that she'd experienced in her years living in the house. She said she tried to do the dishes, but the water pressure was very low. It took a long time for her to get it all done.

She said was later in the living room with her husband when they heard Ed O'Brien yelling outside at their window for help. The Reckleys ran outside and over to the Downing home. Ed entered first, then her husband, Barry, and she followed.

*Q:And what happened next?*

*A:The first thing I saw was the bathroom. And the water was running over the sink. And I turned and looked and saw Janet on the floor. . . . I was a little stunned, to say the least. I stepped back. And I was barefoot at the time. And then there were pictures under my feet. And I stepped back and my heel stepped on the picture, so I looked down between my feet to see what I had stepped on. Uhm, my husband stepped toward me. And he took my arms and said: 'Get out of here. Get him out of here.' I turned to my right and saw Ryan coming in to the entry of the building. So I took Ryan and went out of the*

157 Id., p. 94

*house.*

*I took Ryan out to the front lawn, across the front lawn, over to the driveway side by the fence. . . . When I was taking off Ryan's rollerblades, a Somerville police officer pulled up in front of Janet's car. He got out of the car and walked up the walkway. And he was very casual. And he says, "So, what's going on there?" And I said, "I think you need to go in the house." I didn't want to say anything in front of Ryan. Uhm, he went—he was a little fussy about it, and he said, "Well, tell me what's going on." I said, "I think you just need to go in. There are other people in there." He went into the house.*[158]

On re-direct examination, George effectively pointed out to the jury the total lack of police interest in Virginia's observations.

*Q:Mrs. Reckley, have you ever been interviewed by the police in this case?*

*A:By the police? No.*

*Q:Were you ever interviewed by the District Attorney's Office?*

*A:Yes. I was.*

*Q:And when was that?*

*A:Two weeks ago, two and a half weeks ago.*[159]

George finished by asking Reckley about Eddie. She said Eddie was extremely respectful toward her. She'd never seen him violent or confrontational in the presence of either his peers or Downing.

Reilly asked predictable questions about whether Reckley or Ortiz or Paul Downing Sr. or any of the other people whom she'd seen that night, was bleeding, cut or

158 Id., pp. 97-102

159 Id., p. 93

scratched in any way. She did not recall anyone bleeding or being cut.

Next, he tried to impeach Reckley's timeline of when her daughter left and she went into the living room and then heard Ed O'Brien yelling.

*Q:And that's when [at about nine o'clock] you noticed the water, you weren't getting any—hot water.*

*A:That's correct.*

*Q:And how much longer after that was it that you heard the voice of Mr. O'Brien's father calling for assistance of your husband and you went into the Downing home?*

*A:After I was doing the dishes?*

*Q:Yes.*

*A:A while.*

*Q:Do you recall saying it was a short time?*

*A:A short time from when I finished the dishes and sat down, yes. Probably fifteen, twenty minutes after that.*[160]

Reilly tried but failed to shorten the period of time between 9:00 and when Reckley heard O'Brien calling for help. When Reilly couldn't get more out of this line of questioning, he ended with questions leading Reckley to say that she had not heard anyone knocking at the Downing door, crashing down the cellar stairs or calling "Ed, Ed, nice hiding spot." She heard the boom coming from the bottom of the stairs. She heard nothing from the top of the stairs.

On redirect, George put to rest the time question by simply asking Reckley when she finished the dishes.

*A:Probably about twenty past, 9:30. It was a lot of dishes.*

*Q:Is the reason it took so long because the pressure was gone?*

---

160 Id., pp. 121, 122

*A:Absolutely.*[161]

Reckley's daughter, Christina Flint, was sworn in next. Her testimony comported completely with her mother's about the events of that evening between 6:00 and 9:00. Regarding the noise she heard coming from the Downing home, she said it alarmed her because "it was loud. It was just unusual." Christina had lived in that house and was well acquainted with the noises and voices and you could hear through the common wall if they were loud enough.

*Q:Would you tell the jury what you heard, at that time?*
*A:Uhm, it sounded—we were changing my daughter's diaper, and it sounded like, uhm, when you come down a flight of stairs and you may catch your heel on the last couple of steps, three or four steps. Then you come down . . . and this was just on the lower half, because it was on my mother's, our dining room wall.*[162]

Christina Flint told the jury that she'd been interviewed by the District Attorney's Office on Saturday (two days before she testified). That was the first and only time she'd been asked what she heard the night of the murder.

On cross-examination Reilly attempted to get Christina to agree that the sound could have been someone just coming down the stairs. She did not agree.

*Q:But it was loud?*
*A:It was loud. Yes.*
*Q:And it was over several stairs? At least from wherever you mentioned, the fifth stair, down?*
*A:Yes.*

161 Id., p. 122

162 Id., p. 143

*Q: To the bottom?*

*A: Um-hmm.*

*Q: And it's definitely going from top to bottom?*

*A: Yeah, from—yeah. Not from the very top, but from where I heard it.*[163]

All of this appeared to go well for the defense. It established the time that the loud boom was heard in the Downing home and when the water pressure was first noticed to be low. Eddie's whereabouts at both of these times when things were occurring in the Downing home were clearly accounted for by the prosecution's own witnesses.

Reilly's closing argument, however, would make the jury think otherwise.

163 Id., pp. 148-149

# CHAPTER 37
## THE DEFENSE EXPERT

Dr. John Thornton, a forensic scientist and expert in criminalistics, serology, and analysis of hairs, fibers, bloodstains, paint, soil, glass, fingerprints, tire tracks, and drugs, was hired by Bob George "not quite three weeks" before he testified on September 29, 1997.[164]

Thornton had nine years' experience with the crime laboratory of the Contra Costa County Sheriff's Office in California. After that, and for the next twenty-four years, he taught forensic science at the University of California, Berkeley. After his retirement in 1994, Thornton became the director of Forensic Analytical Specialties, an independent consulting laboratory. He was a distinguished member of both state and national criminalistics organizations, and had published extensively in the field. He had been qualified as an expert witness over 800 times in both state and federal cases.

Thornton reviewed the police reports, the witness statements, Downing's medical records and autopsy report, the crime scene photographs, transcripts of the grand jury testimony of Robert Pino and Detective Femino, as well as the actual space at 71 Boston St., albeit two years after the crime.

In Thornton's opinion, local authorities had unduly limited the scope of the actual crime scene to areas where

---

164 ELEVENTH DAY OF TRIAL, Volume XIV, September 29, 2997, p. 164

there was blood visible. He believed that critical evidence not directly in the blood path could have been overlooked using this method. In this particular case the second floor of the house was never processed for evidence because the blood evidence ended on the fifth step going up (or down) the stairway. There may have been evidence that was overlooked on the second floor. (Although not specifically mentioned by Thornton, the only shower in the house was on the second floor. None of the investigators ever checked to see if the perpetrator had taken a shower to clean off.)

Eddie left the house at 9:20 p.m., and at that time Downing had appeared to him to be dead. She already had the deep wounds on her neck, according to the memory he shared with Spiers back in October 1995. The perpetrator, therefore, would have had almost forty minutes more to clean up and leave the house before Ryan arrived home to find his mother on the dining room floor.

Thornton was critical about the way the crime scene had been processed. In his opinion, crime scene investigators use "the physical evidence to tell a story. If there is physical evidence of a person's presence in the second story, by way of fingerprints or other evidence, that would be useful in understanding the circumstances of the case. If the evidence is not picked up, if it is not documented, if it's not photographed, videotaped, if there's not an exhaustive search, then that evidence is lost to us. It's part of the puzzle that we do not have, ah, to try to complete the puzzle and tell the story of what actually did occur. So, if those, if the crime scene processing is defective, then those aspects of the evidence that might be available are forever lost. Additionally, if we don't understand the scene because of parts that are lost, then aspects that we do see, like very obvious bloodstains, these aspects may not be interpreted correctly."[165]

Based on his review of all of the photographs of the crime scene, it was

Thornton's opinion that if Eddie had murdered Downing, "he would be covered with blood . . . there would be blood from his hair down to his shoes."[166]

Any cleanup would have needed to be exhaustive: taking a shower and changing clothes, including underwear. The amount of blood that would have been thrown about the scene would easily have soaked through his shirt to his underwear. The small stains on Eddie's T-shirt, on the bottom hem of his shorts and on his sneaker were not consistent with perpetrating what amounted to a massacre as depicted in the crime-scene photographs. Thornton testified that in the aftermath of such an attack, he would expect to see blood on the entire body of the perpetrator: in the hair, in the ears, the eyebrows, the nose, both arms, and in the creases of the neck.

Looking at the photograph taken of Eddie at the police station that night, he said: "I think it's essentially obligatory that, ah, the person who inflicted the ninety-some stab and cut wounds on, ah, Janet Downing would have been significantly contaminated, stained with blood. The cleanup, ah, any cleanup procedure that would result in Mr. O'Brien appearing as he does in that photograph, ah, would have to be very exhaustive. It would require, in my view, ah, taking a shower and changing ah, his clothes, including, ah, underclothing to, ah, present the appearance that's shown in, ah, the photograph."[167]

Even assuming—hypothetically—that Eddie had two shirts on that night, the forensic expert was clear that the

165 Id., pp. 170-171

166 Id., p. 183

167 Id., p. 184

amount of blood thrown around the scene would have seeped through the first shirt to the second shirt in great quantities, certainly greater than was visible on Eddie in the photograph. His pants would have been so stained with blood that the seepage would have gone through to his "undershorts" as well. The one small drop of blood on the shin and the small drop of blood on Eddie's sneaker were equally inconsistent with any theory that he'd inflicted these wounds, according to Thornton.

Regarding the wounds on Eddie's right hand, Thornton's opinion was that "the thumb wound in particular was not consistent with Eddie holding the weapon and his hand coming down onto the blade, as if slipping down over the hilt."[168]

George then noted possibility of contamination by the number of people who had been present at the scene without any protective gear on.

*Q:How do we prevent, or how does one prevent that [contamination] from happening at a crime scene?*

*A:Well, there are standards for crime scene processing. Ah, they are generally agreed upon, they are not particularly controversial, that say that a crime scene first must be frozen; that is, it must be preserved. Secondly, it must be documented. And that's done by means of photography—increasingly now by means of videotape. It's done by means of diagrams, and it's done by means of note-taking. And then the scene is—the evidence is collected. And then finally . . . well, the final step is interpretation. Some aspects of physical evidence are susceptible of interpretation at the scene. Others require laboratory analysis prior to their interpretation.*

*Q:And, doctor, when you say "frozen," is that in the immediate aftermath of the body being removed or as the*

168 Id., p. 191

*body is found?*

*A:No. That should take place immediately with the arrival of the first officer. Q:So not five and one half hours later?*

*A:No. No. I am alive to the issues of—of the necessity of the medical personnel, ah, of being at the scene. I have no quarrel with that at all. But that—that's the only exception that is generally conceded with respect to the preservation and freezing of a crime scene.*

*Q:Were the standards, the national standards [for processing crime scenes] followed in this case?*

*A:No.*

*Q:Why?*

*A: Well, there are some—there appears to be some disruption of the crime scene. Photographs taken [at] different [times] in the crime scene processing showed items that had been moved or displaced. Ah, I think there were a couple of physical evidence issues, ah, that could have or should have been resolved, that are still left hanging as a result of a failure to consider these aspects of the evidence. Specifically, I am referring to the photographs, ah, that were found near the front door. And then the stain that was found on the victim's hand.*[169]

With that vague reference about moved and displaced evidence, Bob George ended his direct examination. He did not inquire about the significance of the unknown DNA on the hilt of the knife and the scrapings from underneath the victim's fingernails.

Reilly saw his opening and ran headlong for the goalposts.

*Q:Assuming, doctor, that there is evidence in this case that the victim was sleeping on this couch, in the den; and*

169 Id., p. 196

*assuming further, that there is an ottoman, a piece of furniture knocked over in the area of the living room—would that be consistent, in your experience, with a struggle breaking out in that area, yes or no?*

*A: Well, yes, but I need to qualify my answer.*

*Q: You will have time for that. Yes or no?*

*A: Yes.*

*Q: And doctor, directing your attention to the area of the stairs, assuming, doctor that there is evidence in this case that on the third, fourth, and fifth stairs there is evidence that—blood evidence that is consistent with the victim on the lower portion of the wall, the carpet on those stairs; and assuming further, doctor, that there is evidence in this case that a hair found in that blood is microscopically similar and consistent with the hair of the victim, is that consistent with the victim being attacked in that area?*

*A: Yes.*

*Q: And is it consistent with her head being on those stairs?*

*A: Yes.*

*Q :And, assuming further, doctor, that there is evidence in this case on the second stair, that blood samples taken from that area are consistent with the blood—known blood samples of Edward O'Brien, is that consistent with him being in that area? Yes or no?*

*A: Yes, sir.*

*Q: And assuming further, doctor, that there is a—Edward O'Brien, there is evidence in this case, was seen the night before the murder with a knife, a green knife with a loose hilt, and, assuming further, that he was seen on the morning of the murder with a knife, a green knife with a loose hilt, and that a hilt is found on that third stair near where the victim's blood and hair is, is that consistent–I ask you–is that consistent with that knife coming off, the hilt of that knife coming off the knife attacking Janet Downing?*

*A:I—I think so. Again, I need to qualify my answer. Do you want the qualification now, or—*

*Q:You will have time for that later.*

*A:Sure.*[170]

This is the oldest cross-examination trick in the book: the "you can clarify later, just answer yes or no right now" trick. Of course, the witness never does get the opportunity to clarify the answer. If your witness is the victim of this kind of inquiry, they should have been prepared to respond that they cannot answer the question with a simple yes or no. If you haven't prepared your witness, then you must object and argue that the witness has not finished answering the question. The examiner is cutting him off before he can give his full answer.

Thornton, a veteran of some 800 prior court appearances as an expert witness, should have known this old trick quite well, and he should not have fallen for it. But he was going like a lamb to slaughter here. And where the hell was George?

Reilly continued:

*Q:Is it consistent with a knife, with the hilt of the knife, coming off in an attack, a knife attack on Janet Downing in that location?*

*A:Yes.*

*Q:And assuming further, doctor, that this is where Janet Downing's body is found, and assuming further there is no evidence of any drag marks between the stairs and the area where she is found, is that consistent with her being mobile getting from that area to that area?*

*A:Well, I have a problem with that, okay? I think that's not inconsistent, but in my review of the autopsy, I think that*

170 Id., pp. 199-206

*there is some evidence of—dragging. Right.*

*Q:You saw some evidence that she was dragged from here to there?*

*A:Well, I certainly see some evidence of, ah, abrasions on the backs of, ah, of her, ah, elbows and in the portions of her lower extremities, which forces me to at least consider the possibility that she was dragged. So I—I just don't know whether she made it from the stairs to the dining room on her power or not.*

*Q:But she made it there. Did you see any blood on the floor, or any drag marks on the floor that would be consistent with her being dragged there?*

*A:I don't see any indication of—of, ah, blood drag marks. No.*

*Q:And, doctor, doctor, assuming further that on the inside–on the inside of the door, the left–inside there's a dimmer switch. Below that dimmer switch was found the blood consistent with the victim's blood, is that consistent with her reaching out for that dimmer switch as she's going into that area?*

*A:It's consistent, with a qualifier that would be required.*

*Q:And assuming further, doctor, that on the inside of the front door are found three bloody fingerprints identified as being—belonging to Edward O'Brien, is that consistent with him placing those fingerprints in that area?*[171]

This disastrous cross-examination continued uninterrupted for what seemed like ten full minutes. The same yes-or-no questions about the victim's blood on the cellar stairwell walls, about Eddie's bloody fingerprint on the wooden post, about Eddie's jaunt through the sticker bushes and down Hamlet Street, and finally the single drop of blood consistent (no longer inconclusive in Reilly's mind)

171 Id., pp. 199-206

with Downing's blood on his shin being consistent with Eddie being in the house at the time she was murdered. Yes, yes, yes, yes, all are consistent with that and, no, not one objection from George.

*Q:Assuming there's evidence in this case, . . . inside the front door, blood consistent with Edward O'Brien was found; assuming there was DNA testing done in that location; the blood in that area was found to match a banding pattern of Edward O'Brien, do you have any evidence to offer to this jury that those results were contaminated?*

*A:Nope.*

*Q:And you don't challenge them, do you?*

*A:Well, no. I don't challenge the—the blood typing. But I think the point that is under discussion here is: given the fact that this is the blood of Mr. O'Brien, how did it get there? And the fewer number of people that were at the scene that we could pose that question to, and, if the number is just two or three and both—all those people say, "Well, I know for certain that, ah, I could not have contaminated that, ah, that area with the blood of Mr. O'Brien," then I'd—I'd feel better about the quality ethic, ah, expressed in the crime scene processing. But if there's a large number of people, that may be a bit vague on this issue, then I find it more unsettling.*

*Q:Doctor, would you be very comfortable in agreeing with me that the results of the testing in this case establish that Edward O'Brien's blood is in that house?*

*A:Yes. I have reviewed that work, and I find no reason to disbelieve it.*

*Q:Along with his fingerprints?*

*A:Yes.*

*Q:Along with the hilt of the knife? Well, a hilt of a knife.*

*A:Yes.*

At that point the judge interrupted the questioning and called both attorneys to a sidebar.

*McDANIEL: Sidebar. How long are you going to be?*
*GEORGE: I could go right up to lunch, and I'll go after lunch, darn it.*
*McDANIEL: Okay. When you go to lunch, you do me this favor. You tell Mr. O'Brien I don't want him [Ed O'Brien Sr.] squeezing her [Tricia O'Brien's] hand and all that hugging. He continues to do it. The next time I see him doing it, I am going to tell him, in front of the jury, I'm going to tell him, "Stop hugging and squeezing hands here. This is not a drive-in." Now if he wants me to tell that in front of the jury, I'll be happy to do it.*
*GEORGE: Okay.*[172]

Why on *earth* did McDaniel choose this particular moment to stop the trial and chastise George because Eddie's father and mother were holding hands in the courtroom? George had just experienced the thrashing of his only expert witness. His hired expert had capitulated in the end, lulled into yes and no answers, asserting that he had no proof that prosecution's evidence was contaminated in any way. One wonders if McDaniel was even listening to the testimony.

One would have hoped that all those questions to which Thornton answered, "I need to qualify that answer," would have been duly noted by George or someone at the defense table. In that way, he could systematically go through them and repair some of the damage that the cross-examination inflicted on this witness.

George stood up for redirect examination.

172 Id., pp. 218-225

*Q:Dr. Thornton, you attempted to clarify several of your answers to Mr. Reilly during your direct [sic] examination. Do you remember what things you were attempting to clarify?*

*A:I don't think I remember all of them. There were a number of questions posed that I thought that, ah, a yes or no answer cried out for some qualification.*

*Q:Which is the first thing you remember?*[173]

Come on, Bob George, are you really telling us that you and your team of lawyers at the table took no notes during that cross-examination? Are you really going to make this witness try to remember what was asked of him twenty or thirty minutes ago?

When Thornton couldn't remember, George took another tack.

*Q:Directing your attention to this particular crime scene: Are you particularly comfortable in telling us how you believe blood got from one location to another because of the numbers of people that were in the scene?*

*A:Well, I find that to be troublesome. Yes.*

*Q:Why?*

*A:Well, there—there just isn't documentation of everything that, ah, everyone did or didn't do. And with a small number of people at a scene that, ah, that problem–which is a perpetual problem in any crime scene—but it's kept to a minimum. . . . I don't see my function here, or in any other case, as advancing one theory over another, unless there's some extrinsic means of testifying, ah, testing an opinion. It's one thing to form a hypothesis and give voice to it; but it's another thing to establish a fact by testing a hypothesis. And, in this instance, there are a number of issues*

173 Id., pp. 226, 227

*where I just don't think the physical evidence is going to enable us to test those hypotheses. I think we have wrung out of this scene as much as we can from the physical evidence.*

*Q:Doctor, assuming that the hilt of the alleged murder weapon was found at the scene of this crime on the stairs where Mrs. Downing was attacked, I would ask you to further assume that the third source of DNA was found on that hilt. Other than Edward O'Brien and Janet Downing, is that consistent with a third person being present at the scene?*

*A:Well, I think that it's consistent with, but, I think that my answer calls out for the same qualifier that, ah, I wanted to append to Mr. Reilly's questions: that, although it's consistent, I don't think that it's necessarily exhaustive of the possibilities.*[174]

And then Bob George showed that he hadn't heard the wisdom of Atticus Finch in *To Kill a Mockingbird*: "Never, never, never on cross-examination ask a witness a question you don't already know the answer to. . . . Do it, and you'll often get an answer you don't want."

*Q:Doctor, I ask you to assume the following facts: I'd ask you to assume that Janet Downing was sleeping on the couch on January—on June—on July 23, 1995, at some point in time in the evening hours. And I would ask you to further assume that, at some point, she woke up and at some point ended up in the front foyer of her house, the foyer of the house you were in yesterday, or two days ago. I would ask you to further assume that, at some point, she was involved in a struggle getting to that location, which left remnants at the crime scene, as you have observed in the pictures that you have seen. I would ask that you further assume that,*

174 Id., pp. 228-230

*at some point, Mrs. Downing ended up in the room to the right of the door, where Mr. Reilly directed your attention to earlier. Now, I'd ask you to further assume that Edward O'Brien appeared as he did in the aftermath of this crime, as in the Exhibit No. 50. Doctor, do you have an opinion, to a reasonable degree of scientific certainty, as to whether Edward O'Brien's blood being present at the scene indicates that he was involved in the attack on Janet Downing, taking all of those things into consideration?*

*A:No.*

*McDANIEL: When you say no—no, you have no opinion? His question was, do you have an opinion?*

*A:No. I don't have an opinion.*[175]

Atticus Finch was right. This is precisely what happens when you break the cardinal rule. You get answers you do not want.

With a few more questions about the lack of blood on Eddie's clothing, George rebuilt some of his witness's credibility, but not his own. He had not prepared the witness properly, had not prepared his own questions properly and failed to rehabilitate the witness because he failed to take any notes during Reilly's questioning. Why would George ask this doctor when he'd been hired? It only showed that he was scraping together his defense just as the trial started three weeks ago.

Thornton finished his testimony with his already-overstated opinion. "I think that the idea that a person could inflict that many wounds and not have some very obvious and significant blood on their clothing and body is so slender as to be close to preposterous."[176]

Reilly had not yet spiked the ball in the end zone, and he

---

175 Id., pp. 244-246

176 Id., p. 247

stood up one more time to question the witness.

*Q:Are you aware that prior to that picture being taken, that photograph being taken of Edward O'Brien, he had been home?*

*A:I do recall that from the police reports, yes, sir.*

*Q:And you don't know what he did when he went home before he went to the Somerville Hospital, do you?*

*A:No.*

Yes, it was an unfair question, because this witness did not know that prior testimony proved that Eddie had been seen with the same clothes on minutes before and minutes after the murder without any blood on him. Reilly was really showing the jury that this witness was not familiar with the facts.

The question also suggested to the jury that Eddie could have cleaned up before he went to the hospital, and then to the police station to be photographed. It was as lame as the broken kitchen door theory, but no one on the defense team had picked up on that one either.

George should have thought to subpoena the EMTs who'd come to Mid-Nite Convenient that night, evaluated Eddie's wounds, and believed that there was no need for further treatment. Surely they could have told the jury how little blood was on his clothing and on his body at 10:00—before he'd been home. Surely they could have resolved the continuing questions about what Eddie was wearing that night, what was wet, what wasn't wet, what his demeanor was.

They were independent witnesses, not Eddie's "friends" or "co-workers." Wouldn't it be far better to call them to testify than rely on photographs taken after Eddie went to the hospital?

# CHAPTER 38

## A LICK AND A PRAYER

My mother used a phrase a lot when she didn't have time to do a proper job around the house, and hoped that what she did accomplish would get her through the immediate problem. "I gave it a lick and a prayer," she'd say after a hasty cleanup of the living room before company arrived. A lick and a prayer is a superficial cleaning, a slight and hasty wash.

The next and penultimate witness for the defense was Father Henry Jennings, the O'Briens' parish priest. Thornton had already performed the hasty superficial wash of the crime scene, and now Jennings would provide the "prayer." This, sadly, would complete Eddie O'Brien's defense.

Jennings had been pastor at St. Joseph's Church, next door to the Mid-Nite Convenient store, for thirty-one years. He knew both the O'Brien and Downing families. Eddie had been a student at the grammar school as well as the chief altar boy for the parish. Tricia O'Brien was a Eucharistic minister, and Edward O'Brien Sr. was the head of the parish council.

For many years, Jennings had gone to the O'Brien house every month to bring communion—initially to Big Ed's stepmother and, more recently, to his father, the chief.

Jennings described the O'Brien family: "I would call them an—an excellent Christian family who participated in all of our parish activities, who shared in almost everything we asked of them. They were well-liked and respected. . .

. Eddie was an excellent young man, too, from my point of view. And I think the other priests would corroborate that."[177]

Jennings also knew the Downing family, and first met Janet Downing at the twins' baptism. He said Downing was actively involved in the grammar school. She was not a Catholic at the time, but she shared in all the school functions. She worked very hard for the school. He described her as "an excellent mother. Wonderful." She was present each time the boys served as altar boys and took great pride in her children.

Jennings had had many telephone and face-to-face conversations with Downing over the years, and then she asked him to give her religious instruction because she wanted to convert to Catholicism.

*Q:Did she ever mention Eddie O'Brien to you?*

*A:No. Out—outside of—ah, nothing except what he would be doing with the sons, you know. Different things they may have been doing.*

*Q:Did she ever mention him as a problem in her life?*

*A:Not to me.*[178]

A lick and a prayer. Amen. Go in peace.

Jessica O'Brien, Eddie's little sister, walked up to the witness stand in her Catholic school uniform. Jessie was now thirteen, and the last witness to testify for the defense. Jessie remembered July 23 well, because it was right before her brother got arrested.

George questioned her.

*Q:Did you have a curfew that night?*

*A:Yes.*

---

177 ELEVENTH DAY OF TRIAL, Supra, p. 255

178 Id., p. 258

*Q:What time did you get home that night?*

*A:8:30.*

*Q:And how old were you then?*

*A:Eleven.*

*Q:And when you got home, who was there?*

*A:My brother. Uhm, John Roberts, his kid, Timmy, Megan—Mary, I mean.*

*Q:Do you remember how Eddie was dressed?*

*A:He had long shorts, dark, and a white shirt.*

*Q:I don't know if you remember, but do you remember what time Eddie came into the house?*

*A:No.*

*Q:And where were you—now, the jury's been in your house. Which room was Mary in and which room did Eddie put the tape in for Mary?*

*A:The second room.*

*Q:And where were you when Eddie did that?*

*A:I was, uhm, in like the room beside it.*

*Q:In the front room, looking out to the street.*

*A:(No audible answer.)*

*Q:Was there a television set in there?*

*A:Yes*

*Q:At some point did you go upstairs?*

*A:Uhm-hmm.*

*Q:And when was that?*

*A:Uhm, I went up to my room and put my hair up.*

*Q:And was Eddie up there?*

*A:He came up and went into his room and started listening to music.*

*Q:Okay, and were you listening to that music, too?*

*A:For about five minutes.*

*Q:At some point did you go downstairs?*

*A:Yes, and I went into the front room.*

*Q:And what did you do in that room, when you got*

*downstairs?*

*A:I started watching TV.*

*Q:And were—you don't remember what shows were on?*

*A:No, I was just flipping through channels.*

*QWere the shows already on?*

*A:Yeah—already started.*

*Q:Now, at some point after—how long did you sit downstairs before you saw Eddie again?*

*A:About five minutes.*

*Q:And at some point did Eddie come down the stairs?*

*A:He came downstairs and he said: "Dad, I'm going to—I'm going to go to Burger King."*[179]

Jessie remembered taking a call later from Eddie who was at the Mid-Nite Convenient store, but she could not remember what time that happened. She also could not remember what time Eddie was brought back to the house by the police that night. She testified that her Uncle Doc took Eddie to the hospital when he came home.

And thus the trial ended.

Of course the jury didn't know that yet. George hadn't formally "rested" his case.

The jury was released and the judge conducted a sidebar conference with the attorneys.

*McDANIEL: Who are you going to have tomorrow?*

*GEORGE: Well, based on your—next, I'm going to meet with the defendant tonight about that old issue of him testifying. I also have to take up with the parents, the whole issue of cross-examination with the story and all that stuff coming in. If they—if they take my advice, my advice will be that this case will be over in the morning. I mean, in other words, they will not testify. I hate to say what my advice is*

179 Id., pp. 263-271

*going to be, but the matter is–*

*McDANIEL: Yeah. I want you to say it on the record.*

*GEORGE: I will advise them on cross-examination. Eddie's story about what happened on the premises at Mrs. Downing's house could possibly come in on cross, if Mr. Reilly chose to explore it. To me, that's a significant issue on whether I advise them as to what they are facing. The defendant, on the other hand, is someone I have talked to about just the pros and cons generally. Of course, I will ask you to inquire of him in the morning, as I know you do.*

*McDANIEL: I always do.*

*GEORGE: But, as of right now, I'm advising him not to testify, and the family—He's up in the air. He may want to testify, although I have a feeling that by tomorrow, he won't.*[180]

George is alluding to the fact that Eddie's version of what happened, as recounted to Spiers (i.e., that he was there, that he saw Downing's dead body, that he saw the killer) would come out on cross-examination. That's why he was advising Eddie's parents not to testify.

Why he chose this course of action is, however, unclear and certainly not what Eddie or his parents wanted. Everyone (except George) believed that unless the jury knew the truth of what happened that night, Eddie would most likely be convicted. George, however, seemed to be clearly going with a defense strategy of "you can't trust the crime scene, and the prosecution has not proved to you beyond a reasonable doubt that Eddie was there, or that he killed Janet Downing."

This was, of course, not a defense that had any chance of overcoming the prosecution's case. Eddie's blood, fingerprints, and DNA were at the scene. This would have to be explained to the jury by George in a way that made it

180 Id., pp. 270-272

perfectly clear that, although Eddie was present, he was not the killer.

The three lawyers on the defense team and I met over lunch. Everyone agreed that if the defense did not explain to the jury why Eddie's blood and prints were at the scene, Eddie was "dead in the water." That was the phrase I remember hearing the most at that lunch on September 29, 1997: "dead in the water."

George said, "Okay, I'll argue that in closing, I know I can out-argue him." But opening and closing arguments are not *evidence*. The jury may not consider them in deciding whether Eddie was guilty. Eddie needed his story put properly into evidence, through the testimony of a witness, so the jury could consider it in deciding his guilt or innocence. We all tried to explain this to George.

The defense had failed to adequately refute the blood and fingerprint evidence through its own serology and DNA testing. Its expert witness had turned into a witness for the prosecution. Absent contradictory blood and fingerprint evidence, the defense had to explain Eddie's presence at the scene of the murder.

The lick and a prayer was entirely inadequate.

Hiring an expert on the eve of trial usually indicates that he is the only expert available on such short notice. Experts are hired a year—or at least months—in advance of trial. They help to advise the lawyer and shape the defense. Thornton wasn't even properly prepared for direct examination, let alone cross-examination. He seemed to play no role in shaping any defense theory of the case.

Eddie's parents would have told his story if asked, "What did your son tell you?" They would have testified that weeks after he was arrested, he passed a note to his lawyer saying he was there and he was too afraid to tell anyone because he believed his family would be killed if he talked. Isn't that precisely what everyone but George agreed needed to be done? So why would George advise the O'Briens not to testify because Eddie's story might come out? Eddie's story *needed* to come out!

This jury knew that Eddie was at the Downing home at 9:20, that he had fled the scene, and that he allegedly bled there. There was no reasonable doubt about that.

If the defense did not give the jury a credible explanation for that evidence, the jury would most certainly convict Eddie.

# CHAPTER 39

## BOB GEORGE: CLOSING ARGUMENT

In Massachusetts, the defense presents its closing argument first. Before Bob George commenced his closing on the morning of September 30, 1997, he asked the judge to inquire of Eddie O'Brien as to whether or not he wished to testify on his own behalf.

*McDANIEL: All right. Mr. O'Brien, as I understand it, your lawyer has rested in this case. He will officially do it in front of the jury. That indicates, therefore, that you will not testify in this case.*

*I want you to understand the fact that you have an absolute right to testify or not to testify, that's your choice. And you make that choice after consulting with your attorney. And, in your case, I expect you would have consulted, as well, with your parents. And that this decision was an intelligent decision based on consultation with both your attorney and your parents. Is that right?*

*DEFENDANT O'BRIEN: Yes, it is.*

The reality is that almost no defense attorney will willingly put his client on the stand. It is not done. There's too much risk involved. The preparation time is long and difficult—and Bob George had not given this trial the time or the depth of work it needed. And the risk of the prosecution taking the testimony somewhere the defense team didn't want it to go was just too high.

On television, the defendant will almost always testify. In real life, almost never.

*McDANIEL: And you understand that you cannot come back later and say, "I wanted to testify, but my lawyer told me not to," or "made me not testify." Sometimes that happens. And I want to be certain at this moment in time that your not testifying is something done of your own free will. And that you understand the consequences of not doing so. Because, as I say, it may be too late later.*

*I don't know what the outcome of this case will be, nor does anybody else here know. But, in my experience, people sometimes come back later and say: "I wanted to testify, but my lawyers stopped me from testifying. I kept saying I wanted to testify."*

*So I want to make certain that this is something that you understand what you are doing. You have done it after consultation with your lawyer and your parents. And, in the final analysis, it is you who will say: "After having had those consultations, I do not wish to exercise my absolute right to testify." Is that so?*

*DEFENDANT O'BRIEN: It is.*

*McDANIEL: All right. There are no reservations about it?*

*DEFENDANT O'BRIEN: No.*

Without this colloquy, the defendant could allege on appeal that he was denied his constitutional right to testify on his own behalf. The colloquy has been standard procedure since 1987 when the U.S. Supreme Court in Rock vs. Arkansas held that a criminal defendant had a constitutional right to testify on his own behalf.

*McDANIEL: All right. Bring in the jury, please.*[181]

181 TWELFTH DAY OF TRIAL, Vol. XV, September 30, 1997, pp. 44-47

McDaniel instructed the jury that the lawyers would now deliver their closing arguments. He reminded them that what they said was not evidence. The only evidence the jury could consider was what they heard and saw and learned from the witnesses who testified at the trial, and the exhibits that had been marked as evidence in the trial.

He cautioned the jurors that the lawyers were not permitted to give their opinions in the case. If they said "it's my opinion that . . ." then the jurors were to ignore that statement. The lawyers also were "not to vouchsafe for the credibility of any particular witness. They can comment on credibility or assessment of credibility . . . but they cannot give you the impression that they know, of their own personal knowledge, that a particular witness or witnesses are, in fact, credible."[182]

The lawyers could only argue what they believed the evidence was, together with any reasonable inferences that could be drawn from that evidence. Each lawyer had sixty minutes to argue his case.

George stood and faced the jury. He argued without any notes in front of him. He walked in front of the jury box, looking directly at the jurors. He began by reminding the jurors how the Commonwealth had promised to show that Edward O'Brien murdered Downing in a particular way during a particular time period for a particular reason. The evidence, he said, had shown that the district attorney failed to meet his promise.

District Attorney Reilly, George said, had a theory of the case, which was simply that: his own theory. It was not the jury's theory or the defense's theory, and it was only one theory among many that should be considered in this case. Reilly's theory was that Eddie O'Brien was sexually

---

182 Id., p. 52

obsessed with Downing and on the night of July 23, 1995, when at about 9:10 he crossed the street from his house to the Downing house and stabbed her ninety-eight times. At 9:20 when Marco, Seth, and John arrived, he fled out the basement door, fabricated a story about being mugged in Union Square, and, through forensic testing, was positively linked to that crime scene by blood and fingerprints.

Bob George's theory, on the other hand, was that the investigation into the murder had focused exclusively on Eddie. The question, he said, was "whether it was good police work or not. I am telling you it was poor police work. But why did everyone deny it, until Robert Pino told you it was true? You probably knew it was true. Why did he stand for it? Did Pino lie about it?"

He continued to look the jurors in the eye, to pace.

GEORGE: *They ignored all the other evidence in the case whether it was good evidence or weak evidence or strong evidence. They never followed up on anything that led them away from this boy. And that's true. I don't have to tell you that's true. It's true. The evidence shows it's true. And it taints this case. It's reasonable doubt.*

*The evidence shows that this boy did not have the opportunity within the time frame allowed in this case, based on the evidence, to commit this crime the way the Commonwealth says it was committed. It's impossible to do what the district attorney says he did in the time that he says he did it. It's impossible. And the evidence shows it. Not necessarily with the witnesses that the Commonwealth called. Because they know that if their window of time closes, so does their case. . . .*

*In his opening, the prosecution promised you they would tell you why this happened. Why. We all want to know why this happened. The Commonwealth doesn't even have to prove motive. But they promised. They were certain that they would prove to you that he was sexually obsessed with Janet Downing. That he was focusing on her for weeks and days and months. And he told you how he was going to prove it to you. That evidence is false. It's a lie. And we proved it. There's no motive. And the evidence is clear as to the background of this boy.*

*I'm not asking you to judge this boy by his family. I'm not asking you to judge this boy because I say he's a good guy. He was fifteen-and-a-half years old back then. He was right in the middle of his adolescence. Do you think that if there was a witness out there that could bury him with bad behavior, you wouldn't have heard about it?*

*I'm not telling you he was an angel. But I'm telling you this: He was not of the character, of the background or of the type to commit this kind of horrible crime on his best friend's mother, in his own neighborhood, on a hot summer night . . .*

*The DA's whole case is based on that crime scene. The story he tells is only consistent, possibly consistent, with the way that crime scene was detailed five and one half hours after Janet Downing was taken from that scene.*

*But if you don't trust the crime scene, if you don't believe that the crime scene was exactly as it was photographed at three o'clock that morning, then you can't trust the crime scene as the underlying basis in constructing this case. And that's the foundation of the Commonwealth's case.*

*All the forensics come from there. Their whole theory of the case comes from there.*

*Was there contamination in that house? Was there movement of evidence among the many rooms?*

*Please. You were there. Don't make me put up the board. That was only before midnight that those eighteen people were there. That doesn't count Janet Downing.*

*That doesn't count the dog. That doesn't count Ryan. You have been to that scene. Nineteen people in and out of that house before midnight. Those were the only people we could document. Not wearing protective gear of any kind? Pino has told you that it's all changed now.*

*Nothing on your feet? Nothing on your hands?*

*No diagrams? No photos? No Polaroids? No notes as to where things were?*

*Let's make one thing clear, members of the jury. And it's been said a few times, but I want to make it clear again.*

*I'm not saying that because people tried to save Janet Downing that this scene is wrong. Leave the EMTs out of it. There were fourteen other people there. This room is small. The inside foyer is small.*

*Is there any doubt, from the exhibits in the case, that evidence has been moved? How do rugs move back and forth? And pictures appear and disappear? And papers go up and down stairs?*

*Those aren't markers. Those are tissues being used to do whatever is being done. But you see all kinds of movement in this picture alone.*

*Now does that say anything other than that the crime scene is being moved about? . . .*

*I mean, this isn't some O.J. theory where people are conspiring to move evidence around. This is a sloppy crime scene. Thornton told you that. There are national standards. There are laboratory standards.*

*There is no logbook. No sign-in sheet. Transference. Fancy word. It's for you to decide whether it's a possibility that there was transference, based on what you know about this crime scene.*

*No gloves. No gear. No nothing. Stanford's transferring evidence back and forth in bare hands.*

*Whether these swabs are contaminated or not is not important. How these swabs were kept before they were taken is important. Whether Stanford put them in his hands is important. Stanford had been at that crime scene.*

*The way things are being transported in this case, I would suggest to you, tells you that we have got a problem. It's not being done right.*

*If one of your children was on trial, would you want evidence handled that way?*

*REILLY: Objection!*

*McDANIEL: The objection is sustained. . . . Argue the evidence in this case, sir.*

*GEORGE: Following the blood trail was a ridiculous premise upon which to base a crime scene search. The upstairs was never looked at in any extensive way. The closing of the cellar door–that door wasn't closed. That door was closed when Reilly looked at it. It had been closed.*

*Now, I'm not telling you whose blood this is. That's not the point. The point is someone's at the crime scene, touching things, moving things. It could have been one of twenty people . . .*

*The testing in this case was going on as late as this past June. Does that tell you something? As late as this past June.*

*As late as this past July, results were coming back telling the Commonwealth that blood samples at this scene were coming back consistent with people they didn't want to hear about.*

*I'm not telling you that these people killed anyone. I am telling you that if Edward O'Brien's blood had been sent down, results would have been different in July.*

This statement makes no sense. First of all, Eddie's blood had been sent down to Cellmark. Secondly, how would Eddie's blood have changed the results?

*GEORGE: Two months before trial? That's not right. That's not fair when you're on trial for first-degree murder.*

*Now, there are ways. You have heard from these Ph.D.'s and doctors from Cellmark. There are ways to exclude other possibilities. That is what DNA is all about. It's to exclude. It's to prove innocence.*

*They didn't send any of these things to Cellmark in July. They had an opportunity to send these things to Cellmark and exclude all of these people. And do you know why they didn't? Because it doesn't fit their theory of the case.*

*Up until July, the only blood samples that had gone down to Cellmark, into the Serology Lab, were Eddie O'Brien's and Janet Downing's. And, as late as July when results were coming back that didn't fit into their theory of the case, they were still drawing possibilities.*

*Not that those people killed anyone. But it shows you what these blood tests mean. They could mean a thousand things. And that's reasonable doubt. Why didn't Eddie O'Brien's blood, why didn't other unidentified blood go down?*

(Eddie O'Brien's blood was already down there.)

*GEORGE: Are you trying to tell me DNA couldn't have been done on this? On that hair? Feline? There's human hair on there. On that substance that's on her hand?*

*What about the fingernail scrapings? Have you ever heard such unfair, ridiculous testimony? Fingernail scrapings. They come back as not tying Edward O'Brien to that poor woman's hand. And the Commonwealth would have you believe that he cannot be included or excluded – which means absolutely nothing.*

The written Cellmark report clearly stated that Eddie was excluded as the primary source of DNA. George characterizes Eddie's "exclusion" as "not tying" Eddie to the fingernails. He continues to misunderstand and therefore mislabel this important exculpatory evidence.

*GEORGE: That's the kind of evidence in this case that you're being asked to convict on. It took cross-examination to make her explain what she meant by that.*

*We have no weapon in this case. We have no bloody clothes–although the Commonwealth can tell you and track exactly where Edward O'Brien went–according to their case–from Mrs. Downing's bushes right to the Mid-Nite . . . There is no evidence he washed up at (his) house. That's a lie.*

*But the Commonwealth wants you to believe that lie to explain the biggest problem they have. If Eddie O'Brien were the killer of Janet Downing, he would have been covered with blood. Expert evidence in this case tells you that—from a nationally renowned criminalist.*

*And nothing can take that away . . . And he did not wash up in the manner that was necessary to change his appearance to the point where Doctor Thornton said he could not, and was not, involved in the murder of Janet Downing . . .*

*The Commonwealth would have you believe that nothing transfers, there's no transference. There's no contamination. This can't be happening. Well, what about number 12?*

What number 12? Was George referring to Item #12, the inner door blood swabs? Or was he referring to the number 12 genetic marker on the hilt of the knife that conclusively excluded Eddie as a contributor to that DNA? More importantly, is he suggesting they shouldn't trust the DNA on the hilt because it is contaminated?

*GEORGE: They want you to believe that there's some kind of transference, there's some kind of jumping. That it's not connected to this case–when it proves there's a third human source of DNA on that hilt.*

*You know when they found that out? They tell you on the*

*witness stand. July. July. Two months ago. No further testing.*

*Is that right? Is it right to argue in one breath that this ties someone to a murder scene, but in another breath, not mentioning it to you that there's a third source of human DNA on this? When Eddie's DNA isn't even found on it?*

When he asked the jury, "Is that right?" "Is that fair?" the jury had to be thinking: Wasn't that your job, Mr. George? Why didn't you test all of that "stuff"? You've had two years to analyze that evidence, too, haven't you?

Bob George was over two-thirds of the way through his sixty minutes. Some of his argument was so vague that it was meaningless. Other parts were convoluted and confusing as seen above. He did not make clear what, exactly, he was referring to when discussing the evidence.

George did a decent job when showing the improbability of Eddie having committed this crime without having blood all over him. Eddie was observed at Mid-Nite Convenient at 10:00 by all of his friends, the store clerk, the EMTs, and the police who escorted him home. No one testified that he was covered in blood or even observed blood on his clothing.

Still, the two critical pieces of evidence pointing to the real perpetrator are the unknown DNA on the alleged murder weapon and underneath Downing's fingernails. These deserved more than a passing comment about "unfair" evidence, and possibly transferred evidence.

George went on to criticize the testimony of Jack Arnold and Frank Kling, the store clerks, regarding the loose hilt.

He called Sergeant Stanford, who brought Eddie's clothes back to the scene of the crime bare-handed, a liar.

Eddie's clothes proved he couldn't have committed the crime. Why would Bob George suggest they were contaminated?

*GEORGE: They never searched the second floor adequately.*

If only George told them that the only shower in the Downing house was on the second floor, this might have held greater weight with the jury.

*GEORGE: But, you know, all of that aside, why did I have to call the Reckleys to the witness stand? Why did I have to call Christina Flint to the witness stand? They were the next-door neighbors to Janet Downing. Talk about ignoring other suspects! They were the next-door neighbors. They lived on the other side of a common wall, a few inches thick. They weren't interviewed until last Sunday. . . .*

*They are not lying about what they heard at 8:15. They are not lying about the*

*water pressure being gone about 9:00. Those three thumps you heard were Janet Downing being killed. Not a sound out of that house after those three loud bangs. Not one single, solitary sound. Not the dog. No yelling. No struggling. Nothing. She was being killed. And the prosecution must know that.*

*But why didn't they interview (them) until last Sunday? It didn't fit their case. It doesn't fit their case. Is that right? You know, when I talk about Artie Ortiz and looking for his keys in the backyard and all of that, that came from one of Janet Downing's best friends. The woman who spent her entire last day with her. Am I saying Artie Ortiz killed Jane Downing? Why, no.*

*Why was that ignored? Why is it that the kind of evidence that doesn't weigh anything to these people? Isn't it something you follow up, or look at, or see? Not if it doesn't fit your case. And once again, going back to the hilt: Once they found there was a third source of DNA on the hilt, they never considered any other person as possibly being involved in this case? Please.*

*An equally plausible theory in this case, as consistent, is that after Paul left that house at approximately 8:05 to 8:10, the killer is in the area.*

*It's not plausible; it's true that around 8:15 Mrs. Downing was being killed on those stairs. The Reckleys told you so. And they weren't guessing the time. They were changing the baby on the table. They were looking right at the clock.*

Was Bob George intentionally removing Paul Downing Jr. from the possible suspects by taking him out of the house before the 8:15 stairway noise? Paul, himself, and Michelle Cameron testified he came out at 8:30 p.m. Did he surmise that the jury would not tolerate the prospect of Downing's son having some knowledge or involvement in his mother's murder?

*GEORGE: That a person enters the house, who is not Edward O'Brien, struggles with her, kills her, undresses her, redresses her, and then Edward O'Brien came upon that scene later. Cut or uncut. You don't know how he was cut.*

*We know the wound on this thumb is inconsistent with the attack. We know that his appearance is inconsistent with this attack. We know that the wounds on his hands are consistent with defensive wounds–from the renowned expert.*

*That after he sees what he sees, he panics, he runs–just like any fifteen-year-old would. Huckleberry Finn type of behavior: if you see something, you run. You lie. Marco lied.*

*In fear, you go to the next place, the only place you can go, the Mid-Nite. You call the police. He's a suspect, minutes later.*

*What do we know that is uncontroverted? We know that there's a third DNA on the hilt.*

*We know that the defendant couldn't have committed this crime at the time the Commonwealth says it happened. We know that the Reckleys heard her being killed at 8:15 or between 8:15 and 8:30, if you give it its widest berth. That the Reckleys hear nothing, including the dog, after that time. Not a sound, because Janet Downing is dead.*

*That the water pressure is gone at 9:00 while she's washing her pasta pot.*

*And the defendant is accounted for, for this entire time, by John Roberts, Michelle Cameron, and Jessie O'Brien. John Roberts is lying? Protecting a murderer?*

*Remember, Judge McDaniel is going to tell you about what it means when people testify or don't testify. We don't have to do or prove anything in this case. That boy doesn't have to take the witness stand. He doesn't have to stand up there or sit up there and get terrorized. He has no burden to do that. He doesn't have to do that.*[183]

Bob George had used up almost all of his sixty minutes of argument by now. It was time for him to wrap up the package and deliver it to the jury.

George recounted all the evidence that the Commonwealth provided to prove Eddie's guilt: his "obsession" with Downing, the newspaper with the headline "We're Natural Born Killers" in his bedroom, that he was angry and wanted to hurt someone, that he had a telescope in his room, that he thought Downing was a bad cook, that he saw her undress in front of her bedroom window, Eddie and Marco seeing the woman across the street undressing: "That's not obsessing. That's average, immature, and stupid fifteen-year-old behavior. But it's not obsessing to kill someone."

George reminded the jurors that Eddie wasn't "watching"

183 TWELFTH DAY OF TRIAL, September 30, 1997, Vol. XV, pp. 53-93

Downing on her couch; he went into the room with Joey Dion to play Sega Genesis. Also, Downing had an air conditioner in one of her bedroom windows and her other bedroom window was not visible from Eddie's house. Therefore he could not have seen Janet Downing undressing.

*GEORGE: And do I even have to talk about the "Natural Born Killers"? The lie? . . . Their own photo shows you it's an out and out lie. The whole newspaper was there. That "Natural Born Killers" indicates state of mind—it's a lie. It's false evidence. That Thornton isn't allowed to clarify his answers, but he did on redirect.*

*So in the end it doesn't matter. Because one thing Thornton said, loud and clear, that this boy didn't kill Janet Downing, looking that way. And that the wounds on his hands were defensive wounds.*

*Mr. Reilly, in his opening, told you that this killing was personal. You're not*

*kidding, it was personal. But Eddie O'Brien didn't kill Janet Downing. He's telling you there's a sexual nature to the crime. Well, Eddie O'Brien had no reason to have a sexual obsession, because he had none.*

*That the person who killed Janet Downing was angry and violent and in a frenzy.*

*Eddie O'Brien was never angry. Was never violent. There's no indication he was ever in a frenzy. It doesn't fit who the defendant is.*

*To convict this defendant, to convict this boy, you must believe that he went from switching off green and orange popsicles with a two-year-old boy, calming that boy to the point that he took him home for his father. Minutes later, he was playing with a fake ID with Michelle Cameron, teasing and joking and laughing with his family and with neighborhood friends, talking about one-on-one basketball, football camp, his life . . . in the moments before he walked across the street and stabbed his best friend's mother to death a hundred times?*

*That's what common sense is. That's not what happened. You don't put "Sleeping Beauty" in your tape deck and listen to music and do something like this. Only a monster does this kind of stuff.*

*Now, I'm not ignoring the bloody prints at the scene.*

*The hilt of the knife. He may have been at the scene. He could have been at the scene. It doesn't mean he killed her. And the Commonwealth hasn't proven it.*

*Members of the jury, in closing–I could talk all day–this boy is innocent. He didn't commit this crime. He didn't do it.*

*You're being asked to determine that. You're being asked to find, beyond a reasonable doubt, that he killed that woman exactly the way the prosecution says. In light of everything I just told you, and in light of everything you know, the monster who killed Janet Downing didn't come out of that neighborhood. The monster that killed Janet Downing didn't come out of the house where Edward O'Brien was raised. He came from outside the neighborhood.*

*This boy had no reason to kill her. He had no obsession to kill her. And he didn't kill her.*

*There was no time. He didn't have the opportunity. He doesn't have the capacity. He doesn't have the character.*

*When you are being asked to evaluate whether he's guilty of first-degree murder in this case, please recognize, please recognize that the Commonwealth's case is based on twisted evidence, a compromised crime scene, and ruined lives. Convicting him in this case would only compound the tragedy that happened to Janet Downing, because he's innocent. And the evidence proves it.*

*Thank you.*[184]

---

184 Id., pp. 93-114

# CHAPTER 40

## TOM REILLY: CLOSING ARGUMENT

Calmly, slowly, and thoughtfully, Tom Reilly rose from his seat at the prosecution table. He immediately seized on Bob George's admission that Eddie was at the scene: "It's up to you if you heard him correctly, but now he is finally at the scene. No more Union Square."[185]

Reilly then formally addressed the jury, thanking them for "agreeing" to serve on the jury and for all of the sacrifices that they made over the past weeks to decide "this very troubling case."

Reilly spoke to the jurors quietly and with respect, recounting moments that were sad, painful, funny, and ironic from the past two weeks. He was emotionally drawing them in, with praise for their commitment, and gratitude for their patience and attention, even through the tedious days of fingerprint analysis and DNA testimony. Here was the professional lawyer, not the guy who talked like he was on the street corner with his buddies. Reilly was elevating them to a higher level of discourse that seemed almost empathic at times.

*REILLY: But all of that paled in contrast to the testimony of Dr. Leonard Atkins, this past Friday, as he described, in detail, what happened to Janet Downing. The violence and the brutality.*

---

185 TWELFTH DAY OF TRIAL, September 30, 1997, Vol. XV, p. 106

*All of a sudden, death was no longer an abstract matter. It happened, and it happened in an exceptionally brutal way.*

*You even saw the face of death on Janet Downing.*

*Now, why do I say this to you? I say this to you because it is difficult, it is very difficult, for anyone to imagine how anyone could do this to another human being. Particularly, when it's the boy next door and it's the mother of his best friend. It's hard. It is very hard. It would be much easier for everyone if there were someone else.*

*It would be much easier for everyone if it never happened. But it did. And if it didn't happen, everything could go back to the woman on Prospect Hill. O'Briens in their house and the Downings to their house. Gina Mahoney. On their porches in the summer. But it did happen, and there is no going back.*

*Follow that evidence. Follow that trail of evidence, and I respectfully suggest it will lead to one, and only one, conclusion: Edward O'Brien is guilty of murder. He is guilty of murder in the first degree.*

*Now, where—where does that trail start? I suggest to you that the evidence tells you it starts right at 71 Boston St., on the early evening of July the 23rd of 1995.*

*The evidence tells you, very clearly, what time Janet Downing got home. It was about 6:30. She finished her grocery shopping. The woman was exhausted. She went into that den and fell asleep.*

*Now, the evidence tells you that within the next hour–the next hour—Edward O'Brien twice, not once, but twice, went into that den area looking at Janet Downing.*

*It's before seven o'clock when he comes out. And he tells Paul Downing, who's sitting in a car waiting for Eddie O'Brien's sister. And he said: "What's your mother doing sleeping? Is she okay?" "Yeah. She's just tired." That's the first time.*

The importance of Paul Downing Jr.'s new trial testimony to the prosecution's case is now evident. Placing Eddie in the house alone with Downing made him a creepy voyeur, who was rapidly developing into a monster.

*REILLY: And then, the second time. . . . What's he doing in there the second time, when he already knows she's asleep?*

*Gives you a little view, a little glimpse of what's going on with him that night.*

*Now, where do you see him next? You see him next by . . . that kitchen door, by the lock. You heard the explanation: "Well, it's broken. And someone might get in." Is that what he's really saying? Is that what he really means when you know there is no sign of forced entry in this case? I suggest to you, now you know how he got in that house that night.*

He moved on to the Reckleys' evidence.

*The evidence in this case is that Paul Downing came home sometime between 8:00, 8:30. It's closer to 8:15. It's clear that he's out of there at 8:30. He says it. And he goes with the defendant's sister to Revere Beach. And he tells you his mother is alive. She's sleeping on that couch—8:30.*

*Then, what about Virginia Reckley? What about what she has to say?*

*She comes in here and she tells you at 8:15 she heard a noise. And she can tell you the exact steps: the second, third and fourth steps, right? Third, fourth, and fifth, whatever they are. Right where the evidence is. And ironically, it's the only thing she hears all night. But she tells you the time. And she can't recall the other time when she told–the statement she gave right after.*

*Her daughter. Her husband left at nine o'clock, a short time later. Mr. O'Brien came running across the street. Well, you know it's an hour later.*

*Virginia Reckley, obviously—it will be up to you to make this decision—had a little bit of a tiff with some of the police officers that night. She wasn't too kind to them.*

*And then she comes in and she's going to tell you, she's going to tell you what time the murder happens. And she is going to tell you what time the death occurred. Dr. Atkins couldn't even tell you that; but Virginia Reckley thinks she can. Her own daughter didn't back her up. What did she hear? She heard someone coming down the stairs. Coming down the stairs. And you know from the evidence that a short time before that, a short before time before that, Ryan Downing is in that house coming down the stairs before they leave, and he has rollerblades on.*

This is an egregious misrepresentation of Reilly's own evidence. Ryan Downing testified he left his house at 7:50 p.m. after he put his rollerblades on, but he never said he went down the stairs in them. Virginia testified that it "sounded like someone had fallen down the stairs." She never indicated which stairs. Christine said it sounded like "when you come down a flight of stairs and catch your heel on the last couple of steps, three or four steps, then you come down." And lastly, Virginia said she was doing the dishes between 9:00 and 9:30 with no water pressure. Sometime after that Ed O'Brien came running over.

Reilly knows he's in trouble with these two witnesses because they heard the loud boom like someone falling down the stairs at precisely the time Paul Downing admitted that he was in the house. His next statement is startling and looks eerily like a huge red flag:

*And the only person that you know that is in that house during that period of time is Janet Downing and her son, Paul. And I suggest to you it would be shameful, shameful, even to suggest that Paul is responsible for the murder of his mother.*[186]

George had explicitly eliminated Paul Downing as a suspect in his closing.

Reilly said this to shame any juror who dared to consider Paul's involvement in the murder of his mother and discourage them from even entertaining the thought.

Notwithstanding the credibility issues of Marco Abreu and Anthony Stamatouras (whose clock was twenty minutes off), Reilly pounded away, telling the jurors now that when Marco saw Eddie turn around:

*[Eddie's] eyes are bulging out of his head. He's out of it. He's out of it. Anthony Stamatouras backs up Marco. . . . And what does he tell you? He [Eddie] gets up and over that fence. And it's not easy. And when he gets up and over that fence, that black shirt comes up. And he's got a white shirt underneath. He's changed his clothes. That's what he's done.*[187] *. . . Now we know. And they finally acknowledge he was there. But it's a little bit late.*[188]

Reilly continued on with a dramatic depiction of the murder, Downing hearing something in the hallway, running in there without her shoes, being confronted, "all 113 pounds of her matched up against him." He got her head down on the stairs and inflicted the wounds to her head. That was when the hilt came off. But she got up and ran to the dining room, and reached for the light before he was on her again. Now she's on the floor, face up "where Eddie O'Brien finished Janet Downing off with deep, penetrating thrusts of that

186 Id., pp. 106- 117

187 Id., p. 121

188 Id., p. 123

knife, powerful enough to sever, actually sever the rib."[189]

Downing was tortured, Reilly insisted.

> *The tip of that knife was poking her chin.*[190] . . .
>
> *He tried to slit her throat. She was alive, and he kept doing it, over and over again. And then he removed her bra and sliced it some thirty-six times, before putting it back on her and putting her blouse back on.*

Reilly did not say, but next was presumably when Eddie cleaned up in the powder room so well that it removed all traces of blood from his hair, face, eyebrows, eyes, ears, neck, hands, shirt, shorts, underwear, shoes, arms, legs, and even under his fingernails and around his cuticles. In other words, Reilly would have the jury believe that in the span of just five to seven minutes, while his father sat on a porch directly facing the Downing home, Eddie managed to walk across the street, change his clothes, hide his first outfit, go down into the backyard, walk up the back stairs onto the deck, open a door with a broken doorknob that does not open even when the deadbolt is off, walk through the Downing kitchen and dining room into the hallway, beat, murder, and torture Downing first on the stairs and then in the dining room, inflict ninety-eight wounds to her head and body in addition to the bruises and contusions from the beating, torture her, slit her throat numerous times, undress her, slash her bra thirty-six times, re-dress her, clean himself up thoroughly, close and lock the front door, leave the house through the basement, get scratched up in the bushes, jump down onto Hamlet Street where his friends saw him at 9:20 and finally, go and change back into his old clothes, dispose of the bloody clothes and dispose of a knife.

---

189 Id., pp.126-127

190 Id., p. 127

Nothing at that crime scene was contaminated, Reilly insisted. The police and other personnel did their jobs and they did them well. This was validated by the defendant's own expert, Dr. Thornton, who, according to Tom Reilly, testified: "You're right. You've convinced me whose blood was in that house."[191]

This had to be an intentional misquote of Thornton's testimony.

*REILLY: What about the hilt? Now the hilt—the hilt was found on that third stair. Right above where his blood is and right alongside of where her blood is.*

The blood on the stairs was not conclusively anyone's blood. Its DNA was never tested. Reilly continues to represent blood as belonging to a person. This is again intentionally misrepresenting the evidence. All he can truthfully say is that Downing cannot be excluded as a potential source of this blood.

*The evidence also tells you that that day, that morning, he had the green light—knife—green knife with the loose hilt. What is the suggestion? Because basically, you can see—what is the suggestion? Well, the suggestion is—wait a minute. There's an extra "12," there's an extra 12 on the DNA cap, on the DNA testing on that metal hilt. There's third person at the scene. Who is it? Everyone agrees in this case that testified there's only two people bleeding in that house. And it's Janet Downing and Edward O'Brien.*

*But it's number 12. It can't be him. Well, check the chart. And you check that one, right over there that the defense looked at. Check out the CSF1PO. Edward O'Brien 11 and 12—11 and 12.*[192]

191 Id., p. 129

192 Id., pp. 135, 136

This was such a deliberate misrepresentation of the evidence that it requires a visual explanation of what Reilly did with the jury. Below is the DNA chart to which Reilly directed their attention. What Reilly does is tell the jurors to look at just one marker, the first column. In order for there to be a DNA match, the known DNA must match the hilt's markers in all three columns. The unknown DNA appears in the second column, not the first.

| | CSF1PO | TPOX | THO1 |
|---|---|---|---|
| Item 21 (Knife Hilt) | 11, 12 | 8, 9, 11, 12 | 8, 9, 3 |
| Janet Downing | 11, 12 | 8, 11 | 8, 9, 3 |
| Edward O'Brien | 11, 12 | 8, 9 | 6, 9, 3 |

*DNA Graphic Chart*

The number "12," which represents the unknown DNA on the hilt, appears in the second column, TPOX. To match, Eddie must have a 12 in the TPOX column, and an 8 (not a 6) in the THO1 column. The fact that the hilt has a 12 in TPOX column 2 excludes both and Eddie O'Brien and Janet Downing as contributors to it.

Reilly knew exactly what he was doing; he knew it was unethical and fraudulent. And he did it without even flinching.

*REILLY: Ladies and gentlemen, don't be misled. And don't be distracted.*

*There is a suggestion: Why didn't we test everything? Why didn't we get Artie Ortiz's blood? Ryan's blood? Paul's blood? Paul Downing Sr.'s blood?*

*Well, the evidence will tell you we had Paul Downing Sr.'s blood within days of this.*

True, but they never tested it against any of the unknown DNA.

*That goes to the theory that we didn't look at anyone else. We went where the evidence took us. . . .*

*And your memory will control as to whoever used the word "obsession," "sexual obsession." Or whether the word that I used was "interest," an "unusual interest." A fifteen-year-old young man, mother of his best friend.*

*And who can ever understand, could ever truly understand why this happened? It's well beyond the bounds of normal human behavior, even. No one really knows.*

*But if you look carefully, there are glimpses. Little glimpses, little snippets of information. Little details that give you a clue of what he's all about, what he's really thinking, and what makes him tick. . . .*

*And what's in that room? There's baseball–there's baseball cards. But there's also a telescope on the floor, by the windows. And there's also a newspaper that's a month old with "Natural Born Killers" on it. . . .*

*I suggest to you right then, there's a lot going on in that room. A lot, you may not know it.*

*Now, what about the comments about being a lesbian? . . .*

*And you heard an explanation for it yesterday when Mrs. Bradbury came down from New Hampshire and told you that: "Oh, really, what happened was a year ago. And I was having a conversation, a private conversation with his father. And I said something I shouldn't have said."*

*What does that tell you?*

*It tells you a little bit more. They didn't even know it. They didn't even know it, but he was secretly there, listening to a private conversation between adults. . . .*

*And what about watching neighbors undress? That's a concern. . . . And it's even greater concern that he's watching the mother of his best friend undress. And he tells them.*

*Does he have any boundaries? Does he have any boundaries to what's right? And what's wrong? . . .*

*But I suggest to you, it's one thing to talk about going into Mrs. Kenney's [the elderly neighbor's] house, and it's another thing to actually go in Janet Downing's house, when she's sleeping and she's alone in the dark. It's quite another thing.*

*And I suggest to you it's still another thing to go in there when you are armed with a knife. . . .*

*Why do you take it? . . .*

*I suggest to you, you take it because you're prepared to use it. You are prepared to use it—if you're caught—if you're caught.*

*Ladies and gentlemen, why—maybe Edward O'Brien has been telling us in his own way, right from the very beginning, why. When he told Sergeant Stanford and he told Ryan Downing: "You saw my face, now I must kill you."*

*He got caught in that house, and he did what he had to do. And he did what he was prepared to do. That's how it started. And then the rage and the emotions took over. He didn't stop until it ended. . . .*

*I—I don't dispute that shortly before 9:00 he was at that house, his own house. And he was fine. And he was with those kids. And he probably put that video in of Snow White and then left. By ten o'clock, he's on that telephone line, reporting a crime that never happened. In between, he's massacred Janet Downing.*

What a masterful stretching of the ten-minute window of opportunity to commit the crime to almost one hour. But Eddie left his house at about 9:15 and the three boys saw him shortly after 9:20 p.m. Will the jury remember that?

*REILLY: Now, however the way they want to have it, he's at that scene now. And you listen to that voice [on Eddie's 911 tape].*

*And listen. Listen for any trace, any trace of compassion. Listen for any trace of emotion. Listen for any trace of human feeling, common human decency about what has happened to him. You won't find it. It's not there. That's who he is. Doesn't care. He doesn't care.*

*Ladies and gentlemen: In a short time this case will be yours. . . . And when you render your verdict, you will speak the truth. The truth of what happened to Janet Downing. I respectfully suggest that the truth in this case is the truth anywhere. It's inevitable.*

*And I respectfully suggest the evidence in this case, the truth in this case is Edward O'Brien, on July the 23rd of 1995, went into that house and killed Janet Downing, stabbed and sliced her ninety-eight times.*

*Now, the defendant is entitled to a fair trial. And he is entitled to be well represented. And he has been.*

*I suggest that there comes a time in every person's life that they must answer to the wrong that they have done another. I respectfully suggest that that time has now come for Edward O'Brien.*

*On behalf of everyone that's involved in the prosecution of this case from Officer Blair to me–I ask you to return a verdict of guilty; guilty of murder in the first degree. Murder committed with deliberate premeditation and extreme, extreme atrocity and cruelty.*

*Thank you.*[193]

---

193 Id., pp. 106-149

# CHAPTER 41
## JURY INSTRUCTIONS

Closing arguments ended, and the court took a short recess. It was late morning on September 30, 1995. When the jury returned, the clerk announced that Juror No. 9 would be the foreman. (The judge chooses a foreman at random. He does not give reasons for his choice, and instructs the jury not to speculate on his choice.)

Then, at 12:50 p.m., Judge McDaniel began instructing the jurors on the law.

Jury instructions are long and tedious; they are often repetitious. Jurors cannot take notes, nor will written instructions be provided to them in the jury room. They must remember all of the instructions. McDaniel talked to the jurors nonstop for over one and a half hours, until approximately 2:30.

*McDANIEL: You are the sole and exclusive judges of the facts in the case. It is the jurors and the jurors alone who determine the weight, the effect and the value of the evidence that was offered during the course of the trial. Once you make these determinations of fact, then it will be your duty to apply them to the law that I give to you in these instructions in determining whether the defendant was guilty or not guilty. Of course, one of your most important functions is to evaluate the credibility of the witnesses who have testified in this case.*[194]

---

194 TWELFTH DAY OF TRIAL, Vol. XV, September 30, 1997, pp. 151-218

Because of the length and complexity of the jury instructions, I have excerpted below those legal tenets and concepts that McDaniel covered and are the most important and difficult for the deliberating juror.

- **Presumption of innocence:** *The burden of proof is on the prosecutor. All the presumptions of law, independent of evidence, are in favor of innocence and every person is presumed to be innocent until he is proven guilty. . . . And a defendant is not to be found guilty upon suspicion or conjecture, but only upon evidence produced in this courtroom. The defendant need not prove he is innocent.*
- **Beyond a reasonable doubt:** *The standard of proof is beyond a reasonable doubt, not proof beyond any shadow of a doubt . . . it does not mean proof beyond all doubt . . . that is what reasonable doubt is not. Reasonable doubt is that state of the case when, after the entire comparison and consideration of all of the evidence, the minds of the jurors are left in that condition that they cannot say they feel an abiding conviction to a moral certainty of the truth of the charge. . . . If there is a reasonable doubt remaining, the accused is entitled to the benefit of it by acquittal. It is not sufficient to establish probability . . . that the fact charged is more likely to be true than the contrary. But the evidence must establish the truth of the facts to a reasonable and moral certainty.*
- **Direct and circumstantial evidence:** *Direct evidence generally is the testimony of a witness who asserts actual knowledge of a fact which he or she saw, heard, or in some way was exposed to. . . . All you have to do is determine whether or not you want to believe it. . . . On the other hand circumstantial evidence is proof of a fact where*

*no witness can testify to the fact directly . . . so you have to draw inferences. . . . Circumstantial evidence, therefore, is founded on experience and observed facts and requires establishing a connection between known fact and facts sought to be proved.*

- **Murder:** *Murder is the unlawful killing of one human being by another with malice aforethought. . . . Murder committed with deliberate, premeditated malice aforethought or with extreme atrocity or cruelty is murder in the first degree. Murder, which does not appear to be in the first degree, is murder in the second degree.*

- **Elements of first-degree murder:** *First, it [the Commonwealth] must prove the act of unlawful killing. Second, that the killing was committed with deliberate premeditation. And third, that the killing was committed with malice aforethought. . . . The term "unlawful killing" refers to the absence of justification or excuse for the killing. To find premeditation, you must conclude that the defendant thought before he acted. . . . [T]he deliberation does not require an extended time span. . . . Rather it refers to the purposeful character of the premeditation. . . . It is not so much a matter of time as of logical sequence. . . . [T]he Commonwealth must show that a defendant's resolution to kill was the product of cool reflection.*

- **Malice aforethought:** *Thought before action . . . that is all aforethought means. . . . An intention to inflict injury on a victim, which is not justified . . . is malicious within the meaning of the law. . . .[I]t is contemplation rather than reflex, and it must precede the act.*

- **Extreme atrocity or cruelty:** *Malice aforethought must also include the doing of an act creating a plain and strong likelihood that death would follow. . . . Actual* *intent to kill is not a necessary element of murder under this theory because . . . a reasonably prudent person would have known of the plain and strong likelihood that death would follow a contemplated act. . . . The Commonwealth must prove that the defendant caused the victim's death by a method that surpassed the cruelty inherent in the taking of a human life, considering seven factors: consciousness and degree of suffering of the victim; extent of physical injuries; number of blows used upon the victim; manner and force with which the blows were delivered; instrument employed; disproportion between the means needed to cause death and those employed by the defendant.*

He offered a few more general instructions about listening to one another's thoughts and allowing oneself to be persuaded by a fellow juror's argument "only if you are convinced that your position is erroneous. . . . But do not surrender your honest conviction . . . solely because of the opinion of your fellow jurors."

And with that, the jury was reduced. To reduce the jury, four alternate jurors' numbers were chosen from a box with all of the jurors' numbers in it. These four were then separated from the deliberating jurors, in another room. They were instructed not to discuss the case with one another. If, for any reason, a deliberating juror is excused before a verdict is reached, then one of the alternates would be chosen at random to take that juror's place, and deliberations would begin all over again, as if no deliberations had already taken place.

The jurors deliberated for approximately three hours that afternoon, and asked to be discharged for the night and resume deliberation in the morning.

# CHAPTER 42

## THE VERDICT

On Wednesday, October 1, 1997, jurors resumed deliberation at 9:30 and remained behind closed doors all morning and afternoon. At approximately 3:30, they sent a message to the judge that they had reached a unanimous verdict.

The parties were all called by the clerk and told to be in the courtroom by 5:00 to receive the verdict. The O'Briens came from their house in Somerville, I came from my office in Cambridge, and we all met in an atmosphere of intense fear and anticipation.

Judge McDaniel spoke to the audience:

*As you no doubt have heard by now, there has been a verdict in this case, by the jury. And so, I want to take this opportunity now, just to caution you about any outbursts of any kind.*

*This has been a very difficult case. There is no question that somebody, one side or the other, is going to be disappointed. And that may occasion someone to express that disappointment. Please do not do so. I want no outbursts of any kind. No applause. No hugging. No noise whatsoever, relative to the verdict. Because, after all, this jury is returning a verdict on what it sees as the evidence in this case. And they ought not be embarrassed by any outburst. Now, if there is anybody here who cannot conform his conduct in the appropriate way, leave the courtroom now. Because I will not tolerate any expressions of any emotion. I know that is difficult, but I won't tolerate it. I will deal with it summarily if I have to. All right. Bring the jury in.*[195]

At 5:15 the jurors entered the courtroom to deliver their verdict. They filed in single file, looking down at the floor, which is not unusual, but always feels ominous.

*CLERK: Defendant, please stand. Jury, please stand. Mr. Foreman, has your jury agreed upon its verdict?*

*FOREMAN: Yes, we have.*

*CLERK: Would you hand it to the court officer please, sir?*

As is customary, the verdict was handed to the court officer and given to the clerk, who handed it to the judge. The judge recorded the verdict and returned the verdict slip to the clerk. The clerk handed the verdict slip back to the court officer, who returned it to the foreman.

*CLERK: Indictment 95-1535-001. Commonwealth versus Edward S. O'Brien. Mr. Foreman, is the defendant guilty or not guilty?*

*FOREMAN: Guilty.*

*CLERK: Guilty of what, sir?*

*FOREMAN: Guilty of the first degree.*

*CLERK: Go ahead, sir, read it.*

*FOREMAN: Ah, extreme atrocity and cruelty.*

*CLERK: Members of the jury, you will hearken to your verdict, as recorded by the Court. The jurors upon their oath, do say that the defendant, Edward S. O'Brien, Indictment 95-1535-001, is guilty of the offense as charged, which is murder in the first degree, and extreme atrocity and cruelty. So say you Mr. Foreman?*

---

195 THIRTEENTH DAY OF TRIAL, October 1, 1997, Vol. XVI, pp. 47, 48

*FOREMAN: That's right.*

*CLERK: So say you all, members of the jury?*

*JURY PANEL: Yes.*

*McDANIEL: Mr. Clerk, impose the mandatory sentence.*

*CLERK: Mr. O'Brien, please stand, sir. . . . You will hearken to the sentence the court has awarded against you. The court, having duly considered your offense, orders you to be punished by confinement in the Massachusetts correctional institution for a term of life. Custody, Mr. Officer."*[196]

Eddie then was taken away by the court officer and the audience erupted in loud expressions of disbelief or relief, depending on which side they were on. I stood motionless, watching Eddie's back as he was escorted out the door beside the witness stand and back to the holding cell behind the courtroom.

The entire hallway outside the courtroom was a makeshift pressroom, with each TV station having a desk and phones installed. The print media were three rows deep. Cameras were everywhere. It was chaos. I grappled with the crowds to get the hell away from there without being asked my thoughts. I could not go back to the holding cell to see Eddie because I knew I was not in control of my own emotions. I was angry, upset, scared, nauseated, and sad—all at once. I did not want him to see me until I could pull myself back together and be the support he so needed right then.

Eddie was transported to the Massachusetts Correctional Institution at Concord for classification. It would be his first night in an adult prison. He had just turned seventeen years old. I could not imagine the terror he was feeling.

I went to see him that night in prison. He was numb. He was in shock. He was not present emotionally. He couldn't

196 Id., pp. 48-55

talk. I held his hands and told him I was prepared to do whatever I could to get him out of prison. I told him that if he knew who the man was he saw in Downing's house he needed to tell me, even if he believed his family was in danger. He just shook his head up and down in silent agreement, saying nothing with glassy, distant eyes. He was in a trauma-induced dissociative state.

# CHAPTER 43

## AFTERMATH

One week later, on October 9, 1997, Tom Reilly announced that he was running for the office of Massachusetts attorney general. In an article in the *Boston Globe*, Reilly said he would have the help of U.S. Attorney Wayne Budd, his closest friend, in getting his campaign going. "I haven't focused on the politics of it. Now I need to pay attention to what has to be done to get a campaign up and running."[197] Ironic, because all he'd done for two years was focus on the politics of it.

"Make sure they investigate, investigate, investigate, investigate if I am ever found dead," Janet Downing had demanded of her friend Gina Mahoney on the day she was killed. Mahoney had tried for a year, but could not get the police to listen to her or to further investigate her friend's murder.

The investigation into Downing's murder was anything but professional and thorough. Critical information was ignored; witnesses were not interviewed at all or literally turned away; unknown fingerprints and DNA at the murder scene went untested. Preposterous theories to support the prosecution's view of the case were constructed with conjecture and hunches. Facts needed to bolster that case were simply fabricated. Witnesses were spoon-fed testimony to repeat on the witness stand.

197 Lehigh, Scot, "Pines, Reilly declare for AG's Post," The Boston Globe, October 9, 1997

From the outset, this case had been about one thing only: convicting Eddie O'Brien. It was not about Janet Downing or her horrible death. It was not about the truth. It was not about justice. It was about a political agenda that coincided with a murder that gave the candidate who would benefit from it two years of nonstop media attention and exposure. It was about advocating for monumental changes in a juvenile justice system that, in fact, was quite healthy and not in need of any reform.

Twenty years later, a movement is afoot to return to the juvenile system Massachusetts had before the Eddie O'Brien case: rehabilitation, not retribution. In 2013, the Supreme Judicial Court of the Commonwealth of Massachusetts ruled that imposing a sentence of life in prison without parole on a juvenile was unconstitutional. Parole is now an option. In 2016, the SJC ruled that inmates convicted as juveniles could be moved to a minimum-security facility as a step toward becoming eligible for parole.

This isn't an option for Eddie O'Brien. He hasn't—and won't—apply for parole, because that would involve having to admit to the crime.

A crime he never committed.

The "investigation" into Janet Downing's death and prosecution of Eddie O'Brien was a perfect example of the politics of murder. If the perpetrator had been found to be a drug-addicted twenty-something (or an African-American or Hispanic fifteen-year-old), Reilly wouldn't have prosecuted this case himself. The Downing family would not have had the undivided attention of the district attorney, but would have been dealing with an assistant district attorney racking up jury trials for a résumé to move out of public service and into the lucrative private sector. The Downing family would have been another good family coping with a horrendous crime.

Eileen McNamara, a seasoned reporter at the *Boston Globe*, wrote the following about District Attorney Tom Reilly after his announcement:

*Just days ago, Reilly insisted he had not had time in the last two years to even think about his political future. He was too busy preparing his first-degree murder case against Eddie O'Brien, the Somerville teenager accused in the July 1995 stabbing of a neighbor, Janet Downing. Say this much for Reilly: He thinks fast. Only one week after the jury returned a guilty verdict in that case, the district attorney says he is a candidate for attorney general. Ever since Reilly decided to try the case against O'Brien himself rather than assign it to one of his deputies, he had been fighting a public perception that he was exploiting an emotional and high-profile crime to advance his own political career. O'Brien's overwrought parents, appearing live on Court TV, accused the prosecutor of just that last week as their seventeen-year-old son was being led from the courtroom to spend his life in prison. Reilly, for his part, insists he was motivated to prosecute O'Brien not by politics but by outrage at the viciousness of a killer he has described as a "sexual sadist."*

*Only Tom Reilly knows his own motivations. Given his distinguished career as a prosecutor, he is entitled to the benefit of our doubts, his overnight decision to run notwithstanding. But the district attorney courts public cynicism when he launches his bid for higher office talking not about the regulatory and public-protection role of the attorney general but about capital punishment and child pornography—hot button issues ignited by the latest horrific murder in Middlesex County. We have had enough of legislating by hysterics in this state. In the last decade, we have rewritten the Juvenile Code in Massachusetts to ensure that teenagers accused of murder will be tried as adults, without exception. We did not make these changes comprehensively, after a measured public discussion about the potential for rehabilitation and the need for punishment. We made them piecemeal, in reaction first to the shooting of two boys on a Roxbury stoop by a teenage gang member and then to the fatal stabbing of Janet Downing. Public outrage has its place.*[198]

I don't know who killed Janet Downing on that hot night in July 1995. I only know who didn't kill her. When you have the presumption of innocence, the defendant is not required to prove anything, especially who really killed the victim. At least that's what the law says.

Eddie O'Brien's case was operated outside the law since the very beginning. He never enjoyed that presumption of innocence. He was targeted as the killer hours after the murder, and the Commonwealth spent all its resources trying (and failing, in my opinion) to make the crime fit him. I don't think Reilly cared who really killed Janet Downing. He cared about getting the conviction, changing the juvenile laws and getting elected attorney general.

There are a number of facts I do know, about which there can be little doubt:

- Within a time frame of five to seven minutes it is impossible to do what someone did to Janet Downing.
- Something loud happened between 8:15 and 8:30 p.m. on the stairs in the Downing house. Paul Downing Jr. was in the house when that happened.
- Someone was using a lot of water in the Downing

198 McNamara, Eileen, "Political Capital From a Tragedy," The Boston Globe, October 11, 1997

home between 9:00 and 9:30 p.m.

- It is impossible to slaughter another human being in the manner Janet Downing was killed and not have blood all over one's body, clothes, shoes, and shirt. Even if Eddie's white "Over the Rim" T-shirt had been underneath a black shirt, it still would have been saturated in blood.
- No black shirt was ever found.
- The DNA on the alleged murder weapon is identifiable and is not Eddie's. Reilly chose not to try to identify it.
- There was DNA under Downing's fingernails — Reilly chose not to try to identify it.
- There was no forced entry into the house, and the kitchen door to the home was undisturbed. Because its doorknob was inoperable, it was impossible to enter that door from the deck even with the deadbolt unlatched.
- The dog did not bark at all during what was clearly a violent struggle. There is a strong possibility that the dog knew the intruder or one of the intruders, who quieted the dog. Ortiz, for example, had lived with that dog for over a year.
- Ortiz was present at the Downing house when the first responders arrived. His cab was blocked in by the ambulances and fire trucks. He was parked beside Downing's backyard. His keys were lost in her backyard. The door from the cellar to the backyard was wide open at 9:20 p.m.
- Ortiz had keys to Downing's house, which he refused to return, according to Janet Downing herself. He was observed parked at her house on a regular basis during the week while the house was empty. He was able to enter the house without forced entry.
- Ortiz apparently organized four other cab drivers to surround Downing's car and box her in as she drove home from work just months before the murder.
- Downing was afraid of Ortiz and suspected he was

trying to terrorize her.

Here are a few things I know about Eddie O'Brien:

- Eddie had no history of conflict or violence. He never treated Janet Downing in a disrespectful way.
- Eddie underwent hours of examination by a well-respected child and adolescent psychiatrist, who determined that Eddie did not suffer from any mental illness. He also underwent a battery of psychological testing, indicating the same thing. Normal, healthy, mentally sound fifteen-year-old males are not known to murder friendly neighbors for no reason.
- Eddie keeps his friends close. He talks to his good friends once a week by phone.
- He has engaged in every activity in prison that brings him people and information from the outside world (or the "real world," as he calls it). For years he has attended a group that comes into the prison twice a week to say the Rosary. He goes to Mass every week. He attends a three-day religious retreat given at the prison each year. He refers to himself as a Roman Catholic. He calls his parents every single day, and he speaks to one or more of his siblings every single day.
- Eddie puts his head on his pillow every night with a clear conscience; because of this, he harbors no rage or vindictiveness about his plight.
- He sees his life this way: For reasons unknown to him, he was given a path to walk that was completely unexpected and inexplicable. He doesn't know why he was chosen to walk this path, but he believes there is a reason and a purpose to his life. So he does it with dignity, and with some hope that one day the path will lead him to a more familiar life, one that includes his family and friends, one that might also someday include a wife and some kids. Eddie knows nothing is guaranteed, and he might be in prison for

the rest of his life. He accepts that, and does not let it affect his daily life.

- First and foremost, he lives one day at a time–this, he told me, was the single most important lesson he learned about how to survive in prison. Today is the only day that matters.
-

Defense attorney Bob George played right into the hands of the politicians in this murder case. Perhaps thinking the case would be disposed of in Juvenile Court, he prepared only for the transfer hearings. He did not plan for District Attorney Tom Reilly's appeal of Judge Paul Heffernan's decision. But all the rules of the game changed as the law changed with Eddie's case.

Having been outspent financially by the endless resources of the prosecution, George was caught up short, with only four months to prepare for a murder trial. He had done no independent testing of the evidence; he had no experts and no money to hire experts. He was woefully unprepared. He was not even familiar with the evidence he did have in his possession. Without preparation and the guidance of some experts in DNA and blood evidence, he settled for the nondefense of "he didn't have the motive and he didn't have the time." That would never trump the forensic evidence.

To have any chance of winning this case, it was imperative that Eddie's story come into evidence. When the judge ruled out the tape of Eddie's telling the story to Dr. Spiers before the administration of the truth serum, George had to find another way to tell the story. He simply didn't do it. There are several ways that the information could have come in without Eddie testifying. Did he even consider them? I think not.

He told the judge before he even told the family or Eddie that he wasn't putting any of them on the witness stand. I can only speculate as to why, but here are my thoughts: He never settled on a theory of his defense. At first it was "he was never there, those boys didn't see him." Then, when it was clear that he had to explain Eddie's blood at the scene, it was too late to prepare anyone else to testify. He settled for "he didn't have the motive and he didn't have the opportunity" to commit this crime.

Eddie's first lawyers created a conflict of interest when one represented his father at the grand jury and the other, unbeknownst to him and his parents, tried to work out a plea deal with the district attorney one week after Eddie was arrested.

Eddie's parents were advised to contact Bob Launie, who was right out of law school and had never tried a murder case. Launie called in Bob George, a well-known defense lawyer. George told the O'Briens not to worry about money, that they would hold a fundraiser and get enough money to cover the cost of Eddie's defense. When that didn't happen, he asked the O'Briens for $60,000, then $75,000 more, and finally $50,000 more. Eddie's parents mortgaged their house and were tapped out by then.

The trial was now mere weeks away, and George had no experts and no money.

As for me, I was a seasoned lawyer, and I'd done jury trials, but I'd never done a murder case. Bob George was a well-known and highly respected downtown Newbury Street lawyer, and the truth is that I just assumed he knew what he was doing. I didn't understand that he was as ill-prepared as I see in hindsight he was. I didn't know what the evidence was, because I wasn't given any information about it. Eddie's parents didn't know that Eddie had been excluded as the primary source of DNA on the hilt and under Janet Downing's fingernails until I told them this year!

A ray of light has recently penetrated Eddie's cell at

the Souza-Baranowski Correctional Center in Shirley, Massachusetts. The Innocence Program has accepted his case and has just begun the uphill climb of trying to overturn his conviction. Thousands of inmates are on Innocence Project and Innocence Program waiting lists around the country. He is indeed very fortunate. As Eddie says, "Hundreds of inmates have been exonerated in the United States because of wrongful convictions. I've gotta believe I'm gonna be one of them."

If by telling this story that ray of light in Eddie's cell gets a little bit wider, then this book's goal will have been achieved.

# APPENDIX A

## STATE POLICE CRIME LABORATORY UPDATE

*FBI Begins Review of Crime Lab*
*Downloads DNA data after aide's suspension*
By Jonathan Saltzman, Globe Staff | January 20, 2007

FBI analysts downloaded more than 20,000 DNA profiles over 15 hours Thursday and yesterday, starting a top-to-bottom review of the State Police crime laboratory a week after an administrator was suspended for failing to tell prosecutors of DNA matches in nearly a dozen unsolved rape cases.

The audit, sought by the head of the State Police, is expected to last weeks, if not months, said a State Police spokesman, Lieutenant Detective William Powers.

The two analysts from the FBI crime lab in Quantico, Va., are trying to determine whether Robert E. Pino, the civilian administrator of the state's Combined DNA Indexing System, may have mishandled more DNA test results than the 15 disclosed by the State Police last week, when the agency announced his suspension with pay, Powers said.

State Police have said that Pino received results last year indicating that DNA tested in 11 old rape cases matched genetic samples from convicted felons, but that he failed to report the information to police departments for months, during which the 15-year statute of limitations for rape expired.

In four cases, Pino prepared reports to police saying

that tests linked DNA recovered at crime scenes to suspects, when, in fact, they had not. Pino did not mail all four reports, and no one was arrested because other officials discovered Pino's mistake, Powers said.

"By looking at all the different cases he would have reviewed, [the FBI] will determine whether there were more notifications which he should have made," Powers said. The FBI will also determine whether Pino reported other matches when none existed.

The data being audited by the FBI had been stored in a computerized databank that matches DNA profiles of convicted felons with samples collected at crime scenes and analyzed by civilian scientists at the Sudbury facility or at private labs. A 2004 state law requires anyone convicted of a felony to submit a blood sample, so the lab can identify the DNA.

Pino has declined to comment, saying that he remains an employee and that the allegations are under investigation. However, the Massachusetts Organization of State Engineers and Scientists, the union that represents him, has issued a statement saying the mishandled cases stemmed from years of underfunding and inadequate staffing.

"This investigation shouldn't be about an individual; it should be about an office that hasn't grown with the advances in technology," the union's president, Joseph Dorant, said in the statement released Sunday.

The mishandling of DNA test results is an embarrassment for Colonel Mark F. Delaney, who became superintendent of the State Police in May after running the forensics lab for four years and overseeing what the [Governor Mitt] Romney administration characterized as a dramatic overhaul of the troubled facility.

The legislature increased funding of the lab from $6.2 million in fiscal 2005 to $16.2 million in fiscal 2007, in part to address a mammoth backlog in DNA analyses that reached 1,000 cases in 2005. In addition, lawmakers created the post of undersecretary for forensic sciences in the Executive Office of Public Safety to oversee improvements at the lab and the state medical examiner's office.

Senator Jarrett T. Barrios, who expects to be reappointed as co-chairman of the Joint Committee on Public Safety and Homeland Security, said this week that he wants to hold hearings to determine how the mistakes in the lab happened and who was overseeing Pino.

# APPENDIX B

## ROBERT PINO UPDATE

On January 12, 2007, Robert Pino was suspended from his job as crime laboratory CODIS administrator after an investigation by Colonel Mark Delaney, State Police superintendent. Specifically, Delaney said that Pino failed to make timely and/or accurate notifications of DNA "hits" or matches in several old but still open cases. As a result, in many of the cases, a suspect was identified prior to the expiration of the statute of limitations, but neither the police nor the district attorney was notified in a timely matter, and the statute of limitations passed before the cases could be filed. In a few cases, Pino made notification to law enforcement officials of DNA "hits" on old cases when, in fact, no match had been made.[199]

In April of 2007, Pino was fired from his job of twenty-four years. He responded to his firing by asserting that his superiors should have been fired as well, because they knew about all of these problems. He insisted he was the "fall guy" for a poorly administered laboratory.

Reporters in an exclusive interview with a Boston area investigative team posed the question: Why was Pino taking the brunt of the blame for problems everyone else seemed to know about? "I think all of it's politics," said Pino.[200]

199 Commonwealth of Massachusetts, Department of the State Police, Public Affairs Unit Press Release dated January 12, 2007

200 Boston Globe, "Former State Police Crime Lab Administrator Tells Troubling Story," July 6, 2007

In 2014 Pino's reputation was further impugned due to his forensic work in another murder case from Somerville. Michael J. Sullivan was convicted of murder in 1986, and Pino was the chemist and crime scene investigator in that case as well. In 2014 Sullivan was granted a new trial by the Supreme Judicial Court based on a re-examination of Pino's forensic work in the case.

Specifically, a jacket worn by Sullivan on the night of the murder was examined by Pino who testified at Sullivan's trial that blood was detected on both cuffs of the jacket. He further testified that a hair was found in a pocket of the jacket and that the hair was, in his opinion, "consistent" with that of the victim. The blood and the single hair were the only physical evidence connecting the defendant to the murder.

When re-examined by an independent laboratory in 2012, absolutely no blood was detected on the jacket. Furthermore, the court reiterated that the hair could not be identified as the victim's because hair evidence is not absolute.

# APPENDIX C

## ROBERT GEORGE UPDATE

*Prominent attorney Robert George gets 3½ years in prison for money laundering conviction*
By Brian Ballou and Martin Finucane
Boston Globe staff 10.31.12

A federal judge sentenced prominent Boston criminal defense attorney Robert A. George today to 3½ years in prison for money laundering and related crimes.

"It is a sad day today for the entire legal profession, bench and bar alike," U.S. District Judge Nathanial A. Gorton said as he sentenced George.

George, 57, who was convicted in June of helping a former client launder $200,000 in profits from crimes, insisted on his innocence before he was sentenced in the Boston courthouse.

"I know it pains everyone that I am standing here, pleading for myself the way I have for clients for so many years," George said. "I only sought to do what I could for somebody who asked for help."

"It's hard to drive by many courthouses that I have labored in for so many years," he said. "My fall from grace has been long and hard."

Gorton also fined George $12,500 and ordered him to forfeit his Lexus and $39,000. The judge ordered George to surrender on Jan. 15.

Robert Goldstein, George's attorney, said after the hearing, "I don't think any reasonable person can rebut the assertion" that the informant who played a key role in convicting George had "a plan and that plan was to somehow exact revenge on Mr. George."

Prosecutors had asked for a prison sentence of more than five years, while defense attorneys requested an 18-month sentence. George was convicted of seven counts of conspiracy, money laundering, and structuring bank deposits to avoid government scrutiny.

Ronald Dardinski, who secretly recorded conversations with George while working as a government informant, said at trial that George had voluntarily offered to help him "clean" illicit profits and referred him to a mortgage broker who took 20 percent and split it with George.

In a legal career spanning three decades, George has represented a number of high-profile clients, including organized crime figures and Christopher M. McCowen, a garbage man convicted of the 2002 rape and murder of fashion writer Christa Worthington.

--------

2015 update:

George was released from prison and is monitored with an ankle bracelet by a parole officer. He has been permanently disbarred from the practice of law.

# APPENDIX D

## THOMAS F. REILLY UPDATE

Tom Reilly won the election for attorney general of Massachusetts in 1998 and served for two terms until January 2007.

In 2006 he kicked off his campaign for governor of Massachusetts. He finished third in the primary in September 2006. His opponent, Deval Patrick, went on to win the general election.

Currently Reilly leads the Government Investigations and Defense practice group at Manion Gaynor & Manning LLP. According to their website, he "provides advocacy and strategic solutions to clients facing investigation by federal, state law enforcement and regulatory agencies."

In 2000, Reilly, the then-attorney general, told reporter David Weber of the *Boston Herald*: "Edward O'Brien is a very dangerous young man. I was always fearful that if he ever were released, he would kill again and he would kill a woman. There is no doubt in my mind he was a budding serial killer. That's what he is."[201]

201 Weber, David, "SJC Nixes New Trial for Somerville Killer of Friend's Mother," Boston Herald, October 19, 2000

# APPENDIX E

## WILLIAM WELD UPDATE

William Weld lost the Senate race in 1996 to the incumbent, Senator John Kerry. He was nominated in 1997 by President Bill Clinton to serve as ambassador to Mexico, but because of opposition by the Foreign Relations Committee chairman, Senator Jesse Helms, he withdrew his nomination. He subsequently returned to the private sector and moved back to his home state of New York, where he launched an unsuccessful attempt to be elected governor in 2006.

Weld writes novels for the mass market and has published three books. In 2001, Meryl Gordon, a reporter with New York magazine wrote:

"Four years ago, he was governor of Massachusetts and a prospective GOP presidential candidate. Today, William Weld is living with his girlfriend in New York and has a novel coming out. Talk about your midlife crisis! . . .

"Weld used large chunks of his adult autobiography in dashing off two earlier political thrillers, *Mackerel by Moonlight* and *Big Ugly*. He dictated the books ('ten pages an hour,' transcribed by a secretary) as a lark, starting in 1997, and they received lukewarm reviews. Both feature the exploits of alter ego Terry Mullally, a smart-ass prosecutor turned politician who loves Latin and grammar, takes on the Establishment, excels at snappy patter, and has no qualms about ruthlessly cutting corners to get ahead."[202]

In 2016, Weld became the vice-presidential candidate for the Libertarian Party.

---

202 Gordon, Meryl, "Weld at Heart," New York magazine, January 14, 2002

*The Soiling of Old Glory | Pulitzer Prize 1977*

The author and publisher would like to thank renowned photographer Stanley Forman for the use of his Pulitzer Prize-winning photograph, "The Soiling of Old Glory," in this manuscript.

The winner of three Pulitzer Prizes, Forman has published a book of some of his work, BEFORE YELLOW TAPE, that can be ordered at **www.beforeyellowtape.com**

For more of his photographs go to:

**www.stanleyformanphotos.com**
**www.thesoilingofoldglory.com**

# PREFACE TO THE SECOND EDITION ADDENDUM

May 2026

It has been approximately 10 years since *The Politics of Murder* was published. Much has happened over those years: changes in the law; Eddie O'Brien's transfer to medium security at Northeast Correctional Center Institution at Gardner, Massachusetts; information received and investigated since the publication in 2016. These changes and developments seem to trickle in, with lengthy periods of inactivity in between. This is the reality of how slowly the justice system moves, especially for inmates who are working on post-conviction appeals, requests for reversal, requests for new trials, and requests for clemency for their convictions.

I frequently ask myself whether the needle has moved at all in Eddie's case since the publication of *The Politics of Murder*. Many days, I think not. On other days, I am amazed at how much information we have gathered since then, and how much further along the road to getting some relief from his wrongful conviction we are. Those are usually the days when I speak to Eddie on the phone. His patience and determination carried me through the times when the needle seemed stuck. He hasn't rested for a day during these last 10 years.

Most of what I present in these new chapters is a direct result of the arduous work and the endless hours

Eddie has spent requesting, and then combing through, the often handwritten notes he received from his Freedom of Information Act (FOIA) requests. Hundreds of documents we didn't have access to before were produced, exposing the shameful corruption and deliberate errors in the proceedings which have unjustly kept him in prison for the past 31 years.

We had other help as well. Many readers are familiar with Karen Read, who was charged with the murder of her boyfriend, Boston Police officer John O'Keefe. The re-trial was held in the Superior Court for Norfolk County in 2025. The first trial ended in a hung jury.

During those two trials, unimaginable prosecutorial misconduct and police corruption were exposed on national television. Similar political collusion and corruption I wrote about 10 years ago was playing out live on television daily and viewers were witnesses to it. Such corruption suddenly didn't seem as farfetched as it had in 2015.

Unfortunately, yet another person accused of murder was forced through a life-altering ordeal that robbed her of her liberty, her reputation, her employment, and cost her millions of dollars to defend herself. (Before the second trial began, she already owed five million dollars in deferred legal fees to her lawyers.) The Commonwealth of Massachusetts has such enormous financial and personnel resources that the scales of justice are always tipped in its favor, no matter that the defendant has "the presumption of innocence." If they cannot pay eye-watering amounts of money for a team of defense attorneys, the best forensic experts, and the best scientific labs, then the fight is as lopsided as David and Goliath. I'll take a one-million-dollar defense fund over the presumption of innocence any day! By the time Karen Read got to trial, she had lost that presumption in the press—just as Eddie had. The presumption isn't going to win the case if the defendant cannot access funds for investigators, forensic analyses, several lawyers, and expert witnesses needed to properly defend the case. With funds to hire the small army necessary, at least the defendant has a fighting chance.

The presumption of innocence also cannot fight the blue code of silence of the police or the collusion among the many state offices that participated in Karen Read's prosecution, or should I say persecution. What we all saw in that courtroom was what most people could not see in 15-year-old Eddie O'Brien's courtroom. None of us was ready for that in 1995.

Scores of bloggers and podcasters championed Karen Read's cause and supported her with fundraisers and marches. A whole subculture of groups in the Innocence/Wrongful Conviction and Police Anti-Corruption world joined forces and raised the consciousness of the public to the point where the debacle that was unfolding was undeniable. Without such overwhelming support, I doubt she would have prevailed.

One of those podcasts turned its attention to Eddie O'Brien's case when the Karen Read trial was over. That is when the landscape changed for Eddie; we were introduced to a large community of people who understood what had happened to him. It started with one woman in that community posting a photo of *The Politics of Murder* on Facebook with the comment: "If you thought the Karen Read case was corrupt, you've got to read this book." A podcast picked that up and began researching the case. They live-streamed 38 episodes of their show about the Eddie O'Brien case. A wealth of new information came out of those sessions. That information alone informed investigations into other possible suspects.

On a personal note, I was finally able to accept in my own legally trained mind that the collusion and corruption went even further than just incompetence with a smattering of obfuscation. I now firmly believe that this was a coordinated and carefully executed plan to convict an innocent young boy for a horrible murder, for the sole purpose of advancing personal and political agendas.

I also believe that the police and prosecutors knew Eddie had not brutally murdered Janet Downing. They intentionally refused to look at any evidence that pointed to any other possible suspect; they intentionally withheld exculpatory evidence critical to Eddie's claim of innocence; and they fabricated incriminating evidence to convict him.

In this addendum to *The Politics of Murder*, I'm going to show you how.

# CURRENT STATUS OF JUVENILE LAW

The initial intent of the juvenile court in Massachusetts was to treat juvenile offenders as children needing direction and guidance, rather than as criminals needing punishment and removal from society. Eddie O'Brien's case allowed the Commonwealth and the proponents of the "adult time for adult crimes" to pass the Juvenile Justice Reform Act of 1996 and the Youthful Offender statute, requiring juveniles as young as 14 charged with certain felonies to be tried as adults and subject to adult sentencing. Eddie was 15 at the time of Janet Downing's murder. His sentence was life without the possibility of parole, a now-mandatory sentence under the 1996 law. He was 17 years old when he was sentenced in 1997.

The new legislation was passed during a period of "tough-on-crime" reforms fueled by the now-discredited theory that a new generation of "superpredators" was about to emerge. This theory held that violent teens without morals were going to take over our cities. Harsher, adult-style sanctions were required to combat this anticipated wave of youthful crime. In an earlier chapter, I termed this legislation a " knee-jerk reaction" to a perceived threat, and that is exactly what it proved to be. The superpredators never materialized, and juvenile arrests declined by 71% to 75% from 1996 to 2019. Serious violent crime arrests for youth dropped by 67% during this period—a rate of decline more than double that of adults (31%).[203] This trend had nothing to do with the harsher sentencing legislation. Youthful crimes were already declining between 1995 and 1997, when Eddie was sentenced.

The Supreme Judicial Court of Massachusetts has been consistently critical of the legislation for several reasons, not the least of which was that it was scientifically inaccurate. The law was built on a theory that has since been debunked. Brain science showed that the prefrontal cortex, which is responsible for emotional regulation, reasoning, and impulse control, is not fully developed until a person's mid-20s. New brain science confirmed that children were being punished as adults for acts committed when their brains were often not "adult" enough to form a more adult solution.

Secondly, there was a huge racial disparity in whom the Youthful Offender indictments affected. Data from the Massachusetts Trial Court has shown that Youthful Offender indictments disproportionately affected Black and Latino youth when compared to White youth for similar offenses.[204]

Lastly, studies showed that juveniles placed in adult prisons were more likely to reoffend than those kept in the juvenile system, because they lacked access to age-appropriate education and therapy.

In 2013, the Supreme Judicial Court of Massachusetts ruled that mandatory life without parole for juveniles—a key pillar of '90s-era logic—was unconstitutional, signaling

---

203 Trends in Youth Arrests for Violent Crimes (August 2022). Office of Juvenile Justice and Delinquency Prevention; Who Gets Arrested in America: Trends Across Four Decades, 1980–2024 (December 2025). Council on Criminal Justice

204 I explained the importance of having a White youth as the defendant in this case in the original text of the book. It was of utmost importance, given the racial atmosphere in Boston at the time, that the new legislation not be seen as targeting the Black and Latino communities, even though that was exactly who it was targeting.

a legal shift away from the 1996 act's severity.[205] It violated the Eighth Amendment prohibiting cruel and unusual punishment. The court reasoned that because judges cannot determine whether a juvenile is irretrievably depraved, they also cannot determine "with any reasonable degree of certainty, whether imposition of this most severe punishment is warranted."[206] This decision led to the re-sentencing of all juvenile lifers in Massachusetts to a term of life *with* the possibility of parole, granting 63 inmates immediate parole eligibility after 15 years of time served.

Legislators began to respond to the U.S. Supreme Court and Massachusetts Supreme Judicial Court. In 2018, further relief came from the Criminal Justice Reform Act of 2018, significantly shifting the focus of Massachusetts juvenile law back toward rehabilitation and effectively rolling back several of the most punitive elements of the 1996 Youthful Offender Statute.

In 2024, the SJC expanded protection from mandatory life sentences without parole by raising the minimum age an offender could be subjected to mandatory sentencing from 17 to 20. The court created a whole new class of people, based on the new brain science, called "emerging adults." The court determined that emerging adults share the same neurological characteristics as juveniles, making such sentences unconstitutional for them as well.[207]

Although we have not exactly come full circle, the misguided knee-jerk reaction legislation of 1996 was deemed to be so flawed and unconstitutional that much of it was rescinded within 20 years of its enactment.

Juvenile law has been rapidly righting many of the

---

205 *Gregory Diatchenko vs. District Attorney of Suffolk County*, 466 Mass. 655(2013)

206 Ibid., p. 670

207 *Commonwealth v. Mattis*, 493 Mass. 216 (2024)

wrongs inflicted on the children and emerging adults who were irreparably impacted by it. Can they recover from what was so arbitrarily and cruelly done to them during these 30 years? I think that remains to the seen.

Incarceration in an adult prison at age 17 is a trauma unique unto itself in the kinds of trauma children can suffer during adolescence. Modern research emphasizes that the brain does not develop in a vacuum. The youths we are talking about have had their brains developing in environments and under such stressors that can psychologically defeat fully mature adults.

Trauma can disrupt the coordination between the parts of the brain that can heighten vulnerability to reactive or aggressive behaviors.[208] Because the young adult brain is still under construction, harsh environments like solitary confinement can cause lasting neural alterations. These alterations can affect cognitive processes crucial for assessing complex environmental challenges and implementing effective solutions.

How have the brains of these children and emerging adults been affected by their years of harsh treatment and confinement? Could this cruel and unusual punishment have created the kind of behavior it was trying to thwart?

---

208 The Body Keeps the Score: The Neurobiological Profile of Traumatized Adolescents, Daniela Laricchiuta, et. al. *Neuroscience & Biobehavioral Reviews*; Volume 145, February 2023, 10503

# EDDIE'S ADVOCACY IN PRISON

In his journey through the correctional system. Eddie O'Brien has been housed in several different Massachusetts institutions over the 31 years of his incarceration. At age 17, he went directly from the courthouse to Walpole Prison. He was at Walpole for two years, after which he was transferred to the newly opened "supermax" prison at Souza-Baranowski Correctional Center in Shirley in 1999. He remained there for almost four years, when he was transferred to Old Colony Correctional Center in Bridgewater, at the age of 23.

Eddie was 27 when he was transferred to MCI-Norfolk. He had been at Norfolk for four years when they sent him back to Souza-Baranowski for possession of a cell phone.[209] He spent five years at the supermax before he was permitted to apply for transfer to NCCI Gardner in 2019 when he was 39 years old. He recently celebrated his 46th birthday at Gardner.

In 2017, while housed at the supermax at Souza-Baranowski, Eddie filed a *pro se* lawsuit against the Department of Corrections regarding the denial of his appeal of the disciplinary action against him for possession of a cell phone (Docket No. 1784-1815). On June 19, 2019, after hearings on the Department's Motions to Dismiss the

209 The penalty for this offense for most inmates at Norfolk was two weeks in solitary (the hole). There were some who were also sent to Shirley for having a cell phone but didn't stay a Level A inmate (escape risk) for more than two years. Eddie was in his fourth year as a Level A when he filed the complaint against the Department of Corrections.

Complaint, Judge Douglas L. Wilkins dismissed the case when the DOC removed his Level A classification. Douglas L. Wilkins just happened to be the son of the Supreme Court Justice Herbert Wilkins who, in 1996, ordered a second transfer hearing in juvenile court with a different judge after DA Tom Reilly lost the case in Heffernan's decision.

At Gardner, Eddie became very active in advocating for inmates' needs when the COVID pandemic hit. Inmates were in lockdown most of the time, and visitation with family and friends was suspended. On May 26, 2020, Eddie filed a civil lawsuit *pro se* against the Department of Corrections seeking declaratory judgment that the continuing lockdown of the prison amounted to cruel and unusual punishment, depriving the inmates of rights granted to them under the United States and Massachusetts Constitutions (Docket #2084CV0314). The DOC filed motions asserting that the facility had instituted "modified" lockdown procedures for the pandemic, and that the requested relief was, for all intents and purposes, provided to the inmates.

Eddie opposed the dismissal, stating that as much as the defendants wished the court to believe that things were running smoothly at NCCI Gardner, they were not. The weight room, gym, and outdoor running track were still closed. Recreation time had actually *decreased* since the motion to dismiss was filed. Visitation with family was only permitted one time per week, noncontact, and for 50 minutes. Nevertheless, the court dismissed Eddie's complaint as moot on December 2, 2020. (Eddie filed a new lawsuit regarding visitation rights that were severely restricted during the COVID pandemic in 2022. The case was consolidated with another case he filed, and is proceeding in Suffolk County. A law firm has taken his case *pro bono* and is in the process of conducting depositions of various DOC officials and completing other discovery matters.)

In 2021, Eddie and a few of his friends formed the "Enlightenment Group for Lifers" for inmates who were serving life sentences. It started as a self-improvement program to get lifers out of their cells and into the population; some of the life-sentence inmates preferred to watch TV all day in their cells.

The Lifers Group offered to help inmates working on commutation and clemency issues. They hosted a game night, with card and board games available to play. They started a reading group where inmates read and discussed classical literature. They sponsored a 5K-run fundraiser for the benefit of a shelter for victims of domestic violence in the community.

Every year, they requested the opportunity to strengthen family connections by sponsoring an event where family members could meet other inmates and their family members. They planned it for school vacation week in April, so children, nieces, nephews, and grandchildren could attend and meet other kids with incarcerated relatives.

Visitors of inmates doing a life sentence tend to drop off after their first five years of incarceration, with many only having telephone contact with their families after that. EGL wanted to address that estrangement, but each year the institution denied their requests. Finally, in 2025, EGL sponsored the first "Family Reunification" event for inmates serving life sentences ever in Massachusetts. They had a party with food and beverages, a photographer to take family photos, music, and other entertainment. It was a huge success, and several inmates were able to connect with extended family they barely knew and who now visit them regularly.

EGL has a membership of 104 lifers at NCCI-Gardner with an average of 70% of members participating regularly in their weekly events. EGL has a Facebook presence which describes them as "a self-help group committed to personal growth, accountability, and transformation. Through remorse and self-awareness, we strive to achieve a true understanding of how to live a restorative lifestyle. We believe that meaningful reform begins within—change must be self-seeking and rooted in personal responsibility. Although we operate with limited resources, our commitment to rehabilitation and positive change is strong. We actively seek partnerships and outside resources to help meet the needs of those dedicated to rebuilding their lives."[210]

Eddie has filed a total of eight civil complaints *pro se*, beginning in 2010 when he was at Norfolk Prison. He currently has four open cases with the Department of Corrections, two concerning his work with EGL and retaliatory actions that he alleges were taken against him and the group for filing these lawsuits, and the two consolidated cases regarding visitation rights. He has become the go-to jailhouse lawyer for many inmates seeking advice. His legal skills are quite impressive, and again, all self-taught.

In 2023 Eddie filed a class-action lawsuit on behalf of all inmates regarding programs that the Department of Corrections appeared to offer inmates, but in fact were not providing to them. The class action suit was stayed by the court, so that the parties might settle their differences about these programs. This controversy regarding the Department's deceptive programming, however, was aired on the CBS-Boston television station. Cheryl Fiandaca, the chief investigative reporter and executive editor for WBZ-TV's I-Team, did two shows on the subject.

Thereafter, Eddie applied for admission to the Culinary Arts Program. His application was denied. He had already cleared his attendance with the teacher, who told him a week before that he was on the list and had the right security

---

210 From the EGL Facebook page description of the group.

clearance to attend. Eddie filed an appeal of this decision. The denial was upheld on the grounds that he was already enrolled in an educational program (the college degree program) and he couldn't be enrolled in both an educational and a vocational program at the same time. There is no such regulation prohibiting this, and many inmates participate in both programs, so Eddie re-applied for admission to the program. The second time he was denied because he lacked the appropriate security clearance.

The Department of Corrections frowns upon inmates filing lawsuits and exposing them to the scrutiny of the court. Eddie's advocacy via the judicial system came at a price to him that affects his day-to-day life at Gardner.

Last year, Eddie was suddenly and inexplicably fired from his job in the weight room in the gym by a subordinate employee of Recreation Officer, Jorge Colon. He requested an appeal of that firing, claiming that Mr. Colon was subjecting him to harassment and retaliation for filing his latest lawsuit. Eddie prevailed, and Colon's actions were deemed harassing and retaliatory for Eddie's legal activities. Eddie's job was reinstated.

Other inmates reported that the head of the Recreation Department, Clemente Rivera, was furious that Eddie got his job back and told them that he was now coming for Eddie. Shortly after that, Eddie's request to join the Alternatives to Violence Program (AVP) was denied. He requested a review of that denial, claiming it was harassment and in retaliation for winning his job back.

This time, the administration found that this was not the result of harassment or retaliation: Eddie had simply not been chosen for this program. At the time, however, there were slots available for the program—and no one else who applied was denied admission.

In the summer of 2025, Eddie's *pro bono* lawyers in the

visitation lawsuit were able to depose Richard Morales, the Director of Security at NCCI Garner. Eddie believes that the harassment became more frequent after that, especially with regard to the EGL group. Officers refused to make photocopies for the group or to provide basic materials that any group needs to run a program. When EGL had their Family Reunification Event recently, there was plenty of food and soda left over. The food and beverages had been paid for and provided by the families and friends of the EGL inmates. Since inmates are prohibited from taking any food or beverages back to their tiers, the group decided to use the food to feed the inmates who set up and break down the room for events, who would arrive shortly to clean the room. The guards agreed. However, several inmates saw Clemente Rivera and other correctional officers filling bags with food and drinks and removing them from the room before the clean-up crew arrived.

These actions seem petty because they are petty. In prison, however, petty injustices often can become major problems between inmates and guards, who constantly remind the inmates that the guards have all the power, and the prisoners have none. When petty injustices add up day by day, week by week, month by month, one more petty injustice can turn into tinderbox of resentment, ready to blow up. Massachusetts has weathered four major prisoner uprisings from 1955 to 2017. The most notable recent disturbance within the Massachusetts prison system occurred in September 2024, at the maximum-security Souza-Baranowski Correctional Center. The "max" is now closed.

Eddie was most recently denied admission to the Project Wakeup Program, where inmates speak to emerging adults about life in prison. This is now the third program the administration has denied him in the last two years.

Eddie is planning to file another class action suit

regarding programming this summer.

*Eddie was the speaker for his graduation class*

*Eddie and his parents Ed and Trish O'Brien*

# THE PAROLE BOARD EXPERIENCE

In 2012, the United States Supreme Court struck down mandatory life imprisonment without the possibility of parole for juveniles (offenders between the ages of 14 and 17 at the time of the crime) for violating the Eighth Amendment to the United States Constitution prohibiting cruel and unusual punishment.[211] Their decision was based in part on the "mitigating qualities of youth."[212]

In 2014, the Massachusetts Supreme Judicial Court declared that sentencing a juvenile to life without parole under any circumstances would violate Article 26 of the Massachusetts Declaration of Rights.[213]

The court determined that juveniles must be granted a "meaningful opportunity to obtain release based on demonstrated maturity and rehabilitation." The parole board's mandate is to evaluate the circumstances surrounding the commission of the crime, including the age of the offender, together with all relevant information pertaining to the offender's character and actions during the intervening years since conviction.

Eddie O'Brien was re-sentenced after the U.S. Supreme

---

211 Eighth Amendment (1791). Excessive bail shall not be required, nor excessive fines imposed, nor cruel and unusual punishments inflicted.

212 *Miller vs. Alabama*, 567 U.S. 460 (2012)

213 Article 26 (1780) No magistrate or court of law, shall demand excessive bail or sureties, impose excessive fines, or inflict cruel or unusual punishments. *Diatchenko vs. District Attorney for Suffolk County,* 471 Mass. 12 (2014.)

Court declared that life without the possibility of parole for offenses committed prior to age 17 violated the Eighth Amendment in the *Miller* case. His sentence is now life with the possibility of parole after 15 years served. Because he had already served 22 years by then, he was immediately eligible for parole. But Eddie waived his first two hearings and didn't request one until 2024. To understand why, you must understand how the parole process works in Massachusetts.

The parole board in Massachusetts requires inmates to demonstrate rehabilitation and insight into the reasons for their criminal behavior. Historically, maintaining innocence has been a barrier to parole, as the board views a refusal to admit guilt as a lack of remorse or accountability. Without an admission of guilt, they claim that they cannot assess the level of insight the inmate has regarding their criminal behavior and what led them to commit the crime—which begs the question for wrongfully convicted inmates. The board has created a Gordian knot for those asserting innocence. There is no policy or written procedure offering an alternative to the inmate asserting innocence.

In 2024, the Massachusetts Supreme Judicial Court extended the age of offenders protected by Article 26 to those between 14 and 20 years old at the time of the crime. The court referred to those between 17 and 20 years of age as "emerging adults."[214]

Since 2024, the parole board has released 44 "emerging adults" from prisons in Massachusetts. These "emerging adults" were between the ages of 17 and 20 when they committed the crime for which they were serving the life sentence and were originally sentenced to life without parole. They later became eligible for release pursuant to the Supreme Judicial Court ruling in *Mattis* in 2024. Only one of them claimed innocence; 43 admitted guilt, expressed

---

214 *Commonwealth v. Mattis* 493 Mass. 216 (2024)

remorse, exhibited insight into their criminal behavior and reasons therefor, and embarked on a program of successful rehabilitation. They were released.

Eddie didn't request a parole hearing during the 14 years when he was eligible to go before the board because he did not murder Janet Downing. He cannot and will not admit to a crime he did not commit. He has maintained his innocence since his arrest in July 1995, and never once has he wavered from that position. Even if he was guaranteed he would be paroled if he admitted to this crime, Eddie could not and would not do so. It goes against everything he believes about honor and truth. He would prefer to spend as many years as it takes in prison fighting for an opportunity to prove he is not a murderer.

In 2024, Kevin Francis became the first inmate to be paroled and released while steadfastly claiming his innocence. Kevin and Eddie were friendly in prison. Kevin's case gave Eddie some hope that the there was a possibility that the board would recognize, through his achievements educationally, his work with other inmates and his behavior while incarcerated, that he didn't pose a danger to society if released, even though he denied committing the crime. Prior to Kevin Francis's case, Eddie knew there was no relief for him in the parole process.

Kevin Francis was granted parole at his first parole hearing after 43 years of incarceration. In 1981, he was convicted of the first-degree stabbing murder of his ex-girlfriend. He was 20 years old. He steadfastly maintained his innocence since his arrest. His case was far less complex than Eddie's; the only evidence tying him to the crime was the testimony of two eyewitnesses who said they saw him running after the victim with a knife in his hand. In other words, the case was completely circumstantial.

Eddie's lawyers agreed with him that a parole hearing

was an opportunity he should not waive again for another five years. He had nothing to lose, and everything to potentially gain. The process of preparing for a parole hearing afforded him the opportunity to gather much evidence that he would need when the Superior Court heard his Motion for a New Trial, which was being prepared by his appellate lawyers as he sat at the parole hearing in June 2024. All he has ever wanted was an even playing field and the chance to prove his innocence.

For the parole petition, Eddie needed to have a forensic psychologist evaluate him and his risk of reoffending (otherwise known as a risk/needs assessment). He had to secure employment. He had to work with a social worker to find appropriate community-based programs that he could participate in as part of his parole, and locate a community to move into. Eddie has earned scores of certificates of completion for programs he has participated in while incarcerated that needed to be documented in his parole petition.

He has always taken advantage of every opportunity to earn college credits, participate in enrichment programs, and complete goal-oriented courses for his emotional growth. Eddie has always participated in religious activities. He made his Confirmation while at Walpole Prison, Cardinal Bernard Law presiding. Eddie worked closely with Attorney Jack Cunha, who specializes in parole hearings, to decide how best to present his case for innocence, and all of the "rehabilitative" work he had done while incarcerated. Attorney Cunha submitted a lengthy petition that took months to write. They gathered letters of support.

Eddie had not seen Ryan and Paul Downing for 29 years, making this their first face-to-face contact in nearly three decades. They, too, would have an opportunity to speak to the board.

The district attorney opposed Eddie's request for parole. The opposition is required to submit its argument against paroling the inmate with all of its supporting documentation, days before the hearing so all parties can properly prepare. The DA had not done that, so Eddie's attorney had no information about the substance of their objections.

So, how did the hearing go? In a word, not at all the way it is supposed to go. It became yet another hearing where Eddie seemed to be subjected to unspoken rules that only applied to him and not other inmates seeking parole.

Substantive and procedural errors permeated the hearing. Tonomey Coleman,[215] a board member since 2013, read from the report of FBI profiler Gregg McCrary, hired by Tom Reilly in 1996 to build the motive for the crime which Reilly admittedly hadn't been able to determine. Gregg McCrary didn't testify at trial and his report wasn't included in the trial record. It was not evidence and played no part in the conviction of Eddie O'Brien. In my opinion, this was improper and highly irregular in a parole hearing for a number of reasons.

Procedurally, the board only looks at the evidence from the trial record and the Supreme Judicial Court's decision upholding the conviction when assessing an inmate's readiness for parole. Tonomey Coleman continued to read verbatim and at length from reports and mere allegations that were part of a juvenile transfer hearing but never evidence that was presented at the trial in 1997. By all standards, this material was irrelevant to this hearing. At the very least, Eddie's lawyer should have been notified that the board intended to go outside the official record when they questioned Eddie. It would have been helpful if they had named these documents which were not part of the official

215 Tonomey Coleman was appointed to the board in 2013. He was appointed by Governor Healy to a District Court Judgeship in 2025.

record that may be used at the hearing.

It was an ambush, but one that Eddie handled with intelligence and candor. He showed no animosity toward Mr. Coleman, although he knew Coleman's behavior was improper and meant to arouse Eddie's anger. He was unsuccessful in his attempt to irritate Eddie. Eddie's responses were truthful, forthright, and polite, evidence of the truly mature man who knew not to take the bait.

Three days after the hearing, the Commonwealth provided his defense counsel with the brief and argument that was supposed to be provided *before* the hearing. This contained the reports and allegations that were not part of the official record Coleman had been reading from. Clearly, the DA's office believed their case against Eddie was so weak that they reverted to 29-year-old documents that had played no part in Eddie's conviction. Eddie and his counsel filed an appeal of the parole board's decision based on these irregularities. In an initial victory, on March 22, 2026, the presiding judge permitted Eddie's counsel to expand the record on appeal to include the instructions developed by the parole board for inmates claiming innocence that were only available on inmates' state-issued tablets. They are not written in the official regulations or even in an informational pamphlet.

The board itself hadn't followed those instructions and, because they were digital, there was no way to reference them in the brief. They were also permitted to add a very recent case wherein the parole board had released a man convicted of first-degree murder, who admitted he had instigated the argument and was *among* the group who stabbed a man to death. Attorney Cunha is in the process of preparing the addendum to his petition, and then the Commonwealth will have a certain time to respond. There is no way to predict just how long it will take the board to make a decision on this appeal. Eddie's next parole hearing is scheduled for June 2027. Hopefully, the board's decision will be issued before then.

At the hearing, the board focused much attention on Eddie's disciplinary action for possessing a cell phone while at Norfolk Prison in 2013, which resulted in his transfer to the supermax for a period of five years.

Although it is a well-known fact to those involved in the criminal justice system, I will state for the reader that inmates regularly buy cell phones on the black market in prison. Overwhelmingly, such "contraband" is purchased from correctional officers who bring these items into the prison, where they make a hefty profit on them. A little flip phone burner costs up to $400.00 in prison, and $29.00 on the street. The correctional officers who sell these phones are rarely punished. Inmates are punished with two weeks in the SHU (Special Housing Unit) or "hole" as it is known in prison. Other inmates have been sent to maximum security prisons, as Eddie was. Inmates who name the officer who sold the phone are rare because that makes them not only a "rat" among their peers, but a target for retribution by the guards.

Eddie underwent yet another psychological evaluation, including an assessment of the level of risk he would pose to the general public if released. Dr. Robert Kinscherff, PhD, Esq., who had testified against Eddie at the transfer hearings in 1996. He now submitted a report in favor of Eddie's parole, stating: "There is a strong likelihood if paroled that Mr. O'Brien would live and remain at liberty without violating the law." (Report of Forensic Evaluation, June 16, 2024).

Dr. Kinscherff's clinical assessment was that Eddie did not exhibit any disturbances of thought, emotion, affect or memory, had never been psychiatrically hospitalized, was not on any medication, and had no episodes of substance misuse or need for substance treatment. Eddie's profile was devoid of personality features suggesting any personality disorder.

His risk assessment score placed Eddie at the *lowest* 2.3% among incarcerated males. Dr. Kinscherff went so far as to say that "even if his denial of perpetrating this crime is inaccurate," he "has substantively avoided and/or addressed any criminogenic risk-needs." Eddie's successful employment, educational level beyond 12 years, absence of a history of substance abuse or gang affiliation "all indicate that he is a strong candidate for parole from both a risk-management and recidivism risk perspective… He has achieved the standard indicator for rehabilitation; there is little to suggest that he needs further incarceration." (Report of Forensic Evaluation, June 16, 2024).

*Eddie before the parole board*

# WHATEVER HAPPENED TO ARTIE ORTIZ?

At the time of the murder, Artie Ortiz was Janet Downing's brother-in-law, married to her younger sister Carol. Carol, Artie, and their young son AJ lived with Janet Downing and her family for almost a year before Janet threw them out of the house because Artie was dealing drugs out of her basement.

This is what Janet told her friend, Mary Pereira,[216] and Gina Mahoney, the neighbor with whom Janet spent the last nine hours of her life. Janet told her friends about strange things that had been happening to her and her fear that Artie was essentially stalking and scaring her. You might recall that Janet was emphatic that Sunday afternoon, July 23, 1995, that should anything happen to her, to make sure that the police "investigate, investigate, investigate," even if her death looked like suicide. She would never hurt herself and she truly believed she was in danger.

Artie vacated the house (with his wife and son) but refused to return the housekeys to Janet. Gina Mahoney told Janet Downing that she saw Artie at the house almost daily while Janet was at work.

Artie has remained at the center of any publicity, news articles, social media, or event that concerns Eddie O'Brien, the O'Brien family, my book, or me. When asked why he continues to insert himself publicly in matters concerning Eddie O'Brien, he insists that he has been dragged into this

216 The police report made at the time of the homicide investigation incorrectly recorded her name as "Mary "Reveira."

case for 30 years, and he is doing what he needs to do to defend his name.

Artie started calling me directly. He was upset that his side of the story had never been told. I suggested that he talk with Eddie's attorneys, who would be very interested in what he had to say. He did call Charlotte Whitmore, the head of the Innocence Program at Boston College Law School, which was reviewing the case at the time. What Artie told Attorney Whitmore was consistent with what he had been writing and saying online—that the O'Briens were looking for someone to blame, Gina Mahoney was lying, the book was filled with lies, and essentially he was the only person in the entire satellite of people surrounding this case who was telling the truth.

A favorable review of *The Politics of Murder* was published in a local Somerville newspaper in January 2017, about two months after its release. Artie contributed several rebuttals to the review, personally attacked me as the author, and made statements about Eddie's guilt and his desire to see Eddie "rot in prison."

To this day, Artie continues to return to that article to post renewed denials of his involvement in the crime, even though the article is (as of this writing) nine years old and no one but him continues to write responses.

Perhaps his being blocked from social media sites has led him to continue to vent in this one publication; there were many other reviews of the book in other places to which he didn't respond. I had to block him (and his many other monikers) from the comments page of WildBlue Press, my publisher, because his posts offered little but insults about people who liked the book and assertions about my untruthfulness.

Here is a sample (unedited for spelling, grammar, or language):

*Stone cold murderer, this is a perfect case why Massachusetts needs the death penalty back in law, Politics didn't murder this women, Eddie O'Brien did stop trying to deflect his Guilt with politics...murderer*

*I am the brother in law what they think have they are dead wrong rot in hell Eddie*

*You people can't handle the truth Eddie killed her and you all know it I am no punching bag he will rot in hell dirt bag.*

*So giving blood ,fingerprints, hair, and being interviewed by the state police was not enough, your boy Eddie is a cold blooded murderer, an your old lady is nothing but lair*[217] *trying to help free a murderer, who should be charged with perjury ..... know the true facts not a book of misleading assumptions , hearsay & lies, anyone can write a book an print what they like, but the proof is in the pudding, yum*

*This kids is a cold blooded murderer politics didn't kill this victim Eddie Obrien did, politics didn't pick up the knife an stab the victim 90 times Eddie Obrien did, you have the balls saying this kid was over charged, 1st degree murder fits this crime an he was convicted on all counts justice fit the crime, Margo Nash you have nothing but blood money in your hands, shame on people like you looking to make a buck off a murder case as vicious as this, this family & lawyers are a disgrace to our Court System, He'll answer for his crime by God Almighty himself...*

*Open your pages you cowards, you scared people will hear the truth, your nothing but cowards you started this, you brought an innocent person into your family's darma, we will not go away, you hide down the Cape with your bull crap social readings come up here, your just cowards the whole bunch of you, you want to accuse an innocent person*

217 No matter what name or moniker Artie was using, I would know it was him because he always misspelled liar this way.

*of a crime he had nothing to do with but yet your scared to face them, why ? Cause your running from the truth*

*...but he's not he'll be locked up for life, enjoy your visits, out peace*

*Margo Nash your a classic lair, you think anyone believes a word you say , I'll post my thoughts on any forum post you write in, I'll be right behind you any time you post another lie about our family, I don't need anyone to tell me what to write or to whom, you scumbags started this remember that, for someone that claims to be lawyer you got to be one of the stupidest lawyers around, are you people just taught to lie do you have any morals what so ever, you defend a sociopath murderer whom you know is guilty as all hell, shame on you it's all about the money $$ your just being paid to be the scum you are, open your page i have no problem putting my name stamp on any post i write ( stop blocking me ) you'll never do it your to scared of people hearing the truth, why you preventing people from our side of the story, your all cowards, come on let's debate this you coward, enjoy your jail visits remember life with our parole will stand till he's rolled out of there .... thank you*

*May 25, 2024: Margo, the only support you have is from a bunch of lairs. How are you even wrote this book about what you call the truth you Gina Mahoney and O'Brien seem to get the shit together and figure out the truth and nobody has ever asked me anything about this or my story so I'm not hiding. I never will hide so you can keep hiding your Bri can keep hiding Gina keep hiding, cause you ain't got shit on me.*

The O'Brien family had to block Artie after he repeatedly posted inappropriate comments on Eddie's three sisters' social media accounts.

In August 2020, Artie was interviewed on the podcast

True Crime Garage after it aired a three-part show, called *Trail of Blood,* about the O'Brien case. I wasn't contacted, nor did I or anyone in the O'Brien family participate in—or even know about—this show until Artie's comments surfaced. The host explained that Artie had reached out to them about the podcast and wanted to comment on several things that he believed were untrue in *Trail of Blood.*

Artie sounded as if he was weeping when he talked about how deeply the accusations about him had affected him. Although he was now divorced from Carol, he said he remained friends with her and the entire Downing and Solimene (Janet's maiden name) families.

He made a point of saying that his ex-wife had asked him why he kept talking about this case publicly, and he had told her that he needed to talk about it: "I feel good about this."[218]

Artie is now divorced. He is the father of A.J. and Ashleigh, his children with Carol Ortiz, and the father of Michael and Kerry, his children with his brother's wife, Anne Marie.

Michael, Kerry, and their mother Anne Marie are now all deceased.

218 https://truecrimegarage.com/blogs/true-crime-garage/posts/6410783/off-the-record-episode-103

# THE PODCAST

The second Karen Read trial, which began on April 22, 2025, became—quite inadvertently—a catalyst for Eddie's case. That case highlighted the same questions about corruption, deception, and politics in the judicial system that Eddie's case had raised 30 years ago. Nationally, people were following the day-to-day televised trial and watching the local news to see the next outrageous development in the plot. I must admit that every day of that trial, I felt hope that people would now see and believe what I had been trying to expose 10 years ago about the corruption of justice in Eddie's case.

Eddie's parents and siblings had over the years become faithful participants at every Innocence Project and/or wrongful conviction fundraiser, rally, march, and exoneration hearing. They have connected with a whole network of people similarly committed to overturning wrongful convictions, including the woman who posted to her Facebook page a photo of my book with the comment, "If you think the Karen Read case was corrupt, you've got to read Margo Nash's book." Cherie Lee is a professional photographer for the Harriet Tubman Project and other events that Eddie's family attend. I had no idea who she was or what she did, but I could not have been more thankful to her for connecting these two cases on such a public forum. That one gesture turned a spotlight on the Eddie O'Brien case.

Suddenly, Eddie's family and I were contacted by a podcast that streamed on YouTube. The O'Briens and I talked about this development and asked Eddie whether we should appear on the podcast. My inclination was to stay independent of it (mostly because I didn't understand what "streaming podcast" meant, not being myself a YouTuber).

The O'Briens had been blindsided too many times by mainstream media to fall for another opportunity they expected to be positive before turning to public shaming and vilification of their family and son. But Eddie pushed us to accept invitations to the show. We collectively agreed that I would go first, and—if I didn't get slaughtered—the O'Briens would go next.

Streaming podcasts are live online events in which one or more hosts promote discussions about a topic. They interview people involved in the subject matter and discuss the cases in detail, while the podcast audience comments and asks questions via the live chat function.

In true-crime podcasts, guest speakers are sometimes those immediately involved in the case who can give insights and details unknown to the public, exploring alternative interpretations or options, proposing alternate theories of the crime or scenarios surrounding the crime, and trying to get to the truth of what really happened. Several streaming podcasts emerged during the "Free Karen Read" or "Justice for Karen" movement, focusing on that case, or on the characters involved in the case, the local police, and the State Police Crime Lab.

So, in early November of 2025, I appeared as a guest on the show. The audience greeted me with a lot of enthusiasm, anxious to hear about the case. The live chat was going on while I was being interviewed, but I couldn't look at that and think about what I was saying at the same time. I remember logging off and waiting to hear from our network of friends and family whether the responses had been positive or negative in the chat. I was told that the response was overwhelmingly positive.

Eddie obviously couldn't watch it or listen to it, but he *always* knows things before I do. He called to thank me. I swear there is an invisible direct line from the outside world to inside the walls that is far faster and more accurate than the Internet.

The O'Briens appeared the following night. The show was interested in interviewing anyone who had anything to say about the case.

The hosts didn't take any positions on guilt or innocence. They saw themselves as facilitating a discussion; at least that was the stated intention. It is difficult with this particular case not to take a position one way or the other on Eddie's guilt or innocence. As the shows progressed, certain hosts did express personal opinions of innocence. The audience was totally supporting Eddie's innocence. One host began to raise doubts he had about certain aspects of the case in the name of "playing devil's advocate." After several months, and I'm not clear why, being the devil's advocate turned into speculating about what may have happened, that had no basis in fact. I once felt compelled to call into the show because the discussion centered around a scenario that had been completely disproven at trial. Playing devil's advocate is fine, but you must base your position on some identifiable facts in the case.

Eddie's mugging in Union Square, immediately after finding his best friend's mother stabbed to death on her dining room floor, was extremely hard for them to accept. I couldn't agree more. It was always—and continues to be—difficult to believe that a 15-year-old kid could stumble into a murder scene, only to run out of there and get mugged within the same hour.

Imagine trying to convince 12 people this really did happen.

For Eddie, the mugging is just another "you just can't

make this stuff up" part of his whole story involving the events surrounding his arrest for the murder of Janet Downing. When Eddie and I were discussing the book and got to this part back in 2015, his response to me was, "Margo, don't you think that I could have put together a better story in the 20 years I've had to think through this? I understand how hard it is to believe, but it's the only story I have... because that's what happened to me."

Artie Ortiz chose to be interviewed next by audio only, so the audience couldn't see his face. He explained that he was Janet Downing's brother-in-law and that he had been there the night of the murder because his wife called his dispatcher (he was a cab driver) and told him to call home. When he called his wife Carol, she told him to "get to Janet. Something happened." He said the time was about 9:45 p.m. and he was at the Peter Pan bus station in downtown Boston. He drove directly to 71 Hamlet Street in Somerville, arriving at about 10:00 p.m. This version already deviates from previous statements he has made over the years, including that his dispatcher called him to tell him his sister-in-law had been murdered.

When asked how his wife knew about the incident, he said he didn't know but would ask her. The following day, he came back on the show and said he did ask his wife, and she said Janet's oldest daughter Kerriann—who had not lived with her mother in several years—called and told her. There is nothing in the police reports or neighbor interviews that showed that Kerriann was at the house that night, which raises the obvious question, *how did Kerriann know?*

The notable change in Artie's story now was that he learned about Janet at 9:45 p.m., which was clearly about 15 minutes *before* Janet was discovered by her son Ryan and the police were called. That also means that Carol was called by Kerriann Downing well *before* Ryan discovered his mother's body and *before* the police were notified.

The second disturbing fact in this scenario is that Janet's daughter somehow knew her mother was seriously injured, and rather than calling the police for a wellness check, she called her aunt, who also didn't call the police. Carol called Artie, who was driving his cab, and waited for him to stop and call her back. (There weren't any cell phones in 1995; he had to find a pay phone to make the call.)

Either Kerriann or Carol could have called the police and had EMTs there in minutes.

The police, EMT, and hospital records indicate that the police dispatcher received the call at about 9:55 p.m. and initially dispatched patrol cars at that time. First responders, fire trucks, and ambulances arrived at 10:05 p.m., blocking the streets and any vehicles parked on or around the corner of Boston Street and Hamlet Street. Artie claimed that, when he arrived, there were no ambulances, and that Janet had already been removed from the home to Massachusetts General Hospital. Documented records show that Janet Downing was first attended by EMTs while on the dining room floor. The scene was littered with medical debris. At 10:22 p.m., she was transported 2.9 miles by ambulance to the hospital, where she arrived with no signs of life. She was pronounced dead at M.G.H. at 10:39 p.m.

Witnesses reported that Artie's cab was blocked in by fire trucks and EMT trucks and police vehicles. He has always denied that. However, on November 7, 2025, Artie said he *did* see fire engines, police cars, and EMT vehicles. The same vehicles Artie now admits seeing were the very same ones that blocked him in and made the streets unpassable. In order to have been blocked in by emergency vehicles, Artie's cab had to have been there *before* any first responders arrived. If he had arrived after the first responders, he would not have been able to park at the curb next to Janet's house on Hamlet Street, because those vehicles were blocking all parking spaces.

Janet was most certainly in the house when Artie arrived.

Artie told the podcasters that he tried to get into the house but was prohibited by the police. That was the first time I ever heard that. His prior accounts never included an attempt to enter the house. He said his concern was primarily for his nephews Paul and Ryan, so he walked across the front lawn to talk to Ryan, who was seated in a police car in the driveway, sobbing. Artie then went to Gina Mahoney's front porch, directly across the street from Janet's house, where he went upstairs to 16-year-old Danni's bedroom and smoked a joint with her.

You may remember from Chapter Four that Gina Mahoney was quite clear about Artie's arrival at the scene. She describes Artie coming from Hamlet Street near his cab, which was parked the wrong way on the left side of the street beside Janet's house. His cab was blocked in by emergency vehicles. He walked over to Gina's house, and she reported he looked like he had just taken a shower. Everyone else was hot, sweaty, and bedraggled from days of record heat. He looked fresh and cool.

Artie's story changed every day he was interviewed on the podcast. Already I had learned about a new timeline that conflicted with the facts in the record, and Artie was admitting that he learned about the assault before Ryan discovered Janet on the dining room floor. I now tried to incorporate the fact that Carol Ortiz and Kerriann Downing apparently knew about Janet before 9:45 p.m. In this version, Kerriann and Carol never called the police to get help. Artie also didn't call the police when he was told about the attack even though he wouldn't be able to arrive sooner than a 911 emergency vehicle could.

Where was the "tell" in this latest version of the story?

It was inserting Kerriann into the narrative, when she had never been mentioned before anywhere, by anyone. In this new version, Kerriann called Carol Ortiz, and Carol called the cab company. This would mean that Kerriann was the first Downing child to know something had happened to her mother that night, not Ryan, who came home on rollerblades at about 9:55 p.m. Was Kerriann there at the house? Did she see her mother? How else would she know Janet was injured and needed help? More importantly, why would she call Carol Ortiz—and not the police?

I remembered a telephone call I got shortly after the book was published in 2016.

A private detective called me to tell me about an investigation he did into Kerriann's boyfriend in 1997. I will call the boyfriend M.L. The investigator said that M.L. and Kerriann were in a romantic relationship, but that they had broken up approximately three weeks prior to the 1997 interview. M.L. had known Kerriann since 1990 when he was 20 years old and she was just 16; he knew Janet Downing because Janet had come to his house with the police to take Kerriann out of his apartment and to bring her back home after she had been missing for a few days in 1990. Their relationship seemed to be on and off for the next seven years.

The investigator told me that he discovered between 12 to 24 old letters on M.L.'s computer addressed to Janet Downing. Some of the letters threatened to kill her. Others stated that Janet deserved to die, deserved to be stabbed, etc. The detective interviewed M.L. three times over the course of a week in 1997, two years after the murder. M.L. told the investigator that he kept these letters so that he could keep this in his memory "so I can confess my sins if I ever go to confession." The investigator told me that he called Bob George, Eddie's attorney, to alert him that someone should look at M.L. as a suspect in the murder, but Bob George never returned his call.

M.L. has a long history of substance abuse and serious mental health issues; he has been psychiatrically hospitalized on numerous occasions. Over the past 10 years, based on this tip, I have had other investigators go to his residence to talk with him, but none of them were able to make direct contact. M.L.'s mother told each of the investigators her son was hospitalized on the three occasions they came to her house. Until recently, M.L. had lived—since childhood—in the same multifamily home in Somerville owned by his mother, a house that is approximately three blocks from the Downing house, going straight down Hamlet Street to the other side of the McGrath Highway.

The podcast contacted M.L. within 24 hours of my sharing this tip with one of the hosts. M.L. came onto the show voluntarily and was extremely cooperative in sharing information. His information wasn't always accurate; he very much wanted to place his age at 18 when he dated 16-year-old Kerriann. He repeated several times that the police told him he had done nothing wrong, because Kerriann was of the age of consent.

He claimed his relationship with her ended in 1990, right after Janet and the police came to his home to remove Kerriann. He had previously told the investigator it ended in 1997. M.L. clarified to the podcast audience that they had seen each other now and then over the years, and that their last contact was recent—within the last two years, he said—when Kerriann was stabbed, apparently for being in the wrong place at the wrong time. He denied that he had ever written the letters to Janet Downing or shared his writings with the former PI in 1997. He agreed that he often wrote his thoughts down on paper.

At the time of M.L.'s interviews in 1997, Eddie was in the middle of his second transfer hearing. The investigator asked M.L. about his knowledge of Eddie's case. M.L. knew the case, knew of Eddie, and identified with him because they were both on trial for something. When asked who he thought might have killed Janet, he said maybe her ex-husband. M.L. then said he thought the Commonwealth was guilty, not Eddie. He didn't further explain what he meant.

When M.L. was interviewed for the podcast in November of 2025, he was homeless and living under the McGrath O'Brien Highway, which is where the interview took place. His mother passed away a few years ago and the family home was sold; M.L. found himself homeless and panhandling for cigarettes and food. He spontaneously stated that he was sober and taking his medication regularly. He hoped to be housed in the next few weeks with assistance from a state program.

I'm convinced there is a reason Artie introduced Kerriann into the Janet's death narrative. I now knew that she had an ongoing relationship with M.L. before and after her mother's murder. I had always known how close his house was to 71 Hamlet Street, and that he could walk there in five minutes. I knew from the investigator that he had a long history of violent criminal behavior. I learned through the podcast that his most recent arrest in 2023 involved violence.

I had already heard about Kerriann's problematic relationship with her mother from Gina Mahoney years ago. Both M.L. and Kerriann had documented histories of alcohol and drug abuse, and M.L. characterized their relationship as based on drinking and sex.

There was sufficient information from multiple sources that Artie Ortiz was selling drugs out of the basement of 71 Hamlet Street to the neighborhood kids. Both Kerriann and M.L. have struggled with drug dependance or addiction. The basement door was wide open the night of the murder and again, several sources said that Artie's vehicle was already parked at the house that night before the first responders arrived. There are just too many "what ifs" created by this convergence of details to rule it out as a possibility.

What if Kerriann and M.L. were in the basement buying some drugs from Artie while Janet slept upstairs? Did they suddenly hear someone coming down the stairs as if they were falling? Did they hear the door close as Paul then exited the house? Did they go upstairs to investigate?

Or did they see and talk with Paul that night? Did Paul and Janet have another fight? Did Paul push his mother down the stairs? Did Artie, M.L., and Kerriann come upstairs when Paul pushed his mother? Did Janet threaten to call the police? Did she threaten to have Paul removed to foster care as she had threatened the day before, as she had done with Kerriann? Did Artie, Kerriann, and M.L. panic and further subdue Janet? Did they call someone to help them?

There is one more question that needs to be added to this list: Why did M.L.'s brother commit suicide on July 23, 2001, on the six-year anniversary of Janet Downing's murder?

# FURTHER REVELATIONS FROM ARTIE AND THE PODCAST

Artie continued to interact with the podcasters on the show live. He told the audience that he did enter the crime scene about three to four hours later (2:00 to 3:00 in the morning) on July 24, 1995 "to get the kittens and the kitty litter box." This was a revelation to me.

There were no cats in that house.

Janet's autopsy showed she had something labeled by Robert Pino of the State Crime Lab "feline hairs" on her body and in her hand; he collected them from the scene the night of the murder. But where did these feline hairs come from? Janet didn't have a cat, and neither did Eddie O'Brien's family. For the first time in 30 years, Artie was introducing cats to the narrative of Janet's murder when it was a huge unanswered inquiry at the time of the murder. Again, all my alarms went off. Why was he doing this now? There had to be a reason.

I told the podcasters there were no cats in the home and that this was the first time anyone had ever mentioned this in 30 years. They pushed Artie on his statement, and he returned the following day and admitted he had fabricated the story of the kittens "to see how the podcasters would run with it." Having destroyed his own credibility, Artie became "third-party Artie," the third-party culprit[219] who may have murdered his sister-in-law by admitting he had seen the crime scene and wouldn't wish "anyone to see what I saw that night."

The narrative only got worse, as Artie tried to redeem his credibility by saying he actually went in the next day during the daytime to get the dog food. (The Downings did have a dog.) But in trying to understand where the dog was taken that night, and who had asked him to retrieve the dog food, this story also quickly fell apart, and he went back to the kitty litter story again.

Artie boasted, "I've never been arrested in my life," causing them to investigate this assertion. They learned that this was not only untrue, but that his criminal record reflected domestic violence he had perpetrated on Carol Ortiz, his wife.

The truth of what happened between Artie and Carol is that in March 2005, 10 years after her sister was murdered, Artie threatened Carol with a kitchen knife, prevented her from calling the police, and held her against her will. Carol screamed from a window and asked someone to call the police. The abuse had been ongoing throughout their 16-year marriage, according to Judge Leilah Keamy, who presided over their divorce. Carol obtained a restraining order against Artie on March 9, 2005, in the Malden District Court.

That restraining order was in effect for over two years. Artie violated the restraining order by parking outside Carol's residence and yelling at her, continuing to threaten her, and placing her in fear of imminent physical harm. According to the judge's findings, the children witnessed the kitchen knife incident as well as other incidents of their father's violent

219 Third-party culprit evidence—evidence that someone else committed the crime charged, or had the motive, intent, and opportunity to do so. Massachusetts Guide to Evidence, Section 1105.

outbursts.

Artie was ordered to complete a state-certified batterer's treatment program, to participate in weekly drug and alcohol counseling sessions with a licensed therapist, and to complete random drug screens for no less than six consecutive months in order to petition the court for visitation with his two minor children. As of May 3, 2006, the judge found him in arrears on his court-ordered child support by $1,425.73. He was currently unemployed, having been fired from his job at Home Depot for violation of the employer's substance-abuse policy.

Carol Ortiz was granted a divorce on the grounds of cruel and abusive treatment by Aristides Ortiz and granted sole legal and physical custody of the children.

I saw Carol and Artie at Eddie O'Brien's parole hearing. They didn't speak. Carol stayed a long distance from Artie the entire time we waited to be admitted to the building, and they certainly did not appear to be "friendly" in 2024, despite what Artie told the podcast audience.

Artie's insistence on continuing to comment on social media, to call in to radio shows and podcasts where the subject of the Downing murder was being discussed, and "to post his thoughts in any forum that [Margo Nash] is in…" exploded in wake of his appearance on the podcast in November 2025. I learned more about Artie there than I had ever discovered in my own research. The majority opinion in the chat toward Artie Ortiz was decidedly negative following his first appearances. After that, he refused to respond to the podcast phone calls and requests that he come back on the show to finish telling his side of the story.

He was always in the chat, always listening to the show, but he remained silent. In late April of 2026, I appeared briefly by telephone to correct a misunderstanding about a document they were discussing. Artie answered questions in the chat the following night. On or about April 22, 2026, he typed into the chat:

*so even if I did it what can you do now nothing*

He simply cannot stop himself from his need to stay in the mix.

# THE BLOOD EVIDENCE CHAIN OF CUSTODY

I have always been skeptical about the blood evidence in this case. Robert Pino was the field technician who gathered 106 items from the crime scene. Mary Kate McGilvray was the chemist who tested the blood on the items. Both worked for the State Police Crime Laboratory.

In Appendix A and Appendix B of the book published in 2016, I updated the State Police Lab and Robert Pino information to include the fact that Pino was fired from his job of 24 years for mishandling DNA results in 2007. After Pino was fired, Mary Kate McGilvray was appointed acting director of the laboratory in April 2007. An audit released a damning report of her tenure as acting director:

*Specifically, before being appointed as the acting Laboratory Director she neither had significant laboratory management experience nor proven leadership skills. Her management style tends to be heavy-handed and intimidating. Since the start of her tenure, she has not been able to create an atmosphere of trust among Laboratory employees in the Forensic BiologyGroup. The management style adopted by the Acting Laboratory Director is not conducive to building an effective, cohesive, respectful environment... information only flows from the top down. By virtue of their current lines of administrative authority,the analysts at the Laboratory are today not well insulated from the theories of an investigator or district attorney in comparison to analysts in a more independent laboratory framework.*[220]

Mary Kate McGilvray voluntarily resigned in April of 2009 from the lab where she had worked for 24 years. This information caused me more mistrust in the forensic work that was done by Pino and McGilvray on Eddie's case.

Of the 106 items collected by Pino, 59 of those items tested positive for human blood.

Considering all the blood and the number of blood samples taken, only three items eventually implicated Eddie O'Brien and connected him to the murder scene:

a.) swab from the bloody fingerprints on the front foyer door above the doorknob;
b.) swab from the wooden post at the bottom of the cellar stairs "at or near" the fingerprint;
c.) swab from the pink dress hanging in the cellar.

All three specimens contained faint results of the presence of a third DNA from another individual in addition to Eddie O'Brien and Janet Downing. This is found in McGilvray's notes but not in her official written report. Each blood sample was missing one of the bands from Janet Downing's DNA banding pattern. (In paternity/forensic testing, this is considered a non-match.) In the Cellmark Labs data, its significance is never explained.

District Attorney Reilly's theory was that Eddie was injured by the same weapon used to stab Janet Downing when the hilt fell off and his right hand slid down the blade, cutting his hand in the process. If his theory was correct, then Eddie's blood would certainly have been all over Janet's clothing and on the hilt of the knife. But it wasn't. Eddie was

---

220 Mary Kate McGilvray and the problems in the State Police Laboratory (from the audit of 2007 done jointly by Dr. Cotton and Office of Inspector General).

excluded as a contributor in the ABO testing results of the blood on Janet's body, Janet's blouse, bra, shorts, fingernail clippings, and the metal piece/hilt of the knife.

The absence of any bleeding evidence on or around Janet Downing that can be linked to Eddie O'Brien makes Reilly's theory of the case virtually impossible. Remember, Eddie had no blood on his shorts, white T-shirt, or sneakers, all of which he'd had on all day long. His blood was detected in three extremely limited places at the Downing home and in minute quantities. Two of the items were located in the cellar, where blood was smeared all the way down both walls of the cellar stairway. The blood on the wall was not Eddie's. His DNA was allegedly detected in a droplet of blood on the pink blouse hanging on the clothesline. Two other items of clothing hanging on the clothesline with the pink blouse did *not* contain Eddie's DNA.

Eddie's blood was not found on the cellar door latch leading out to the back yard.

The only explanation for the lack of any significant Type O blood at the scene is that Eddie was not injured when he went into 71 Hamlet Street at approximately 9:15 p.m. on July 23, 1995. The man who held a knife to his throat did not cut or nick him. I'm sure Eddie had Janet's blood on his fingers from turning her over to see if she was alive. He pushed the front foyer door closed behind him with his middle right fingers, which were tainted with her blood. But I have serious doubts that the blood was a mixture of Janet's blood and Eddie's blood, simply because he wasn't bleeding then.

Many people cannot accept the idea that Eddie's right hand was cut in Union Square when he defensively grabbed the double-edged knife of the youth who lunged at him and took his 17 dollars. As I said before, statistically the chances of these two things happening to a kid within one hour are very low. I understand their doubts completely.

But that doesn't mean it didn't happen.

There is evidence that another victim was robbed by similarly described youths in Union Square that night at about 8:30 p.m. I have also reviewed reports of the attacker's girlfriend telling her counselor that her boyfriend admitted to the robbery of Eddie that night. Neither is admissible as evidence at trial because it is hearsay. But having read these reports myself, I believe them to be true and I believe that Eddie was confronted in Union Square and was injured there.

The three small cuts on Eddie's right hand, consistent only with a two-sided blade, didn't bleed profusely. A possible diluted stain on his white T-shirt was noted, but it isn't visible in photographs of the shirt. When the Somerville Police assessed the wounds, they deemed them so minor as to not require any medical treatment, and they drove him home from Midnight Variety. It was Eddie's grandfather's suggestion that he get a tetanus shot that prompted him to go to Somerville Hospital with his uncle Doc that night.

But as Eddie always reminds me, there is what you know to be true, and there is what you can prove in court. These are two separate issues.

How do I prove the blood samples at or near his fingerprints were either tampered with or contaminated at some point along the long and undocumented journey from Hamlet Street to the Massachusetts State Police Crime Lab in July of 1995, to the FBI lab in Quantico, Virginia, in January of 1996, back to the State Police Crime Lab in June of 1996, and then finally to Cellmark Labs in Maryland for the DNA testing in September of 1996? I cannot prove it, because I don't know how many people had access to the evidence from July 1995 to July 1997, when the last of the blood was tested for DNA by Cellmark.

The three items tying Eddie to the scene with DNA

were, in fact, gone from Massachusetts for six months but because there was no chain-of-custody log on the items that went to the FBI lab in January of 1996—not even a letter of transmittal or the name of the trooper who came to the State Police Lab in Sudbury to pick them up—I cannot even begin to speculate how the evidence could have been contaminated or tampered with and when that might have happened.

In January 1996, the Massachusetts State Crime Lab sent 15 items for testing to the FBI lab in Quantico, Virginia. There was no chain-of-custody log showing who handled this evidence at each facility, where and how it was stored, who accessed it during the time it was in the custody of that lab, or how and when it was transported back and forth from Massachusetts to the Virginia lab.

The prosecution's most damning evidence placing Eddie O'Brien at the scene of Janet Downing's murder was unaccounted for from January to June of 1996, some *six months*. If Eddie's blood hadn't been found at that murder scene, Tom Reilly would not have secured his conviction. There would be no physical evidence linking Eddie to the crime. Even if the hilt of the knife could have been positively identified as belonging to Eddie, his DNA wasn't on it—but an unknown male's DNA was. During the time this evidence was allegedly somewhere out of state, the State Police Crime Lab had no contact with the FBI lab.

Mary Kate McGilvray, the state lab chemist who packaged the evidence along with known samples of Eddie's blood and Janet's blood, testified that she handed the package off at the state lab to a state trooper whose name she couldn't remember. She believed the trooper was going to drive it to Quantico.

The package wasn't received at the FBI lab in Virgina until three days later.

Where the unnamed trooper stored the evidence during

that time is unknown. McGilvray did not know why it took three days to get there and had no further communication with the FBI while the items were out of state. She testified that sometime in June of 1996, the package reappeared at her lab without any testing results. She did not know why no testing was done by the FBI or how it arrived back at her lab.

Failure to use the proper protocol for tracking of all evidence breaks the chain of custody. A chain of custody is an essential element in establishing the reliability and authenticity of the evidence.[221]

Some states will not admit items into evidence at trial without a chain of custody. In Massachusetts, however, failure to log chronologically each person or entity that handles physical evidence doesn't render that evidence inadmissible at trial. Most Massachusetts courts will allow the evidence in, and the lack of documentation of the chain of custody goes to the weight of the evidence. It is up to the jury to determine whether the break in the chain of custody has compromised the integrity of the evidence and made it less credible than it would have been if securely tracked by the custodians of the evidence.

How much weight would you give to evidence that was in the sole custody of one state police trooper for three days, then out of the Commonwealth for six months, allegedly held by a federal facility that failed to document how the evidence was stored, who had access to it, if and when anyone signed it out, why the evidence wasn't tested, and then returned it to Massachusetts, how it was transported back to the Commonwealth, who had custody of it during transport, or who delivered it to at the state lab? If I were the district attorney prosecuting this case, I would want to be damned sure that I could prove that evidence was secure

221 M.G.L. c.6, sec 184A(i) The board shall develop protocols to ensure proper chain of custody of evidence.

every minute it was in state custody, and that the regulations were strictly enforced. Why wasn't this important to DA Tom Reilly? Is it possible he wanted the chain of custody to be obscured in order to tamper with it?

When there are breaks in a chain of custody, or there is no written chain of custody, it is incumbent on defense counsel to question the custodian about whether each of the regulations was followed. It is defense counsel's job to show the jury why they can and should give little weight to the evidence due to it being mishandled by the police and prosecutor. In the O'Brien case, defense counsel did question the lack of chain of custody. But the second part of the process—why the jury should give little weight to it—was not addressed.[222]

I personally have never had a case where the chain of

---

222 515 CMR 7.10,7.11,7.12 states:

**7.10 Safety**

(1) Access to evidence storage areas shall be limited to those personnel designated by the proper authority at the custodial agency.

(2) Custodial agencies shall maintain a list of authorized personnel who have access to storage locations and this list shall be easily available, if requested.

(3) Custodial agencies shall document personnel who enter each storage location by means of a manual or electronic log or security system.

**7.11 Chain of Custody**

(1) Chain of custody must be maintained when evidence is removed from a secure storage location. The item(s) of evidence transferred, personnel making the transfer, and the new custody location of the evidence must be documented contemporaneously by date.

(2) Evidence shall be tracked through a manual log or entered into an electronic tracking system database contemporaneously.

**7.12: Documentation of Evidence Retention**

(1) Security logs indicating access to the evidence shall be maintained and retained for the period of time equivalent to the evidence retention period.

(2) Temperature and humidity control logs shall be maintained and retained for the period of time equivalent to the evidence retention period.

custody was in question. But in a highly publicized case such as this one, where the district attorney was personally trying the case (for the first time in his elected career), where the only forensic evidence tying the defendant to the murder scene was in that package, I would expect the evidence would be as secure and meticulously documented as possible.

The total lack of such security and documentation creates a glaring opportunity for contamination of that evidence, making it significantly less reliable. As a juror, I would want to know why chain of custody was not documented, how biological evidence should be stored to prevent deterioration of the sample, and whether the lack of chain of custody was caused by incompetence or was intentional.

Knowing everything I now know about this case, the many social and political forces at play (which caused a judge to be removed because "higher-ups" didn't like his decision, which caused a governor to stand with the Downing family at the State House to announce new legislation for juvenile murderers, and which permitted a district attorney to hold press conferences on an almost daily basis about the case he was trying in juvenile court), I have no trouble believing that this evidence was contaminated or tampered with in some way, either intentionally or unintentionally.

The weight of the evidence required for proof of guilt beyond a reasonable doubt must be considerable, authentic, and reliable. It is the Commonwealth's burden to prove that it is.

If I were a juror, the way this evidence was handled by the police and prosecutor would give me no confidence that it is reliable and free from alteration or contamination. I certainly would not vote to send a 15-year-old boy to prison for the rest of his life based on this evidence. If the jury really understood the unexplained and questionable circumstances surrounding the blood evidence, would they have had doubts about its reliability? Would they have deemed it dependable enough to convict Eddie O'Brien of a horrific murder when he had no motive to harm Janet Downing? I think not. I certainly hope not.

Unlike the correspondence between the Cellmark Lab in Maryland and the State Police Crime Lab in Massachusetts, communication didn't go through Mary Kate McGilvray. The FBI's response to Eddie's 2017 FOIA request included Page One of a letter addressed to Thomas Reilly, DA, at 40 Thorndike Street in Cambridge. This letter proves there was direct communication between the FBI lab and Tom Reilly in March 1996, while the items were at the FBI lab. The letter assigned a case number, a case manager, and other telephone numbers Mr. Reilly could call directly to speak with lab scientists assigned to the case. There is no second or signature page with the letter. This is the sort of letter that is usually sent directly to the State Police Crime Lab. The custom is that the sending lab communicates with the receiving lab regarding all the evidence to be tested. That protocol was used with Cellmark Labs. But with the FBI lab, communication was not with the lab scientists but with the prosecuting district attorney himself.

The FBI did acknowledge that there had been more materials and files in its possession related to the O'Brien case, and that they most likely would have been produced, but they could not be located even after a diligent search. I assume the signature page is among the missing files.

Mary Kate McGilvray testified that Mr. Reilly had the final authority over what was tested and what wasn't tested. McGilvray, Robert Pino, and District Attorney Reilly met several times to discuss what evidence was collected and which items Reilly wanted tested.[223]

While these evidentiary items were allegedly with the

223 Trial Transcript, Volume 12, pages 125-207

FBI in Virginia, Eddie's first transfer hearing proceeded in Massachusetts without the benefit of the results of those forensic tests. The fact that no testing was done, even though chemists had been assigned by the FBI to do the testing, coupled with the facts that there is no chain of custody documentation and Tom Reilly had direct access to the lab, requires me to question whether Reilly instructed the lab not to do the testing. I must consider this possibility because Reilly *did* discontinue testing of the metal hilt of the knife and Janet Downing's bloody fingernail clippings in 1996 and 1997, when it was determined through preliminary testing that the DNA was not Eddie's.

The Cellmark DNA testing was completed and sent to the defense just days before the trial was to begin. The results on both of these items *excluded* Eddie O'Brien and detected a full DNA profile of an unknown male on both items. Reilly was informed that the initial extraction on these items showed an absence of Eddie O'Brien's DNA, before he halted all testing.

In November 1996, which was five months after the FBI had failed to do any testing, Reilly stopped Cellmark DNA testing on the metal piece/hilt. This evidence had now been in possession of the prosecution for 15 months and had not yet been tested. If Tom Reilly hadn't discontinued the test, the results would have been available for the second transfer hearing with Judge Gailey, a hearing which began in April of 1997. Obviously, those exculpatory results would have changed the course of that hearing by proving that Eddie hadn't handled the murder weapon, giving credibility to his claim of innocence.

On June 25, 1997, Reilly stopped DNA testing on Janet Downing's fingernail clippings after he was told that preliminary testing showed an absence of Eddie's DNA on them. Eddie's trial in Superior Court was scheduled for September 1997. Nevertheless, testing was canceled, knowing that the testing would take at least four to five weeks to complete. There can be no dispute that the longer the defense remained in the dark about this exculpatory evidence, the better for the Commonwealth. The Commonwealth had had possession of the evidence now for over two years. By not releasing the exculpatory evidence to the defense, it shortened the time defense had to prepare for trial or hire DNA experts to explain to the jury how this exculpatory evidence supported Eddie's defense.

It also prevented the public from learning about information which supported Eddie's claim of innocence before the trial started.

Was this a violation of the Brady Rule by the district attorney?

The Brady Rule requires the prosecution to hand over all exculpatory evidence to the defense once it discovers such evidence. Reilly knew these two critical pieces of evidence would exculpate Eddie O'Brien due to the preliminary extractions performed on them. By halting all further testing, Reilly was withholding this exculpatory evidence from the defense. Prosecutors may believe they don't have to disclose exculpatory evidence until the testing is complete and the results are in writing. That reasoning is flawed, however, because it violates Rule 14 governing discovery.[224] The duty to notify the defense tolled on November 27, 1996, when the Cellmark Lab wrote the following to Mary Kate McGilvray:

RESULTS*: An extraction procedure was performed on the thread labelled metal piece on third stair (item 21).*

224 Mass. R. Crim. P. 14(C) When the prosecutor learns of items or information subject to disclosure which cannot be promptly copied or made available for inspection by the defense, the prosecutor has a duty to promptly notify the defense of the existence.

*Testing on this item was discontinued at the request of Mr. Tom Reilly in November 1996.*

Similarly, testing on the bloody fingernails from Janet Downing was sent to Cellmark in November 1996. On June 25, 1997, Mary Kate McGilvray, in a Supplemental Submission to Cellmark Lab, wrote:

*Please HOLD the enclosed blood stained fingernail clippings from Janet Downing until you receive authorization from DA Tom Reilly or Mary Kate McGilvray.*

If defense counsel had been provided with exculpatory evidence when the prosecution was required to do so, it would have been fatal to Reilly's case. Another man's DNA was underneath Janet Downing's fingernails as well as on the hilt of the knife the prosecution was calling the murder weapon. Eddie had been steadfastly insisting he did not commit this crime.

Given those findings, it was now highly likely that he was not the perpetrator.

By halting all testing on these crucial items until the eve of trial, the prosecution gave the defense no time to engage a DNA expert to review the findings and provide expert testimony on how this evidence proved that Eddie was not the perpetrator of this crime to the jury.

### A Note on the Fingerprint Evidence

On July 25, 1997, pre-trial motions were heard in Superior Court. The defense moved that all unidentified fingerprints found at the scene be run through the FBI's Automated Fingerprint Identification System (AFIS) to search for a match. Assistant District Attorney Tom O'Reilly (District Attorney Reilly was on medical leave that summer) confirmed on the record that there were no other fingerprints taken from the scene.

On August 7, 1997, Trooper Wayne H. Riley submitted a report stating clearly that two latent fingerprints and one palm print lifted from the scene had been compared with those of all family members, Artie Ortiz, Carol Ortiz, and Eddie O'Brien. They could have been identified but never were, because they were not put through AFIS to check for a match.

When all the fingerprint testimony was taken, the final count included five identifiable but unidentified prints lifted from the scene. Even though Bob George didn't waive his motion for the AFIS fingerprint evidence, and ADA O'Reilly told the judge that the Commonwealth had no problem with this request, *these prints were never run through AFIS.* The defense failed to raise the request again when the prosecution finally admitted that there were other unidentified prints at the crime scene that had been taken into evidence.

At that same hearing, on July 24, 1997, ADA O'Reilly told the judge that the prosecution still had discovery material it would be "unable to provide for possibly another four or five weeks."[225] DNA testing was "initiated last Tuesday, the fifteenth [July 15, 1997]," he explained, and would take that long to be completed. What O'Reilly did *not* tell the judge was that these tests were initiated in January 1996 (not July 15, 1997) and re-initiated *in a different lab* in November 1996.

However, the district attorney himself had halted all further testing of these items for the past two years. In fact, he stopped all testing on one of them (fingernail clippings) just three weeks prior to that day, knowing there was a trial

225 Transcript July 24, 1997, p. 32

date just weeks away.

The results of the DNA testing on the metal piece/hilt and Downing's bloody fingernail clippings were finally mailed to the defense on September 9, 1997, six days before the trial began. Both tests excluded Eddie as a contributor to any DNA found on them. Both items did have unknown and unidentified male DNA on them. That male has never been identified. His profile has never been run through the national database for DNA (CODIS) to see if there was a match.

Evidence that a male handled the murder weapon and a male's DNA was also found under Janet's fingernails during her fight for her life was indisputably established by the Commonwealth's own evidence, yet the district attorney didn't even attempt to identify the male DNA. His decision to ignore the man whose DNA was found on these items is unconscionable—especially for a prosecutor who is supposed to be searching for the truth.

Tom Reilly, the *elected* district attorney, showed no interest in finding the man who really killed Janet Downing. His sole interest was in convicting Eddie O'Brien.

# NEW EVIDENCE OF MISREPRESENTATION: BLOOD TYPING TESTS

What did the Commonwealth do with the blood samples belonging to family members and Artie Ortiz during its investigation? Tom Reilly requested only ABO blood typing from the State Crime Lab. He never requested DNA testing on the family members or on Artie Ortiz.

Blood typing tests are used as an exclusionary tool to exclude those persons not detected in the sample. The process is called "ABO" blood typing. Blood types are referred to as Type A, which has A antigens; Type B, which has B antigens; Type AB (which has both A and B antigens); or Type O, which has neither A nor B antigens but has H antigens. The foundation to ABO blood typing is the H factor, which is the antigen found in greater concentrations in Type O blood, but is also found in type A, B, and AB blood in lesser intensities.

Ted Yeshion, an expert in serology and DNA testing, explained to me that just because a sample of a mixture of bloods yields an H factor, it doesn't automatically mean this is Type O blood. The intensity level of the H factor must be further analyzed to determine whether it is coming from the other blood types in the mixture, since all blood types have the H factor in them. In order to more particularly identify the source of a blood sample, certain subtests are conducted to look for additional antigens, unique to the person in question.

McGilvray's third report, dated August 7, 1997, included the test results on blood samples from Janet Downing,

Eddie O'Brien, Paul Downing Sr., Paul Downing Jr., Ryan Downing, and Artie Ortiz. Janet Downing had Type AB blood. Eddie O'Brien had Type O blood, the most common blood type in the ABO system. Paul Downing Jr. and Artie Ortiz had Type B blood, and Ryan Downing had Type A blood.

In 1995, crime laboratories in the United States were largely not independent and faced significant concerns regarding institutional bias. Most labs were administratively and financially tied to law enforcement agencies, a structure that critics argued compromised scientific objectivity. This is still true of the Massachusetts crime labs, even though two audits strongly recommended that they be separated from the state police, first in 2007 after Robert Pino was fired from the lab for mishandling DNA test results, and again in 2017, after the Annie Dookhan and Sonja Farak scandals caused tens of thousands of test results to be voided, over 35,000 cases dismissed, and up to 20,000 prisoners released. (Dookhan and Farak tampered with evidence and falsified the drug certificates of defendants for over a decade early in the 2000s.) Annie Dookhan went to prison for falsifying lab results by "dry labbing" drugs, i.e., she did not actually do any testing, she simply certified them as controlled substances. Sonja Farak was an addict who, for almost nine years, stole the drugs that were submitted to her for testing, thereby making her certifications unreliable.

Forensic crime laboratories were intended to be unbiased, independent scientific laboratories to avoid the obvious assumption, if not the reality, that any results would favor the state police, who ran those labs. Unfortunately, Massachusetts has refused to adopt the recommendations of the audits, and questions about the objectivity of the labs still linger.

New evidence received in 2017 revealed that blood typing

results had been manipulated by Mary Kate McGilvray, the chemist at the State Lab. Her handwritten contemporaneous notes were produced in the FOIA request. Until then, the only data available was in her official reports. A comparison between the handwritten notes and the written reports revealed important discrepancies between the two.

Specifically, there are several instances when she found a mixture of two blood types, indicating that there were two contributors to the sample, and subsequently changed that finding to a single source contributor in the report. Mixtures of type A and type B blood turned into AB blood coming from a single source. The only person with AB blood in the family was Janet Downing. Every time Ms. McGilvary changed a mixture of A and B blood into AB blood, she eliminated anyone with Type A or Type B blood contributing to the mixture. This means that Ryan Downing, Paul Jr., and Artie Ortiz were all eliminated as potential contributors, as well as any unknown suspect with Type A or Type B blood.

In McGilvary's handwritten notes, when AB blood was detected, it was recorded as AB. The source of the sample came from one person who was type AB blood. If there was a mixture of A and B blood detected, it was recorded A,B. In other words, the source of the sample came from two or more people one with Type A and one with Type B blood.

Changing the blood type in her reports to AB made Janet Downing the single source of the blood and eliminated any contribution from Type A or Type B blood as a source in that specimen. Thus, a specimen that could have been a mixture of Janet Downing and Artie Ortiz, for example, was reported as coming only from Janet Downing. The seriousness of such misrepresentation cannot be overstated. It challenges every finding and all potential sources of the blood handled by McGilvray. What else might have been changed, either intentionally or unintentionally, that eliminated other potential suspects? Two of the items that were misrepresented in this way were:

1. The V-neck blouse worn by Janet Downing: notes indicate A, B. Report says AB.
2. Picture of grapes found on floor of hallway: notes indicate A, B. Report says AB.

Each time A, B is changed in the report to Type AB blood, it eliminates the contribution of at least four potential suspects in this case: Paul Downing Jr. and Artie Ortiz, both of whom have Type B blood; Ryan Downing, who has Type A blood; or an unknown perpetrator with Type A or B blood.

To obtain more specific information about the origin of the blood, additional testing is normally done to break down immune system characteristics and to detect enzymes, antigens, and proteins. This further narrows the potential pool of suspects prior to doing any DNA analysis.

Two tested items critical to the case were identified by blood type, but no further testing was done which would have further narrowed the source of that blood. One was the drop of blood from Eddie's right shin, swabbed at the hospital the night of the murder. The handwritten notes state that the subtests weren't performed on this swab. However, the written report states the subtests were "inconclusive." The results cannot be inconclusive if they weren't done. The lab notes show no values in the boxes provided for these subtests:

**C95-704 Somerville Supp -2- August 7, 1997**
**SEROLOGY RESULTS: QUESTIONED SPECIMENS**

**Sample Description ABO PGMsub EAP ADA AK Poss. Single source contributors**

**Item 6. Right shin (AB) - -- -- -- JD AO, PD, RD, PD, Sr (Edward O'Brien).**

This single drop of blood and the presence of Eddie O'Brien's fingerprints on the back of the front door caused DA Reilly to precipitously arrest Eddie 48 hours after the murder and prior to any real investigation by the state police homicide unit. The ABO test on the shin specimen showed it was AB blood, consistent with the blood type of Janet Downing.

This is *not* proof that it was Janet's blood; it is only evidence it was her blood type.

If subtests were done but were inconclusive, then the blood cannot be considered "consistent" with Janet Downing's blood. If no subtests were done, basing an arrest on this drop of blood was at best imprudent, and at worst, intentionally deceptive because there was no proof that it was the blood of the victim, Janet Downing. Media reports quoted the DA as saying it was consistent with Janet Downing's blood. That is not true. It was consistent with every person who has AB blood because no subtests were done.

McGilvray ABO type-tested only 29 of the 59 items that tested positive for the presence of blood.[226] Ryan Downing and his twin brother Paul couldn't be excluded as possible contributors to the blood from Janet Downing's shorts, Janet's V-neck blouse, the front door above inside knob, the swab from Eddie O'Brien's right shin, the wooden post, behind the cellar post, the blue blazer and green shirt from the cellar laundry line, the cellar door by the deadbolt, and the back and the front of the picture of grapes on the hallway floor.

Artie Ortiz couldn't be excluded from five items, including the swab from Eddie's right shin, the front door

226 No explanation was given as to why more items weren't tested. The notes indicate that Tom Reilly had the final say over what did and didn't get tested. The items were discussed in meetings between Mary Kate McGillvary and Reilly.

above the inside knob, the cellar door by the deadbolt, Janet Downing's V-neck blouse, and Janet's shorts... and he could have been the single source of the blood from behind the cellar post.

Eddie O'Brien was *excluded* as a contributor to the blood on Janet Downing's shorts, her V-neck blouse, and the cellar door by the deadbolt.

If Eddie had been injured by the knife when the hilt broke and his hand allegedly slipped down over the blade of the knife, as DA Reilly theorized, it would be impossible to prevent his blood dripping onto Janet's shorts and V-neck blouse, which had some 38 stab wounds to it. Eddie's blood (and DNA) was not found on Janet's clothing, skin, hair, or under her fingernails. He was *excluded* as a contributor of DNA on the hilt of the knife. Forensically, there is not a shred of evidence that Eddie was the perpetrator of this horrendous murder.

That makes the blood evidence "mixture" on the front door above the inside doorknob and the wooden post highly suspicious. The only basis for asserting that Eddie was bleeding at the scene is Tom Reilly's theory of the case. If Eddie wasn't bleeding at 71 Hamlet Street on July 23, 1995, his blood cannot have gotten into that mixture above the inside doorknob, the wooden post in the cellar, or the pink dress hanging in the cellar. These three forensic specimens are the only evidence tying Eddie to the murder scene. Without them, he would not have been convicted of Janet's murder. And if he wasn't bleeding, those specimens were either contaminated inadvertently or intentionally. (The police did remove the wooden post and bring it to the lab.)

Mary Kate McGilvray also switched her findings regarding the two fingerprint mixtures. Eddie's fingerprints were reported to be *in* the blood on the front door, whereas his fingerprints (left index finger and left thumb) were "*at or near*" the blood smear on the post. The handwritten notes for both of these blood specimens read "A, B, H," indicating a mixture of Type A, Type B, and Type O blood. In the report, the results are changed to "AB, O." With that switch, Paul Downing Jr., Ryan Downing, Artie Ortiz, or an unknown perpetrator with either Type A or Type B blood were all eliminated as possible contributors.

It is also important to note it was Eddie's right hand that was cut by the knife in Union Square. Even in Tom Reilly's proposed scenario—that Eddie was injured at the house—it wasn't his left hand that was bleeding, so there is no reason why his left thumb and index finger would deposit any blood on the post.

It is also critical to remember that the DNA results of all three swabs (door, post, and pink blouse) contained a faint DNA profile of yet another person, further suggesting contamination.

McGilvray concluded that there were at least two bleeders at the murder scene.[227] Clearly, the handwritten notes we were able to view in 2017 indicate that there were a Type-B bleeder and a Type-A bleeder present in addition to the AB-bleeder, Janet Downing. The police didn't examine Ryan Downing (Type A), Paul Downing Jr. (Type B), or Artie Ortiz (Type B) for wounds or blood on them. Even if they were carefully examined, the blood may not have come from a visible wound. Nosebleeds, for example, produce a lot of blood, and there would be no evidence of a nosebleed after it stopped. The suspect who held a knife to Eddie's throat at the front door may have been an A or B bleeder.

A lot of potential suspects were eliminated by McGilvray when she changed her initial finding from A, B to AB.

---

227 In his closing argument, Tom Reilly incorrectly insisted that McGilvray testified that there were only two bleeders at the scene, a gross misrepresentation of the evidence.

# CONNECTING THE DOTS

In 1995, District Attorney Reilly was nearing the end of his eight-year second term.

Middlesex is the largest county in Massachusetts, and this office is often considered the one to hold if you aspire to higher offices in the Commonwealth. Three of the last five attorneys general in Massachusetts were formerly district attorneys of Middlesex County.

For Tom Reilly, the next step in the ladder was the position of attorney general, and then—hopefully—on to the governor's office. His campaign manager for all his campaigns was Wayne Budd, a childhood friend, attorney, law partner, and a Republican. Reilly ran as a Democrat, because Democrats dominate the voting public in this state; one's chances of being elected for a statewide office become much slimmer if one runs as a Republican. I know of no other candidate in history who has a member of the opposite political party managing his campaign.

Mr. Reilly's agenda, on the other hand, has always supported Republican ideas and initiatives. He wholeheartedly embraced the "superpredator" agenda and the change in juvenile laws.

Tom Reilly and Wayne Budd formed Budd and Reilly, a Boston-based law firm, in 1976.

Reilly left the law firm in 1983 to work for Middlesex County District Attorney Scott Harshburger's administration as first assistant district attorney.

Wayne Budd left the firm in 1989 when he was appointed

by President George H. Bush as the United States Attorney for the District of Massachusetts. Budd succeeded William Weld, who had been appointed U.S. Attorney for the District of Massachusetts by President Ronald Regan in 1981. Weld was thereafter appointed Associate Attorney General in the Justice Department in 1986. In 1992, Budd was appointed Associate Attorney General in the Justice Department where he oversaw, among other divisions, the Bureau of Prisons.

Tom Reilly is the godfather of Wayne Budd's daughter, Kimberly Budd. Kimberly Budd is now the Chief Justice of the Massachusetts Supreme Judicial Court, who will ultimately hear this case. The personal and professional entanglements are unprecedented and still present in Eddie's case.

In 1995, William Weld was the Governor of Massachusetts, Tom Reilly was the Middlesex District Attorney, and Wayne A. Budd was working as a senior partner at the Boston law firm Goodwin, Procter & Hoar, LLP. Budd was considered an ally and influencer of Weld, [228]with political pundits suggesting Budd influenced Weld's appointments during his time as governor. They were both prominent Republican figures in Massachusetts and key figures in the Massachusetts GOP, with reporters also noting that they were close friends and part of the same professional circles.

Governor Weld and Tom Reilly were both believers of the superpredator predictions. They both had law-and-order agendas in their political campaigns. Weld wanted to change the juvenile laws, making kids do adult time for adult crimes. There is little doubt in my mind that the three men, either

---

228 In 1992, Governor Weld appointed Ralph G. Martin II District Attorney for Suffolk County. Ralph Martin was a junior attorney in the firm of Budd and Riley. He left the firm to work for William Weld in the U.S. Attorney's office.

formally as office holders/campaign managers, or informally as friends, discussed how to pass the Juvenile Offender Act to boost Reilly's chances in his run for attorney general in 1998 and to enhance Weld's legacy for his run for the U.S. Senate in 1996.

The night that Janet Downing was murdered in a mostly White, close-knit neighborhood just outside Boston's inner city was a pivotal moment for Weld and Reilly. The prospect of blaming a White 15-year-old altar boy gave the politicians an unexpected windfall. It provided an opportunity for them to push their agendas, capitalize on public fear, and use the case for political gain without being seen as racist. A plan was born.

It was terribly flawed in its execution, however, even though it ultimately succeeded.

The dead giveaway[229] was the total refusal to interview the witnesses who contradicted the prosecution's theory of the case: Gina Mahoney, Virginia Reckley, and Barry Reckley. It wasn't oversight. It wasn't poor police work. It wasn't that they weren't known to the prosecution.

Handwritten statements of what they saw and heard that night were provided to the district attorney by Eddie's defense attorney two weeks after the murder. There is no excuse for not interviewing percipient witnesses and no excuses were offered, which is why it is the dead giveaway.

The prosecution didn't want the facts that these witnesses had to tell because they directly contradicted the narrative fashioned by the district attorney (and, in my opinion, a narrative shared with Governor Weld, Wayne Budd, his campaign manager, and perhaps an influential judge) a mere

---

229 In slang, a giveaway is an unintentional, obvious sign that reveals a secret, truth, or guilt. It is often used in the phrase "dead giveaway" to mean a clue that makes the truth undeniably clear. (Merriam-Webster Dictionary).

48 hours after Janet Downing's death.

Reilly must have assured them that he would be able to bring this one home. He would do the job personally. He would get the political exposure he needed for his campaign, and Weld would benefit politically from the legislation in his run for Senate. More importantly, with Reilly spearheading the prosecution, they would contain the plan; the fewer people involved, the less risk of a leak.

But a plan is only as good as its execution, and this one was terrible. Would it have been so difficult to send someone from the Somerville Police up to Boston Street under the pretense of taking statements for the record? That would have been much less suspicious. The absolute refusal to meet and jot down a few notes from the woman with whom Janet had spent the last nine hours of her life was completely and utterly suspicious.

That Barry Reckley was the first witness to observe the murder scene in its "pristine" condition, before the EMTs, before the fire personnel, before the police, and before the neighbors flooded in, is unheard of—even in a shoddy criminal investigation.

These are critically important interviews to conduct, especially since we now know that no perimeter was established, no log of personnel in or out of the crime scene was set up, and no attempt to preserve the crime scene or the evidence was made. Reportedly, 17 individuals went in and out of that house before the perimeter was secured. None wore protective gear, protective foot coverings, or hair nets.

If Reilly had talked to Virginia Reckley, she would have told him that she went into the house in her bare feet and stepped on the grapes painting, leaving a bloody footprint that had to be ignored because there couldn't be *six* unidentified prints in blood. These were bad decisions because they polluted the entire criminal investigation... and the foul odor from those decisions still reeks after 31 years.

There was no need for a rush to judgment. Janet's funeral services had not yet occurred. The community was in an uproar; people needed to mourn and process. Fifteen-year-old Eddie wasn't going anywhere; he could be arrested anytime. Some semblance of an investigation should have been done before Eddie O'Brien became the *only* suspect.

It took 16 years after the passing of the Juvenile Offender Act of 1996 to have it declared unconstitutional by the U.S. Supreme Court.[230] Eddie's case was a response to the "adult time for adult crimes," movement of the 1990s that proved to be so ill-conceived that it was reversed in relatively short order. In 2012, the court finally, through science and not fear, was able to declare that children between 14 and 17 did not have fully developed brains, capable of the mature reasoning necessary to make sensible decisions when confronted with life-altering situations.

Why is it, then, that people still ask why Eddie didn't go to the police right away? The parole board should understand the adolescent brain science, as they have approved the release of 55 individuals who were previously serving life sentences for murder since the *Mattis* case.[231] Yet one of the board members actually asked him that question! To that board member I say: because he wasn't a mature adult. He was a 15-year-old boy who thought he was going to be responsible for the death of his family if he went to the police.

If that sounds too childish, it is because he was a child. He was a child who came within an inch of becoming this killer's second victim that night in July of 1995. Why do these people continue to expect that he should have walked outside and yelled to his friends, "There's a murderer in

230 *Miller v. Alabama* 567 U.S. 460 (2012)

231 *Mattis*, Supra

there! Janet is dead. I'm going to the police station!"

The prosecution's failure to investigate anyone but Eddie O'Brien as a potential suspect was, by far, the worst mistake in the case. There are no police reports or notes of any interview of Artie Ortiz, who did have a lot of anger toward Janet, who was stalking her, and about whom she expressed fear to at least two of her friends. Tom Reilly's handwritten notes of his interview with James Stanford, the second Somerville Police officer on the scene, show that Stanford spoke to Artie Ortiz outside the Downing home the night of the murder. We don't know what he said, because there were no notes or reports about the conversation.

If you spoke to Artie Ortiz today, he would tell you he didn't arrive at the house until long after Janet's body had been removed. Would Detective Stanford corroborate that statement? Did he ask what Artie was doing there? Did Artie tell him?

If the district attorney or the Massachusetts State Police ever interviewed Artie Ortiz, defense was not given a copy of that interview. And failure to turn that over, we know, would be grounds for granting a new trial.

If you asked Artie in 1995 why he went to the Downing home on the night of the murder, he would have told you what he told the neighbors then: his dispatcher at the Green Cab company radioed him and told him his sister-in-law had been murdered.

If you asked him in 2016, after the book was published, he would have told you his wife called the cab company and asked the dispatcher to tell him to call home.

Then, if you asked him in November of 2025, he would have told you Kerriann called his wife Carol, who called the cab company and asked them to radio him and tell him to call home. He spoke to his wife at about 9:45 p.m. and went straight from South Station to the Peter Pan bus station pay phones in downtown Boston to 71 Boston Street in Somerville. He arrived just about 10:00 p.m.

But if you asked him in April of 2026 how he knew to go to Janet's house, he would have told you that he doesn't know the exact time he talked to his wife, and she didn't tell him what happened to Janet; all she said was that she was on her way to the hospital to be with Janet, but that he should go to Janet's house. Why should he go to Janet's house? Why not meet her at the hospital?

We do know what he did at 71 Boston Street when he got there, and he doesn't dispute this part: he lost the key to his cab on Janet's back lawn, he borrowed Gina Mahoney's telephone, and he went upstairs with Gina's 16-year-old daughter to smoke a joint, all while his wife was with her dead sister at Massachusetts General Hospital. That is the man District Attorney Tom Reilly protected from any investigation.

All versions make it clear that Artie knew about Janet before her body was found by her son Ryan at 9:55, when the police were called. In the latest version, Artie knew, Carol knew, and Kerriann knew. Why did none of them call the police? Weren't they all mature adults, capable of making adult decisions? Didn't they want to get help to Janet immediately?

Not only did Tom Reilly refuse to consider Artie Ortiz a person of interest or potential suspect, he stood at his press conference after the trial and said:

*"A terrible injustice has been done by bringing in even his name, a man who is totally innocent, and injecting his name into this case. That's wrong. That is fundamentally wrong and extremely unfair to him. There is absolutely no indication no no no (sic) item of evidence or anything that would point in that direction."*[232]

232 Video, October 1, 1997, from WBZ Newscast

No item of evidence or anything that would point in Artie's direction? He said that?

Reilly *knew* that the State Police Lab couldn't rule Artie out as a contributor to the blood at the crime scene on five tested items, including the front door above the inside doorknob, the cellar door by the deadbolt, the left wall to the cellar, and the blood behind the cellar post. The report said he could have been the single source of the blood on the back of the wooden post in the cellar. And if we add Artie's blood type back into what Mary Kate McGilvray removed when she switched A, B blood to AB blood, Artie couldn't be eliminated from Janet's V-neck blouse or her shorts either.

If the DNA on the hilt of the knife and under Janet's fingernails comes back with Artie's DNA, the damage to Reilly's professional reputation will exceed the errors he made while structuring this case around the narrative he needed to secure the conviction.

Does that make the DA a third-party culprit by proxy—something like Munchausen by proxy? (Munchausen by proxy refers to a mental illness wherein a caregiver invents health problems in another person, so that the patient will get more attention. Very often, this person is their child. Sometimes, people injure their children, or they change test samples for one that will give a different, more serious result.)[233] It is uncanny how many of the signs of Munchausen by proxy precisely correspond to what happened to Eddie:

- The child (Eddie) is referred to multiple health care providers (psychiatrists, psychologists) and has been in the hospital (detention);
- The child (Eddie) often has had many tests, surgeries, or other procedures (psychiatric exams, psychological tests, blood tests);
- The child (Eddie) is reported to have strange

233 Wikipedia

symptoms that do not fit with any disease (mental defect or disorder). The symptoms do not match the test results.

- The child's (Eddie's) symptoms are reported by the caretaker (district attorney). They are never seen by health care professionals (mental health evaluators, family, friends, teachers, priests, coaches);
- The symptoms are gone in the hospital (in the home, school, or detention setting);
- Blood samples do not match the child's (Eddie's) blood type.

Tom Reilly, now 84 years old, continues to defend a man who has spent the last 31 years cyber-stalking any person that even mentions either this case, *The Politics of Murder* book, Margo Nash, or the O'Brien family. Artie Ortiz is the only member of the Downing family who has kept all the poor choices made in the construction of this case alive and well. The deconstruction of the case has taken years, but you can thank Artie for repeatedly reminding everyone that he didn't do it. Those decisions look even more suspect today and the stench smells worse as each layer is peeled away and the truth is exposed.

Hopefully, the former DA has been told about how Artie took a knife to his own wife, Janet's sister, in 2005, held her against her will, and prevented her from calling the police. The judge who presided over his divorce found that he had been violent toward Carol Ortiz for the entirety of the 16 years they had been married. Mr. Reilly did not see anything about Artie that concerned him, because it distracted him from the suspect he wanted to convict, the suspect he *needed* to convict. If he interviewed Gina Mahoney, she would have told him that just a few hours before she was murdered, Janet was terrified of Artie and clearly believed her life was in danger.

Many people suggested to me that Artie Ortiz must be a confidential informant for a district attorney to publicly protect him so fiercely. I like the theory, but Artie is too unreliable to be a CI. He can't keep his mouth shut, and he is a pathological liar. It has been 31 years, yet he still cannot get one story or one timeline right and stick to it.

More importantly, he cannot help inserting himself into this case.

Offenders insert themselves into cases for several reasons: to monitor the progress of the investigation, sometimes to steer the investigation toward other suspects. Artie is a narcissistic thrill-seeker who enjoys the excitement of hiding in plain sight. He feels a sense of superiority over the victim and the investigators. He craves attention and, right now, he is angry and frustrated that he hasn't gotten the respect and notoriety he deserves for what he considers his greatest achievement.

Have you seen any of these personality traits in Artie Ortiz?

- Pathological lying and manipulation: Skill in weaving complex false narratives and steering people toward false leads.
- Callousness and lack of remorse: A complete absence of guilt, which enables him to act as a "concerned citizen" or even comfort victims' families.
- Sensation-seeking: A drive for the thrill and "adrenaline of fear" associated with being close to the investigation without being caught.[234]

---

234 *Psychopathy*, Law Enforcement Bulletin, July 1, 2012, by Paul Babiak, MS, PhD; Jorge Folino, MD, PhD, et al. in *Behavior Analysis*, How We Investigate, Federal Bureau of Investigation, Official Website of the United States Government.

It is my opinion that Tom Reilly knew, or at the very least suspected, that Eddie hadn't murdered Janet Downing when he prosecuted this case. I have been involved in this case since 1995. I have interviewed witnesses, I have read and re-read the official files and transcripts and the latest information received in the FOIA requests, I have seen the autopsy photos and crime-scene photos. I have read all the police reports and lab reports. More than ever, it appears to me that Tom Reilly tightly controlled the investigation, the forensic testing, the witness interviews, the witnesses' testimony preparation, and the decisions on what evidence to test and what to refrain from testing; and it was Tom Reilly alone who decided to ignore any evidence inconsistent with his theory of the crime. It was Tom Reilly who ordered testing stopped on Janet's bloody fingernails and the hilt of the knife when he learned that preliminary tests showed the DNA did not belong to Eddie O'Brien.

The notes from his training of young prosecutors provide a unique way of building the picture of the defendant: "reverse profile" your suspect.

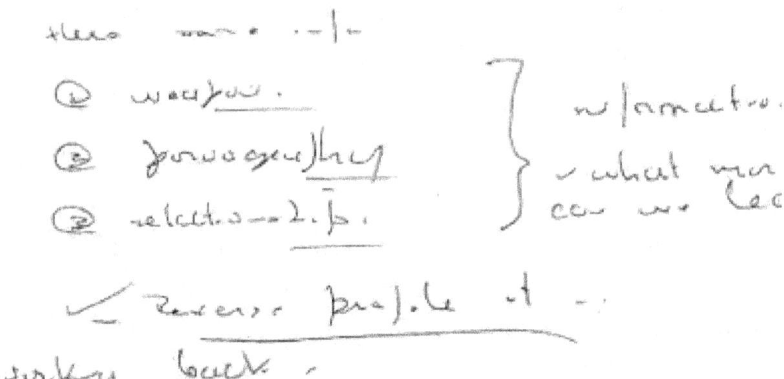

*Need*
*Is there more info*

*1 weapon -- w/?*
*2 pornography*
*3 relationship --what more can we learn*
*-Reverse profile it –*
*working back*

Working back, look at the murder and decide what kind of person commits such a crime, and back your suspect into that profile. This is precisely how Reilly turned Eddie O'Brien into a murderous sexual predator with the help of Gregg McGrary, the FBI profiler. Get more information about pornography and relationship—what more can we learn—Reverse profile it—working back.

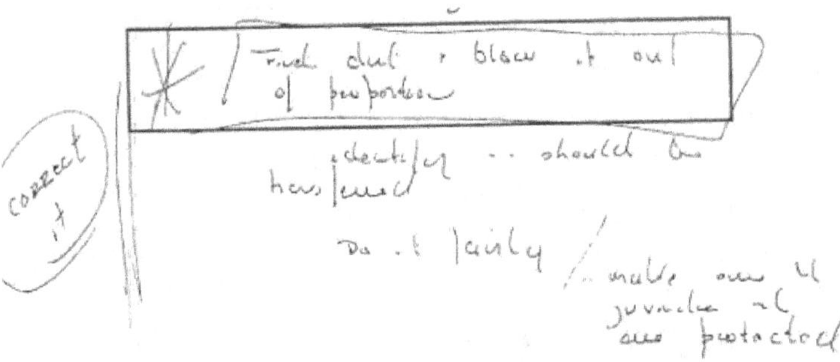

**Find dirt and blow it out of proportion*
*check for ...should (?)*
*correct it -- have found*
*Do it fairly/ .. make sure 4 (?)*
*juveniles (?)*
*are protected*

The only "dirt" Tom Reilly could find on Eddie was seeing a Black woman undress while he and a friend sat on his front porch. That got blown out of proportion to Eddie allegedly telling Ryan Downing that he saw Janet Downing undress from his bedroom window with a telescope. (Janet's bedroom window is not visible from Eddie's bedroom window and the telescope in his room was broken, so it was never taken into evidence.)[235]

235 Handwritten notes of Tom Reilly

# CONCLUSION

Eddie will never get back his teenage years, or his 20s or his 30s or even his early 40s. Those years are all behind him now. What he *can* get is the opportunity to have all the evidence heard by an impartial jury that hasn't been saturated with two years of nonstop news reels, stories, and articles about an Eddie O'Brien that Tom Reilly constructed by reverse profiling; a public that hasn't been subjected to daily press conferences by Tom Reilly.

Will the judicial system, Tom Reilly, or William Weld ever admit that they got this one wrong? Not a chance. The only relief the Commonwealth of Massachusetts can provide is a new trial for a defendant who is now old enough to assist his lawyers in defending himself, who has competent lawyers and the financial resources to hire the forensic experts to dispute the Commonwealth's flawed evidence.

Consider these alarming statistics about what part "official misconduct" has played in wrongful convictions. In 2024 alone, official misconduct occurred in 104 of the 147 wrongly convicted cases. Most of these cases involved more than one kind of misconduct such as:

1. failure to disclose exculpatory evidence to the defense (95 cases);
2. witness tampering (43 cases);
3. perjury by an official actor (39 cases);
4. knowing presentation of perjured testimony (11 cases);
5. police misconduct in interrogations (9 cases);
6. prosecutorial dishonesty in court (8 cases);
7. forensic misconduct (5 cases).[236]

236 [34] National Registry of Exonerations, 2024, p.4

In the coming months, we will see whether the public's growing awareness of official misconduct and outright corruption within today's criminal investigatory processes and judicial systems will inspire those who seek truth and justice to speak out and demand to be heard.

Eddie is filing a Motion for Post-Conviction Relief in the summer of 2026. This is his first substantive appeal of his conviction, and he has worked for the last 10 years preparing his case. It is political, and it is personal. It is about official misconduct; it is about finding the truth. It is about righting wrongs and holding people accountable. It is about what we are willing to accept and what we refuse to accept.

This case can change what we do about official misconduct that leads to wrongful conviction. Why should prosecutors, police, and politicians be immune from prosecution for their corrupt actions? How can we hold them accountable? How can we allow 71% of all wrongful convictions based on official misconduct to continue to be the norm?

It is time to take action.

If you wish to be part of the solution, please join us by:

Reviewing the actual documents in the case,
police reports, timelines, witness statements
at **thetruthabouteddieobrien.com**

Following the progress of the appeal on
**www.thepoliticsofmurder.com**

Signing your name at **https://www.change.org/p/support-a-positive-parole-decision-for-eddie-o-brien** to support Eddie's next Petition for Parole

Donating to Eddie's defense fund by:

Clicking on the Help button on
**www.thetruthabouteddieobrien.com**

Directly donating through:
Venmo **@Edward-OBrien-29**
CashApp **$EdwardObrien6**
**www.givesendgo.com**

*For More News About Margo Nash Signup For Our Newsletter:*
http://wbp.bz/newsletter

*Word-of-mouth is critical to an author's long-term success. If you appreciated this book please leave a review on the Amazon sales page:*
https://wbp.bz/pom2r

## ALSO AVAILABLE FROM WILDBLUE PRESS

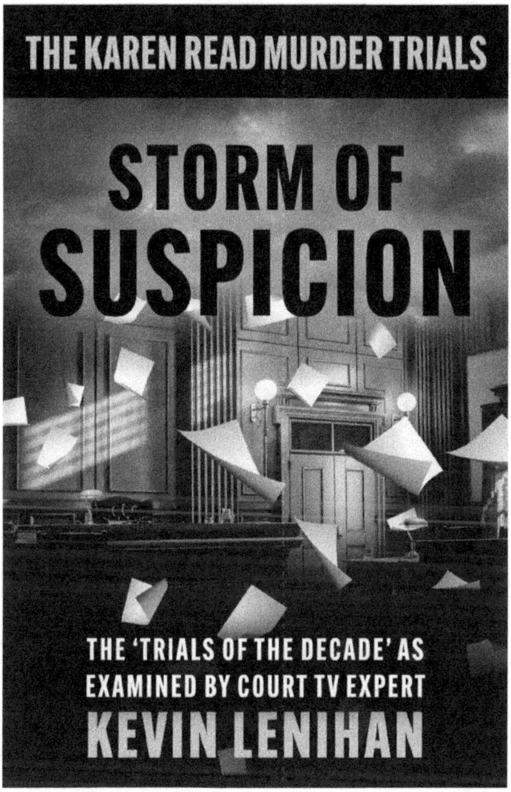


http://wbp.bz/sos

www.ingramcontent.com/pod-product-compliance
Lightning Source LLC
LaVergne TN
LVHW010320220926
848484LV00004BB/818
*9781970361391*